The 7 Lively Arts

SAGAMORE PRESS INC · NEW YORK

"For there are many arts,
not among those we conventionally call 'fine,'
which seem to me fundamental for living."

HAVELOCK ELLIS

THE 7 LIVELY ARTS

BY GILBERT SELDES

PN 22/21
S 46 5

To My Father

and now to my daughter

and to her daughter

In Memoriam : A. H. S.

Contents

Note

This book was written while on holiday some three thousand miles away from data, documents, and means of verification. It is written from memory and, although I have had time and have tried to check up, I feel sure that the safest thing is to let it go as cautious merchants do when they send out statements—with the *caveat:* E. and O.E.—errors and omissions excepted. I haven't tried to write a history of any of the lively arts, nor intended to mention all of those who practice them. I should, however, feel sorry if I have omitted anyone who has given me intense pleasure, even though the omission has not, in any way, the countenance of a slur.

Everything else that properly belongs in a preface has found its way into the two chapters: *The Great God Bogus* and *Before a Picture by Picasso*—and the acknowledgments are numerous and serious enough to need a place for themselves in the appendix.

G. S.

Ile St Louis—New York City
March 1923—February 1924

Note to this edition

Except for the omission of some matter in an Appendix—useful in 1924 when the literature of entertainment was less copious—the text of this book has not been altered. I have added an introduction for the historically minded and inserted comment here and there. The new matter is indented and set off by florets, like this ✺, at the beginning and end of each insertion.

G. S.

New York City—Truro, Mass.
November 1956—May 1957

The 7 Lively Arts

A personal preface

Small good, it seems to me, can come from pretending that *The 7 Lively Arts* was a youthful indiscretion. Before it was published I had enjoyed the privileges and fulfilled the duties of the adult citizen: I had voted for President (twice) and served in the Army (once) and paid taxes. Professionally, also, I had reached the years of discretion. I had rather precociously been an editorial writer on *Collier's* and, during the time the book was written, served not so precociously in various capacities on *The Dial*—and neither my connection with these magazines nor my departure from them had anything to do with their ultimate disappearance. Whatever critical faculties I have were, I should suppose, pretty well developed by that time: I was a practising book reviewer and dramatic critic. The faults in *The 7 Lively Arts* are, I am afraid, as permanent a part of my makeup as the abiding enthusiasm I have for the arts and entertainments I celebrated in this book. I knew what I was doing— but quite obviously I didn't know how to make my intentions clear to my readers.

For in the two areas of chief importance to me, the book was taken to signify almost the exact opposite of what I had meant. In one case, the misunderstanding was a nuisance, in the other intensely satisfactory.

The four words, "the seven lively arts" were first put together as a single phrase—as far as I know—on a late winter evening in 1922 at the corner of 54th street and Broadway.

They were spoken by myself to John Peale Bishop and, I think, Edmund Wilson, although I'm not sure that Wilson was there. I am sure about John Bishop because I remember his comment.

It was proper that this utterance should have been made in the presence of one (or two) of the editors of *Vanity Fair* because that publication had in a way midwifed the book which was eventually published. The circumstances, otherwise of interest to myself alone, have some bearing on the nature of the book. And of my failure to make its nature known.

In February, 1922, a ballet based on George Herriman's comic strip *Krazy Kat,* was produced at Town Hall, in New York: music by John Alden Carpenter, with choreography by Adolf Bolm. I had met the immortal Kat long before. When I was serving my apprentice years on the Pittsburgh *Sun* (also defunct) Krazy Kat edged his way into a comic strip called, I think, *The Family Upstairs* which we were running. Later, when I was on the *Evening Ledger,* in Philadelphia, I met Walter Hoban, the artist of *Jerry on the Job,* and through him, George Herriman. When I heard that Carpenter (a manufacturer of awnings in Chicago, a direct descendant of Priscilla Mullens and John Alden, and composer of the attractive suite, *In a Perambulator*) was going to do a ballet on *Krazy Kat,* I offered to help with publicity. By that time I had met the young Princeton men who were running *Vanity Fair* under the eye of Frank Crowninshield, and proposed to them a piece on Krazy Kat and the comic strip. It was published. The ballet was enchanting. The scenery, by Herriman, unrolled like a sideways roller-towel; the scenario was a distillation of a hundred strips (a rhapsodic text appears after the chapter on *Krazy Kat*); I gather from re-reading my report that the reception was short of total enthusiasm.

The thing I couldn't know then was that, in a way, the Krazy Kat ballet demonstrated both the essence and the eccentricity of what I was going to be doing for several years. My theme was to be that entertainment of a high order existed in places not usually associated with Art, that the place where an object was to be seen or heard had no bearing on its merits, that some of Jerome Kern's songs in the *Princess* shows were lovelier than any number of operatic airs and that a comic strip printed on newspulp which would tatter and rumple in a day might be as worthy of a second look as a considerable number of canvasses at most of our museums. Before I got this simple thing said I apparently let my intemperate addiction to controversy get the better of me and found that I was setting up a sort of rivalry between the arts.

But not at first. Obviously the appearance of a comic strip character in an art-form as remote and chic as ballet (years before Agnes de Mille and *Oklahoma!* showed us that we were all *balletomanes*) gave me an opportunity to back into my subject. It was as if the ballet had thrown a cloak of dignity around Krazy Kat—which was not the way Carpenter himself felt about it. The very thing I was to protest against —the grading of the arts and placing some of them forever at the lower table—was taking place. But I was not as dogmatic then as I later became and it wasn't until some time after, when I wrote a piece about Joe Cook (which developed into *The Damned Effrontery of the Two-a-Day* in this book) that my propaganda began to show.

It was after a few other pieces had been published or discussed that (as I recall it) I took Bishop [and Wilson?] to see what I meant about Al Jolson. We saw one of the last performances of one of his weakest shows, but toward the end, when Jolson, working hard against a cold house, came to his "You ain't heard nothin' yet" the electric spark sprang from him to the audience and as we walked away from the theatre I said I'd use the pieces I was writing as the point of departure for a book which I would call "The Seven Lively Arts." Bishop pointed to the Spearmint electric sign with its galvanic jumping men, and asked, "Including that?" I said I

3

didn't see why not. (I never did write the book about the advertising arts which I once planned.)

At every step of the way, the history of the book illuminated one point or another I was trying to make. After the high-art of the ballet and the chic of *Vanity Fair,* the next element was pure highbrow. Recently escaped from academic halls, Henry Seidel Canby was scouting for books for Harpers and, shortly after I had committed myself to write a book, he asked me to give it to him. I took a year's leave of absence from *The Dial,* did some errands for the magazine in Berlin and Prague, and settled down in Lewis Galantiere's apartment in Paris to write. Except for a folio of George Herriman's *Krazy Kat* and a few clippings, I don't recall having with me any notes, data, or documentation. The whole book was written, in a sense, from memory—for the most part a fond memory. I have enjoyed writing other books, but none was as easy to write as this one.

I can't, at this distance, remember what I expected the reception of the book to be. I do remember that one line of attack afflicted me with a sense of injustice. I was, for the first time, receiving, instead of launching, the slings and arrows of outrageous criticism and, for the last time, suspected that the critics were wilfully misrepresenting what I had written. I can, to tell the truth, still work up a bit of retrospective, or nostalgic, fury against those reviewers who said I was "discovering" what everyone was already familiar with, my point (as I understood it then) being that "everyone" did indeed know vaudeville and the movies and Ring Lardner's stories in *The Saturday Evening Post*—everyone, that is, except the critics (including those who were traducing me). The critics had been snobbish about these things, and it was my point precisely that "everyone's" taste was, in these matters, surer than the critics' judgment. I thought of myself as *un-* not *dis-*covering merits in what was, by definition, popular, hence well-known.

This misconception of my intent was a nuisance. The

4

more serious criticism of the book revealed a fault in its structure. As a piece of propaganda, it did not sufficiently identify the enemy. The final chapter, in which the influence of the art-world of Paris is clear, apparently comes too late. Long before the reader has come to it, he has—he had in 1924 at least—received a strong impression of hostility to the fine arts. The distinction I tried to make between the great arts and those I called the *faux bon* is not sharp enough, perhaps because I couldn't find an exact name for them in English. (I still can't. "Arty" is close, but doesn't convey the exact sense I wanted, the sense that these are damned hypocrites among the arts, imitating the great styles, having nothing to say that justifies their pretensions. They are high-class trash. I'm not sure I chose the best examples at the time and poor Puccini, for whom I now have an almost apologetic liking, seems to have been an obsession of mine. But the thing still exists.)

The late Ernest Boyd was a highly professional critic and he knew what I was trying to say and, knowing also that I hadn't quite said it, attacked the book from the title page to the index. He said that by calling these arts lively, I implied that the others were dull. I could only reply that dull was not the only antonym of lively, that an un-lively tennis-ball was generally called dead, and that although liveliness was not the quality to which above all others great classic arts aspired, they were not dull, but could be made to appear so by pedantry. It was no use. I had critics on my side, too, but for years the book was fair game and there was no closed season.

It is hard for me to believe, at this moment in 1957, in the full current of rock'n'roll and Elvis Presley, that the jazz represented by Paul Whiteman and Vincent Lopez should have been so desperately feared, so violently attacked, as the enemy of music. (By later standards this jazz is "square"—the cool word for the *faux bon*.) It is hard to believe that the appearance of George Gershwin, playing

5

his own songs, at Aeolian Hall and of Paul Whiteman in the same hall, to introduce *The Rhapsody in Blue*, were considered desecrations of those sacred premises. I can, with some effort, make allowances for critics who seriously discussed the art (they really did) of Hergesheimer and James Branch Cabell, but their failure to recognize, at that time, that Ring Lardner was more than a baseball reporter who wrote stories in slang, still goes beyond my retrospective power to forgive. The battle for jazz, for Lardner, for Chaplin and the Keystone cops was won long ago, by them and by the swift movement of events more than by the critics who saw their true worth. But the critics helped and I am glad I was one of them.

I failed to identify the enemy and this was all to the good for one particular group among those who read the book. In all the happy circumstances surrounding *The 7 Lively Arts* none has given me greater satisfaction than the discovery, many years later, that it had been read by young people, particularly by college students, and nothing has surprised me more than the parallel discovery that for them the book was one of the massed guns in the assault against "the genteel tradition." (The heavy artillery was Mencken.) I found this out some five years ago, after I had published *The Great Audience* and several reviewers, notably Edmund Wilson, had referred back to the iconoclastic spirit of the earlier work, and D. W. Brogan had said much the same thing. I didn't believe it and made it a point to enquire. I discovered that it was so. It hadn't seemed to me that my adversary was Hamilton Wright Mabie and it certainly wasn't Paul Elmer More. The critics I was attacking were those who had long emancipated themselves from the gentility of the 1890's, who were acclaiming Eugene O'Neill and Strawinsky, but had not yet recognized the existence of the popular arts. It was gratifying to know that I had scored a bull's-eye, but I would have been happier if it hadn't been on the wrong target.

6

(Once, but only once so far as I know, this book became a prop in a romantic event. The original edition had photographs of some of the people it celebrates. About the time it was published one of them met and fell in love with a young woman whose parents were seriously opposed to the marriage. Forbidden the consolation of having the man's photograph in her room, she constantly carried a copy of *The 7 Lively Arts* with her, making herself a sort of walking advertisement for the book—until her private motive was disclosed. Eventually the marriage took place, so did a reconciliation within the family, my book was placed on a shelf, and all was—and is—well. The young woman was Ellin Mackay; the photograph was of Irving Berlin.)

The book was not a sensational success on the publisher's sales-sheet, but its side-effects were excellent and I found myself acceptable to, if not eagerly sought-after by, large-circulation magazines. I continued to write about popular entertainment, but as I have a phobia about reprinting magazine articles, I didn't publish a book on the subject for some five years when I was commissioned to do a kind of introductory book about the movies—it was ready for the printer when Warner Brothers released *The Jazz Singer* and a chapter on sound was rather hastily added. Some years later I wrote a book about American movies for an English publisher.

In the intervening years the history of *The 7 Lively Arts* is largely the history of its title. I have confessed the truth, that it "came to me." The great luck was that it provided a sort of shorthand for any number of cumbersome phrases and it "became a part of the American language"—which I put in quotes because that phrase also is a part of the American language. (As Brogan and others indicate, my phrase is used also in England.) As shorthand it became generalized, it lost its own slant, it meant popular entertainment without any critical attitude—which, again, is all right with me. Five radio programs, two magazine departments, and other enterprises used the name (the last try was for a charm bracelet)—and in most cases the title was abandoned when I muttered something about using it myself, which I did in *Esquire* and elsewhere. Some years later Billy Rose bought the title for a revue and then gave it back to me. In 1956 the Columbia Broadcasting System leased the title, without reference to the book, for a televison program.

One thing should, perhaps, be made clear about the phrase. There were those who thought (correctly) that you couldn't find seven and there were those who felt (stuffily) that the seven were not arts. Lively was for the most part unchallenged. The sacred 7 came from the classics, from "the seven arts" (which was also the name of a magazine recently defunct) and I never tried to categorize the contents of the book to conform to the figure. If you tried you could make seven, counting feature movies and Keystone comedies as one or you could make ten if you counted all the forms of music separately. I never took a position in the matter.

But I had taken the position that these entertainments not only merited, but needed, critical examination. Within a few years their merit was generally accepted and certain events, unsuspected by me or by anyone else except a few technicians, made the need an urgency. Six months after the book was published I stood in an open square in Boston and *heard* reports on the election returns, coming not from a man with a megaphone, but from a loudspeaker. Radio had arrived.

It took me a long time to discover the significance of the event. I was aware of radio, to be sure. In a casual way I drifted into the business and—the conspicuous mistake of my professional life—drifted out of it—and it was ten years before I could return. A friend was promoting *The Theatre Arts* magazine by talking about shows in New York once a week over WEAF and when he had to leave the city asked me if I would take over. I date this roughly as 1927. Even at that early date I should have recognized the extraordinary power of the instrument I was using. Friends I hadn't heard from since we went to high school together wrote to me and strangers wrote. I branched away from the legitimate theatre into my own favorite kinds of entertainment and I enjoyed the work—facing the mike with an assurance I was never to recapture until, in the earliest days of television, knowing we had no audience, I MC'd some experimental broadcasts. But summer was coming on, we were going out of the city, I suppose I had to earn some money, and I refused the invitation to continue the series. (It was, essentially, an invitation to fill the quarter hour because in those days broadcasters were under pressure to find something or anything to put on the air. I was acceptable, not sensational.) The far shrewder men who stuck with it at the time became the great men of radio—and held their positions for nearly a generation.

Not seeing the opportunity for myself, I failed also to see the essential difference between broadcasting and all earlier forms of entertainment. It was after the blight of Hitlerism and the menace of war had forced all of us to look again at the things we used to take for granted that I began to see radio and, with it, all of our entertainments in a new aspect. I had a page in *Esquire* every month at that time and made my discovery known there. It was more important to me than to anyone else. In simple terms I said that if the American people were going to fight for their rights, the right to have free entertainment was certain to be among them. For purposes of shock, I said we would be more likely to fight for entertainment on the air, untrammeled by a central government, than for the older freedoms we enjoyed as a gift from our ancestors.

This led me to a total reassessment of what entertainment meant. Within a year or so I was working in the field as head of the program department of CBS television which consisted then of myself and a secretary, neither of us with any work to do. Before our studio was equipped and we went on the air, I had ample time to think. Several years later, after a tour of duty with Paramount, my thoughts were sufficiently organized for me to publish (in 1950) a study of the consequences I could not have foreseen in 1924.

In brief, the lively arts had turned into the mass media. They had become part of our daily lives and the pivot on which this revolution turned was the radio receiver, the box in the home which, as far back as 1915, David Sarnoff had predicted—and described as a "domestic utility." Out of it, he said, would come music and news; he did not say advertising would come out of it and, in fact, resisted the influence of the commercial for a considerable time. In a way the commercial was needed to integrate radio completely into our everyday business of living: with the news it created the frame in which entertainment occurred—the daily event on one side, the daily purchase on the other.

The significance of all this has no place in this record of what happened to a book. What really happened was that the subject of the book was transformed and when I came to look at it again, I was so impressed by the effect of the mass media that I couldn't see in them precisely those qualities I had originally blamed others for not seeing: their sparkle and snap, their inner life which corresponds to the brighter and better side of American life, their impertinence and good cheer, and above all the strong creative current which in them has found a native, not borrowed, form for itself. *The Great Audience,* in which my misgivings about our popular entertainments were recorded, was published in 1950. It was in an unexpected way more effective than *The 7 Lively Arts*—it got on the list of required or supplementary reading in college courses in Communications. It strikes me as a glum book and by 1956 I tried to balance my two themes—the delight I take and the fears I experience—in *The Public Arts.* Getting away from the grim words "mass

10

media," finding a new name for them, connecting their social effects with the pleasures they give—was for me an act of simple justice.

I have mentioned the good fortune attending the title of my book. The greatest good fortune a writer can have is to chance, early in this professional life, on a subject which interests him and then to have that subject grow in significance, to start with a report on his own satisfactions and then discover the existence of tremendous underlying forces. It is something to have played a part in changing the attitude of thoughtful people toward popular entertainment, but it is professionally something more to have begun, almost accidentally, with a subject that had its own capacity to grow and to transform itself. When I began to be a critic, I wrote about books and plays, and I suppose if the field of popular entertainment had had a dozen good critics at the time, I wouldn't have turned to it. I wasn't casting about for an undiscovered subject, I was following my own bent and it led to pleasant places. More important for me, it led me away from work for which I was not suited, at which I would have been permanently second-rate. I had neither the equipment nor the temper of mind to be a good critic of the major arts, but my pleasure in them and the sense all of us on *The Dial* felt, at the time, that the great arts, the very core of our general civilization and of our private satisfaction in life, were being undermined in our materialistic civilization and needed to be defended, would have led me, were leading me, into a blind alley. I was becoming belligerent because I didn't know enough; I was quick, so I picked up a jargon, but I was unwilling to do the fundamental brain work that philosophic and aesthetic criticism demanded. I was a good propagandist, and didn't need a thorough grounding in my subjects—merely enough for argument. If I had continued I should have become merely pedantic. From this, the only contemptible kind of intellectualism, my interest in the lively arts and my success in dealing with them, saved me. I have reason to be grateful.

Returning now to the text of the book, to annotate it rather than to criticize, I am aware of its faults—and perfectly willing to leave them uncorrected. Except for a few omissions—such as lists of movies and songs which are now to be found in more complete form elsewhere—the text is that of the original. I know that there are some purple passages and that, out of the context of their time, some sections will seem overwritten. My own comments are scattered through the text—not to bring the book up to the present time, which would require several new books, but to indicate my feelings now about what I felt when the book was written. I can't feel the same kind of happiness now any more than I can remember, when I shave in the morning, what the young man looked like who wrote this book. But I know he and I are the same person and I can be grateful that what he did with so much pleasure has lasted to give so much satisfaction to me.

G.S.

The keystone
the builders rejected

For fifteen years there has existed in the United States, and in the United States alone, a form of entertainment which, seemingly without sources in the past, restored to us a kind of laughter almost unheard in modern times. It came into being by accident; it had no pretensions to art. For ten years or more it added an element of cheerful madness to the lives of millions and was despised and rejected by people of culture and intelligence. Suddenly—suddenly as it appeared to them—a great genius arose and the people of culture conceded that in his case, but in his case alone, art existed in slap-stick comedy; they did not remove their non expedit from the form itself.

Perhaps only those of us who care for the rest know how good Charlie is. Perhaps only the inexpressive multitudes who have laughed and not wondered why they laughed can know how fine slap-stick is. For myself, I have had no greater entertainment than these dear and preposterous comedies, and all I can do is remember. The long, dark, narrow passage set out with uncomfortable chairs; the sharp almond odours, the sense of uncertainty, and the questionable piano; and then upon the screen, in a drab grey and white, jiggling insecurely, something strange and wonderful occurred. It was mingled with dull and stupid things; but it had a fire, a driving energy of its own—and it was funny! Against all

13

our inhibitions and habits it played games with men and women; it made them ridiculous and mad; it seemed to have no connexion with the logic of human events, trusting to an undecipherable logic of its own. A few scholars found the commedia dell'arte living again; a few artists saw that the galvanic gestures and movements were creating fresh lines and interesting angles. And a nation cared for them intensely until the remorseless hostility of the genteel began to corrupt the purity of slap-stick. That is where we are now: too early to write an epitaph—late enough to pay a tribute.

Lest the year 1914 should be not otherwise distinguished in history, it may be recorded that it was then, or a year earlier, or possibly a year later, that the turning point came in the history of the American moving picture. The first of the great mergers arrived—an event not unforeseen in itself, a "logical development" the press agents called it— seeming to establish the picture as a definitely accepted form of entertainment. It was a moment when a good critic might have foretold the course of the moving picture during the next decade, for at that time the Triangle of Fine Arts (D. W. Griffith), Kay-Bee (Thomas H. Ince), and Keystone (Mack Sennett) was formed. Two of these names were already known, and of the two one was to become, for a time, the most notable name in the profession; the third was hidden behind the obscure symbol of the Keystone; it represented one who had acted in, and was now directing, the most despised, and by all odds the most interesting, films produced in America. Mr Griffith was already entered on that road which has since ruined him as a director; he was producing *Intolerance,* and, if I may borrow a phrase from the Shuberts, his personal supervision was not always given to the Triangle-Fine Arts releases; Mr Ince was presently to meditate upon the possibility of joining the word "super" to the word "spectacle," thus creating the word "super-spectacle"; and Mr Sennett—by a process of exclusion one

14

always arrives at Mr Sennett. He is the Keystone the builders rejected.

I know nothing more doleful as a subject of conversation than the social-economics of the moving picture; what was remarkable about the Triangle was not its new method of distribution, its new hold on the timid exhibitor, or its capacity for making or losing fortunes. The thing to note is that the two "serious" producers, and the hard-headed business men who invested money in their efforts, thought it well to associate with themselves the best producer of vulgar slap-stick comedy. More than that, they combined in a peculiar ratio for the scheme provided that there was to be released each week either a Fine Arts or an Ince picture; and that with each of these was to be shown a Keystone comedy. So that those who were perpetually being caught in the rain, or missing the eleven-o'clock from Philadelphia to New York, saw twice as many Keystone comedies as (a) Fine Arts or (b) Kay-Bee releases. The recent all-hailing of Mr Chaplin as an artist because of his work in *The Kid,* the bright young reputations of Harold Lloyd and Buster Keaton, indicate that most critics of the moving picture caught the train and missed the shower. They certainly missed the comedies; for the Fine Arts and Ince pictures were in their time the best pictures produced; and the Keystone comedies were consistently and almost without exception better.

This is not the place to discuss the shortcomings of the feature film; for the moment, let the dreadful opulent gentility of a Cecil De Mille production serve only to sharpen the saucy gaiety of the comic, the dulness of a Universal set off the revelry of slap-stick. There is one serious point which a good critic (Aristotle, for example) would have discovered when he regarded the screen as long ago as 1914 and became aware of the superiority of the comic films. He would have seen at once while Mr Griffith and Mr Ince were both developing the technique of the moving picture, they were

15

exploiting their discoveries with materials equally or better suited to another medium: the stage or the dime novel or whatever. Whereas Mr Sennett was already so enamoured of his craft that he was doing with the instruments of the moving picture precisely those things which were best suited to it—those things which could not be done with any instrument but the camera, and could appear nowhere if not on the screen.

This does not mean that nothing but slap-stick comedy is proper to the cinema; it means only that everything in slap-stick *is* cinematographic; and since perceiving a delicate adjustment of means to end, or a proper relation between method and material, is a source of pleasure, Mr Sennett's developments were more capable of pleasing the judicious than those of either of his two fellow-workers. The highly logical humanist critic of the films could have foreseen in 1914—without the decade of trial and error which has intervened—what we see now: that the one field in which the picture would most notably declare itself a failure would be that of the drama (Elinor Glyn-Cecil De Mille-Gilbert Parker, in short). Without a moment's hesitation he would have put his finger on those two elements in the cinema which, being theoretically sound, had a chance of practical success: the spectacle (including the spectacular melodrama) and the grotesque comedy. Several years later he would have added one word more, that grotesque tragedy might conceivably succeed. For it is not only the fun in the Keystones which makes them successful: it is the method of presentation.

* ◄§ It is a shock to read that the most notable failure of the movies would be in the drama, but this was written about the silent picture and at a time when drama was represented by such writers as are here so contemptuously named. The movies had developed their own way of tell-

* The portions of the text enclosed between ◄§ §► are the 1957 additions.

ing a story, which was not the way of the theatre, and was best demonstrated with non-theatrical subjects. Before this style had matured, sound came in and a whole new body of techniques had to be invented.

Almost equally shocking is the following reference to the "rightness of the spectacle film" which sounds like a prediction of CinemaScope. The shock comes from trying to hold two ideas in mind at the same time: film is the right place for spectacle, and spectacles, in 1957, have almost killed the movies as we have known them from 1927 to the coming of *Bwana Devil* and all the satanic 3-D imps that followed. The intervening years were those of the great dramatic film, of superior comedy, of the gangster cycle, of everything the word "movies" has meant for two generations. If spectacle is fundamentally right for the movies, the wide screen should be its natural culmination—and if this is so, the dramatic movie may be destined to disappear. As its equivalent may persist in television, the cinematic art may divide into two segments: spectacle for the theatre-screen, drama for the TV screen.

When sound first appeared I wrote a piece for *Harper's* which the editors or I entitled "The Movies Commit Suicide"—and for twenty years I was not allowed to forget this. I am therefore chary of predictions. I know that within three years of the arrival of the wide screen, Charles Brackett produced *A Woman's World,* a gay and sophisticated comedy which was as good as any flat-screen comedy of the 1940's. The viability of the wide screen as a medium for a comedy-drama was demonstrated and the mastery of the new dimensions had been accomplished promptly. It took a longer time for the movies to recover from the shock of sound, to put dialogue in its proper place, to free the camera and restore movement to the screen.

But if the big screen can accommodate a small comedy, the movie-house has still to compete with television. And

17

the only way to bring the customers in is to give them something they miss on their 21" screen which, in 1957, meant size, depth, and (for nine-tenths of the receivers) color. ࡍ

The rightness of the spectacle film is implicit in its name: the screen is a place on which things can be *seen,* and so long as a film depends upon the eye it is right for the screen —and whether it is right in any other regard depends upon taste and judgment and skill. Omit as irrelevant the news reels, animated cartoons, educational and travel films—all of them good; omit equally those printed jokes and clippings from the *Literary Digest* which are at once the greatest trial *and* error of the screen. What remains? The feature film and *The Cabinet of Dr Caligari.* This—the only film of high fantasy I have ever seen—is the seeming exception which proves the rule, since it owes its success to the skilfully concealed exploitation of the materials and technique of the spectacle and of the comic film, and not to the dramatic quality of its story. The studio settings in distortion represent the spectacle; they are variations of scenery or "location"; the chase over the roofs is a psychological parallel to the Keystone cops; and the weak moment of this superb picture is that in which the moving picture always fails, in the double revelation at the end, like that of *Seven Keys to Baldpate,* representing "drama."

ࡍ Someone ought to write a history of taste in America, and particularly a history of the vexing relationship between highbrows and the popular arts, using *Caligari* as the point of reference. When this film was first shown, it overwhelmed even those who hated it—it is the only picture I ever heard hissed for its technique, not for its subject matter or political ideas. It arrived at a moment when the American movie was at a low point, it was revolutionary, it seemed to us to point a way out of the blind alley in which Hollywood had abandoned us. In our excitement we did not see that *Caligari* was to a degree going against the grain of the movies, that our movie-makers could learn something from it, but didn't have to unlearn everything they knew.

Something of the natural snobbery of intellectuals was in our attitude—here was a foreign stick with which to beat the native dog. Here was something with reference to a new movement in the major arts. And, as its thudding failure proved, here was something the average moviegoer couldn't understand and didn't want at any price.

There followed a swing away from this extreme attitude to the point almost of denying *Caligari* its great virtues. As we discovered the technical delights of the American movie and especially when we found out that the aesthetes of Paris were admiring our Westerns and discovering Dada in our slapstick, we turned against the "arty" tricks of *Caligari*. By that time it had become a museum piece (at the Museum of Modern Art, at least) and so many people wanted to see it that it was successfully shown in an art house.

There are a few critical mentions of *Caligari* in another chapter. In the years since I last saw it, I have come back almost to my earliest stage of admiration. I cannot think of half a dozen movies which have left so many clear images in my mind and can think of only one recent film that I expect to remember as vividly after fifteen years: Tyrone Guthrie's production of *Oedipus Rex*. Both are completely divorced from the surface reality of the common film, both seem to have been made intentionally to defy the canons of good movie-making, with a kind of independence, as if the producer in each case had said, "Don't tell me what can and cannot be done on film, let's try everything and find out."

There is another facet of interest in *Caligari*. It is the story of a somnambulist in a madhouse, it seemed even in

1923 to say something about Europe which could not be said in words. After World War II had come and gone, *Caligari* seemed to have predicted the event. *From Caligari to Hitler,* by Siegfried Kracauer, is an interesting development of the theme. &

No. The drama film is almost always wrong, the slap-stick almost always right; and it is divinely just that the one great figure of the screen should have risen out of the Keystone studios. He came too early; Chaplin spoiled nearly everything else for us, and he is always used by those who dislike slap-stick to prove their case. Their case, regrettably, is in a fair way to be proved, for slap-stick is in danger. The hypothetical critic mentioned above has not yet occurred; Mr Bushnell Diamond, the best actual critic of the movies, is without sympathy for Mack Sennett and calls him a Bourbon, in the sense of one who forgets nothing and learns less. What Mr Sennett has needed long since is encouragement and criticism; and stupid newspaper critics (who write half-columns about a new Gloria Swanson picture and add "the comedy which ends the bill is *Down in the Sewer*") have left slap-stick wholly without direction.[1] At the same time the tradition of gentility, the hope of being "refined," has touched the grotesque comedy; its directors have heard abuse and sly remarks about custard pies so long that they have begun to believe in them, and the madness which is a monstrous sanity in the movie comedy is likely to die out. The moving picture is being prettified; the manufacturers and exhibitors are growing more and more pretentious, and the riot of slap-stick seems out of place in a "presentation" which begins with the overture to *Tannhäuser,* and includes a baritone from the imperial opera house in Warsaw singing *Indian Love Lyrics* in front of an art curtain. In Paris there are one or two Chaplin films visible nearly every day; in

[1] Except that supplied by the professional journals—often excellent.

20

New York the Rialto Theatre alone seems to make a habit of Chaplin revivals and of putting its comic feature in the electric sign. The Capitol, the largest and rapidly becoming the most genteel, of moving picture palaces (but who ever heard of an opera palace?) frequently announces a programme of seven or eight items without a comedy among them; and you have to go to squalid streets and disreputable neighborhoods if you want to see Chaplin regularly. He could ask for no finer tribute, to be sure; but it is not much to our credit that the greatest mimic of our time has no theatre named after him, that it was in Berlin, not in Chicago or New York, that the first Chaplin festival took place, and that *Tillie's Punctured Romance,* a film intensely important in his development, was last billed in a converted auction room on the lower East Side of New York, where Broadway would find it vulgar.

There were always elements in the Keystone which jeopardized its future—it lacked variety, it was often dull, its lapses of taste were serious. (I transfer the name of Keystone to the *genre* of which it was the most notable example; it was for long, and may still be, superior to most of the others.) But, while there is still time, its miraculously good qualities can be caught and possibly preserved. The ideal comedy of Mack Sennett is a fairly standardized article; too much so, perhaps, but the elements are sound. They include a simple, usually preposterous plot, frequently a burlesque of a serious play; more important are the characters, grotesque in bulk, form, or make-up; and, finally, the events which have as little connexion with the plot as, say, a clog dance in a musical comedy. In the early days of the Keystone, it is said, the plot was almost nonexistent in advance, and developed out of the set and the props. The one which was called, in revival, *The Pile Driver,* must have been such a film, for its plot is that two men meet a pretty girl near a river and they find a huge mallet. It is a film full of impromptus—not very brilliant ones, as a matter of fact—in which Sennett and Chaplin and Mabel Normand each occasionally give flashes of their qualities. A few years later you see the same thing when the trick of working up a film from the material in hand has become second nature. *His Night Out* presents Ben Turpin and Charlie Chaplin as equal comedians: two men on a drinking party, stumbling into a luxurious hotel, reverting automatically to the saloon from which they have been thrown, mutually assisting and hindering each other in a serious effort to do something they cannot define, but which they feel to be of cosmic importance. Later, one finds a more sophisticated kind of comic. *Bright Eyes* has to do with a gawky young man, reputed rich, received into a wealthy family, engaged to the daughter, denounced as an impostor, reduced to the kitchen, flirting there with the maid, restored to favour, and, nobly refusing the daughter's hand, marrying the maid. Here Ben Turpin had good moments, but much of the gaiety of the film depended upon Chester Conklin (or one who much resembles him) as another servant in the house, bundling himself up in furs like Peary in the Arctic, bidding farewell at an imaginary outpost of civilization, and striding into— a huge refrigerator, to bring back a ham before the adoring eyes of the cook.

∾ I was on location once with Charlie Chaplin when he was shooting *Modern Times* (which was his protest against the coming of sound, disguised as a protest against the machine age). Chaplin looked sadly at all the paraphernalia surrounding him and said, "We used to go into the park with a stepladder, a bucket of whitewash, and Mabel Normand, and make up a picture."

This is as good a place as any to say something about the lovely, greatly gifted, tragic figure of Mabel Normand. She was one of those rare apparitions, a woman with high sexual attractions who is also a great slapstick comedian. There have been two others in our immediate time:

Carole Lombard, who died young in an aeroplane accident, and the most dazzling of the three, Lucille Ball. Mabel Normand, arriving at the very beginning of the movies, was the simplest of them, a blessed hoyden, totally unquenchable in spirits, bright without effort. The face of a mischievous boy and the body of an acrobat and the excitement at being alive of a kitten were mingled with a remarkable sweetness of disposition which radiated through every movement she made.

In the time of the great scandals in Hollywood, she was known to have called on William Desmond Taylor, a director, on the night he was murdered. There wasn't a glimmer of evidence to connect her with the crime, but organized virtue turned against her and for a time she couldn't work in pictures. She had a bad time. When I met her she had undergone a cure. I had, then, the rights on Sherwood Anderson's beautiful story, *I'm A Fool*, and asked her if she would play in it. She was enchanted by the story and, to my great surprise, came to see me a few days later to discuss plans for the production. A short time after that she died of tuberculosis at the age of 34.

Something of her story is told in Mack Sennett's autobiography, but only half-told, because Sennett goes genteel and over-reticent. But he communicates the essential truth about an enchanting person whom, quite clearly, like everyone who knew her, he loved immeasurably. ಀ

The comic film is by nature adventurous and romantic, and I think what endears it to us is that the adventure is picaresque and the romance wholly unsentimental—that is, both are pushed to the edge of burlesque. For the romance you have a love affair, frequently running parallel to a parody of itself. The hero is marked by peculiarities of his own: the Chaplin feet, the Hank Mann bang and sombre eyes, the Turpin squint, the Arbuckle bulk; against these oddities and absurdities plays the serene, idle beauty of a simple girl (Edna Purviance or Mabel Normand in her lovely early days), and only on occasions a comic in her own right like Louise Fazenda or Polly Moran. In some five hundred slap-stick comedies I do not remember one single moment of sentimentality; and it seems to me that every look and gesture of false chivalry and exaggerated devotion has been parodied there. The characteristic moment, after all, is when the comedy is ended, and just as the hero is about to kiss the heroine he winks broadly and ironically at the spectators. Our whole tradition of love is destroyed and outraged in these careless comedies; so also our tradition of heroism. And since the moving picture, quite naturally, began by importing the whole baggage of the romantic and sentimental novel and theatre, the moving-picture comedy has at last arrived at burlesquing its silly-serious half-sister. Two years before *Merton of the Movies* appeared, Mack Sennett, with the help of Ben Turpin's divinely crossed eyes, had consummated a burlesque of Messrs Griffith, Ince, and Lubitsch, in *A Small Town Idol,* far more destructively, be it said, than Chaplin in his *Carmen,* and with a vaster fun than *Merton.*

Everything incongruous and inconsequent has its place in the unrolling of the comic film: love and masquerade and treachery; coincidence and disguise; heroism and knavishness; all are distorted, burlesqued, exaggerated. And—here the camera enters—all are presented at an impossible rate; the culmination is in the inevitable struggle and the conventional pursuit, where trick photography enters and you see the immortal Keystone cops in their flivver, mowing down hundreds of telegraph poles without abating their speed, dashing through houses or losing their wheels and continuing, blown to bits and reassembled in midair; locomotives running wild, yet never destroying the cars they so miraculously send spinning before them; airplanes and submarines in and out of their elements—everything capable of motion set into motion; and at the height of the revel, the true

24

catastrophe, the solution of the preposterous and forgotten drama, with the lovers united under the canopy of smashed motor cars, or the gay feet of Mr Chaplin gently twinkling down the irised street.

And all of this is done *with the camera, through action* presented to the eye. The secret of distortion is in the camera, and the secret of pace in the projector. Regard them for a moment, regard the slap-stick as every moment explains itself, and then go to the picture palace and spend one-third of your time reading the flamboyancies of C. Gardner Sullivan and another third watching the contortions of a famous actress as she "registers" an emotion which action and photography should present directly, and you will see why the comic film is superior. There is virtually no registering in the comedy, there is no senseless pantomime, and the titles are succinct and few. In *Bright Eyes,* as the marriage of convenience is about to take place, the mother sweeps in with these words, "Faint quick—he's dead broke." An absurd letter or telegram is introduced to set the play going; the rest is literally silence.

What I have said about Chaplin regards him as a typical slap-stick comedian.[1] The form would have succeeded without him and he has passed beyond the form entirely. The other practitioners of the art come out of his shadow, and some of them are excellent. What makes Chaplin great is that he has irony and pity, he knows that you must not have the one without the other; he has both piety and wit. Next to him, for his work in *His Bread and Butter* and a few other films, stands Hank Mann, who translates the childlike gravity of Chaplin into a frightened innocence, a serious endeavour to understand the world which seems always hostile to him. He was trained, I have been told, as a tragic actor on the East Side of New York, and he seems always stricken with the cruelty and madness of an existence in which he alone is logical and sane. If he, walking backward

[1] But there is more to say; a little of it occurs on page 35.

to get a last glimpse of his beloved (after "A Waiter's Fare-well," as the caption has it), steps on the running board of a motor instead of a street car, he is willing to pay the usual fare and let bygones be bygones. His black bang almost meets his eyes, and his eyes are mournful and piteous; his gesture is slow and rounded; a few of the ends of the world have come upon his head and the eyelids are a little weary. He is the Wandering Jew misdirected into comic life by an unscrupulous fate.

  ❦ Chaplin recognized Hank Mann's exceptional quali-ties and cast him, as well as Chester Conklin, in *Modern Times* and found place not only for old cronies, but for rivals—as he did for Buster Keaton in *Limelight*. ❧

His most notable opposite is Harold Lloyd, a man of no tenderness, of no philosophy, the embodiment of American cheek and indefatigable energy. His movements are all di-rect, straight; the shortest distance between two points he will traverse impudently and persistently, even if he is knocked down at the end of each trip; there is no poetry in him, his whole utterance being epigrammatic, without overtone or image. Yet once, at least, he too stepped into that lunatic Arcadia to which his spirit is alien; not in *Grandma's Boy,* which might just as well have been done by Charles Ray, but in *A Sailor-made Man.* Here the old frenzy fell upon him, the weakling won by guile, and instead of fighting one man he laid out a mob from behind; something excessive, topsy-turvy, riotous at last occurred in his ordered existence. He is funny; but he has no vulgarity; he is smart. He amuses me without making me laugh, and I figure him as a step toward gentility.

Ben Turpin has progressed, fortunately without taking that step. In *Bright Eyes* he was mildly absurd; in *His Night Out,* with Chaplin, he was tremendously funny; and what he learned there of the lesson of the master he imported into his private masterpiece, *A Small Town Idol*. Like Chaplin, he disarms you and endears himself; unlike him, and often to Turpin's advantage, he knows how to be ridiculous. One always sees Chaplin's impersonations as they see themselves. Is he a count or a pretender, or an English gentleman, or a policeman, or a tramp, the character is completely embodied; Chaplin never makes fun of himself. The process of identification is complete and, apart from the interest and the fun of the action, your chief pleasure is in awaiting the inevitable denunciation. Ben Turpin, who has only a talent for Chaplin's genius, makes the most of it and lets you see through him. His exaggerations do more than reveal—they betray, and above all they betray the fact that Turpin is aware of the absurdities of his characters; you see them objectively, and through him you see through them.

When he returns home as the Wild West screen hero, and his own picture is shown before those who so recently had despised him, his deprecating gesture before the screen on which his exploits are being shown is so broad, so simple-silly, that it is more than a description of himself as he thinks it is, and lets us perceive his absurdity. He is exactly a zany.

Three other buffoons of the old Keystone days retain their capacity to be amusing: the galvanic, jack-in-the-box, Al St John; Mack Swain, and Chester Conklin; they are exactly as they were ten years ago, and one fancies they will never be great. The difficult person to be sure about is Buster Keaton, who came to the pictures from vaudeville, and has carried into his new medium his greatest asset, an enormous, incorruptible gravity. He never smiles, they say, and I have sat through some of his pictures—*The Boat*, for one—without seeing any reason why he should. It was a long mechanical contrivance with hardly any humour, and was considered a masterpiece; while *The Paleface*, in which Keaton played an entomologist captured by Indians, passed unnoticed. It had nearly everything a comic needs, and there were certain movements *en masse*, certain crossings of the lines of action, which were quite perfect. Keaton's intense preoccupation and his hard sense of personality are excellent. In *Cops* he took a purely Keystone subject and multiplied and magnified it to its last degree of development: thousands of policemen rushed down one street; equal thousands rushed up another; and before them fled this small, serious figure, bent on self-justification, caught in a series of absurd accidents, wholly law-abiding, a little distracted. I do not think one will soon forget the exquisite close of that picture: the whole police force forming a phalanx, hurled as one body into the court-yard of the station—and then the little figure which, having been trapped within, seems doomed to arrest, coming out, itself accoutred in uniform, and quietly, quietly locking the huge doors behind it. It, yes; for by that time Keaton has become wholly impersonal. So affecting Larry Semon has never been; nor Clyde Cook; and behind them, but *longo intervallo,* come the misguided creatures who make the kind of slap-stick which most people think Sennett makes. I am sure there are other good comedians; but I am not trying to make a catalogue. No one, in any case, has been able to impose himself as these few have; and most of the others are so near in method and manner to these that they require nothing fresh to be said of them.

  ◄§ A few months ago one line from the preceding was quoted in a Cinema 16 program: "I do not think one will soon forget the exquisite close of that picture." I had forgotten. But reading the description I remember—and it was worth remembering. ᵹᴗ

It seemed for a moment, in 1922, that if a confessed murderer were set free by a jury, he or she went into the movies; but if a moving-picture actor was declared innocent, he was barred from the screen. The justice of this I cannot discuss; yet a protest can be made against the æsthetically high-minded who said that the real reason for barring the films of "Fatty" Arbuckle was their vulgarity and their dulness. For "Fatty" had gone over to a comedy more refined than slap-stick long before 1922; and in 1914 he was neither stupid nor dull. Once indeed, in *Fatty and Mabel Adrift* (Mabel being Miss Normand) he came near to the best of slap-stick, and the same picture was as photography and printing, for sepia seascapes and light and shade, a superior thing entirely. The fatuous, ingratiating smile was innocent then, in all conscience, and as for vulgarity—

Let us, before we go to the heart of that question, look for a moment at the comedy which was always set against the slap-stick to condemn the custard-pie school of fun—the comedy of which the best practitioners were indisputably Mr and Mrs Sidney Drew. In them there was nothing offensive, except an enervating dulness. They pretended to be pleasant episodes in our common life, the life of courtship and marriage; they accepted all our conventions; and they were one and all exactly the sort of thing which the junior class at high school acted when money was needed to buy a new set of erasers for Miss Struther's course in mechanical drawing. The husband stayed out late at night or was seen kissing a stenographer; the wife had trouble with a maid or was extravagant at the best shops; occasionally arrived an ingenuity, such as the romantic attachment of the wife to anniversaries contrasted with her husband's negligence—I seem to recall that to cure her he brought her a gift one day in memory of Washington's birthday. These things were little stories, not even smoking-room stories; they were acted entirely in the technique of the amateur stage; they were incredibly genteel, in the milieu where "When Baby Came" is genteel; neither in matter nor in manner did they employ what the camera and the projector had to give. And, apart from the agreeable manners of Mr and Mrs Sidney Drew, nothing made them successful except the corrupt desire, on the part of the spectators, to be re-fined.

  ȺȺ Yet these genteel comedies were, I suspect, the fore-runners of the highly diverting "screwball" comedies of the early 1930's. ȺȺ

Nothing of the sort operated in the far better (feature film) comedies which Douglas Fairbanks made when he was with Fine Arts. To suit his physique, they were almost all adventurous; they were always entertaining. *Flirting With Fate*[1] presented a young man who had decided to die and gave "Automatic Joe," a gunman, his last fifty dollars to "bump him off" unexpectedly. Once the agreement was made, the tide of fortune turned for the young man, and, desiring earnestly to live, he felt the paid hand of the assas-sin always upon his shoulder. At the same time the gunman had reformed; his one object was to return the unearned fifty dollars. And the cross-purposes, the chase and flight, were within short distance of high farce. The comedies of Charles Ray were also unpretentious, and also used the camera. These and others were always perfectly decent; but none of them was refined.

And there, essentially, we are back at slap-stick; for the refined comedy was pretentious, and what is pretentious is vulgar in any definition of the word; while slap-stick never pretended to be anything but itself and could be disgusting or tasteless or dull, but it could not be vulgar. I consider vulgar the thing which offends against the canons of taste accepted by honest people, not by imitative people, not by snobs. It is equally bad taste, presumably, to throw custard pies and to commit adultery; but it is not bad taste to speak of these things. What is intolerable only is the pretense, and it was against pretentiousness that the slap-stick comedy had

[1] Scenario by the adroit Anita Loos.

30

its hardest fight. It showed a man sitting down on a lighted gas stove, and it did not hesitate to disclose the underwear charred at the buttocks which were the logical consequence of the action. There was never the slightest suggestion of sexual indecency, or of moral turpitude, in the Keystones; there was a fuller and freer use of gesture—gesture with all parts of the human frame—than we are accustomed to. The laughter they evoked was broad and long; it was thoracic, abdominal; it shook us because it was really the earth trembling beneath our feet. The animal frankness and health of these pictures constituted the ground of their offense. And something more.

For the Keystone offended our sense of security in dull and business-like lives. Few of us imagined ourselves in the frenzy of action which they set before us; none of us remained unmoved at the freedom of fancy, the wildness of imagination, the roaring, destructive, careless energy which it set loose. It was an ecstasy of comic life, and in our unecstatic lives we fled from it to polite comedy, telling ourselves that what we had seen was ugly and displeasing. Often it was. I am stating the case for slap-stick, but I do not wish to make myself responsible for the millions of feet of stupidity and ugliness which have been released as comic films. I have seen Ham and Bud and the imitators of Charlie Chaplin; I have seen an egg splattered over a man's face with such a degree of nauseous ugliness that it seemed I could never see a comic again. But as like as not, on the same bill was the James Young screen version of *The Devil* with George Arliss, or Geraldine Farrar in *Carmen,* or the *" 'Affairs of' Anatol."* And when people who have seen these "artistic" films, or the barber-shop scene in a Hitchcock revue or Eddie Cantor in a dentist's chair, exclaim (falsely) that moving-picture comedians do nothing but throw pies, I am moved to wonder what on earth they are expected to throw. They are using the eternal materials of their art, precisely as Aristophanes used them and Rabelais, with already far too many concessions to a debased and cowardly and artificial taste. At the two extremes simple and sophisticated people have looked directly at the slap-stick screen and loved it for itself alone; in between are the people who can see nothing without the lorgnettes of prejudice provided by fashion and gentility. The simple ones discovered and prospered the slap-stick screen long before the sophisticated were aware of its existence; they took it for what is was and cared nothing for the fact that it was made by inartistic people and shown in reeking rooms for a nickel. For long the poison of culture was powerless to enter; but not long enough.

I feel moderately certain that the slap-stick comedy is a good thing for America to have; yet, being neither an apostle of pagan joy nor a reformer, I have to put my plea for slap-stick on personal grounds. It has given me immeasurable entertainment and I would like to see it saved; I would like to see a bit more of its impromptus, its unpremeditated laughter; I would like to do something to banish the bleak refinement which is setting in upon it.

Seven years ago, in an imaginary conversation, I made Mr David Wark Griffith announce that he would produce *Helen of Troy*, and I made him defend the Keystone comedy. It seemed to me then as now that there is nothing incongruous in these subjects; properly made, they would be equally unrefined, but *Helen of Troy*, being in the grand manner, would be called "artistic." Mr Griffith has not made *Helen of Troy*, and the pre-eminent right to make it has passed from his hands. The Keystone, with its variations, needs still an authoritative defender and an authoritative critic. It is one of the few places where the genteel tradition does not operate, where fantasy is liberated, where imagination is still riotous and healthy. In its economy and precision are two qualities of artistic presentation; it uses still everything commonest and simplest and nearest to hand; in terror of

32

gentility, it has refrained from using the broad farces of literature—Aristophanes and Rabelais and Molière—as material; it could become happily sophisticated, without being cultured. But there is no fault inherent in its nature, and its virtues are exceptional. For us to appreciate slap-stick may require a revolution in our way of looking at the arts; having taken thought on how we now look at the arts, I suggest that the revolution is not entirely undesirable.

⋙ If it were my intention to improve this book by rewriting it, I might be tempted to try an analysis in greater depth of the Keystone comedy. But I'm not sure I could do it well and some of the discussions I have read, in terms of various schools of analysis and also of economics, have brought me closer to sets of abstractions than to the Keystone in its natural essence. There have also been some good ones, by critics who kept their eye fixed on the events transpiring so madly and so profusely on the screen and related them to general ideas.

Clearly I am satisfied with this account in its general outlines. The belligerent tone was justified at the time and the undertone of apprehension, of fear that the Keystone's qualities would pass forever from the screen, has been justified by events. A few television comedians occasionally use slapstick well, but it is terribly premeditated, it lacks the conviction Sennett and his boys and girls brought to the art. Red Skelton is, I suppose, the best practitioner of the style and while I have no affection for him, I frequently admire him, as I do not admire Lewis and Martin, who are galvanic enough, but whose electric charges come from the baseplug of formula, not from the lightning stroke of genius. The one place genius asserted itself in comedy, after the Keystones, was in the work of The Marx Brothers. It has always seemed to me that *A Night at the Opera* is one of the few great films.

33

When Chaplin said he'd like to throw a pie again, but he wouldn't do it right, he wrote the epitaph of slapstick in this particular phase. You have to feel that it is the only right way to say what you want to say, you have to believe in it utterly, if it is not to become tiresome and what the Keystone never was, vulgar. ❧

"I am here to-day":
Charlie Chaplin

For most of us the grotesque effigy dangling from the electric sign or propped against the side of the ticket-booth must remain our first memory of Charlie Chaplin. The splay feet, the moustache, the derby hat, the rattan walking-stick, composed at once the image which was ten years later to become the universal symbol of laughter. *"I am here to-day"* was his legend, and like everything else associated with his name it is faintly ironic and exactly right. The man who, of all the men of our time, seems most assured of immortality, chose that particularly transient announcement of his presence, "I am here to-day," with its emotional overtone of "gone to-morrow," and there is always something in Charlie that slips away. "He does things," said John S. Sargent once, "and you're lucky if you see them." Incredibly lucky to live when we have the chance to see them.

It is a miracle that there should arise in our time a figure wholly in the tradition of the great clowns—a tradition requiring creative energy, freshness, inventiveness, change— for neither the time nor the country in which Charlie works is exceptionally favourable to such a phenomenon. Stranger still is the course he has run. It is simple to take *The Kid* as the dividing line, but it is more to the point to consider the phases of Charlie's popularity, for each phase corresponds to one of the attacks now being made upon his integrity. He is on the top of the world, an exposed position, and we are all sniping at him; even his adherents are inclined to say that "after all" he is "still" this or the other thing. One goes to his pictures as one went to hear Caruso, with a ghoulish speculation as to the quantity of alloy in the "golden voice." It is because Charlie has had all there ever was of acclaim that he is now surrounded by deserters.

That he exists at all is due to the camera and to the selective genius of Mack Sennett. It is impossible to dissociate him entirely from the Keystone comedy where he began and worked wonders and learned much. The injustice of forgetting Sennett and the Keystone when thinking of Chaplin has undermined most of the intellectual appreciation of his work, for although he was the greatest of the Keystone comedians and passed far beyond them, the first *and decisive* phase of his popularity came while he was with them, and the Keystone touch remains in all his later work, often as its most precious element. It was the time of Charlie's actual contact with the American people, the movie-going populace before the days of the great moving pictures. He was the second man to be known widely by name—John Bunny was the first—and he achieved a fame which passed entirely by word of mouth into the category of the common myths and legends of America, as the name of Buffalo Bill had passed before. By the time the newspapers recognized the movie as a source of circulation, Charlie was already a known quantity in the composition of the American mind and, what is equally significant, he had created the first *Charlot*. The French name which is and is not Charlie will serve for that figure on the screen, the created image which is, and at the same time is more than, Charlie Chaplin, and is less. Like every great artist in whatever medium, Charlie has created the mask of himself—many masks, in fact—and the first of these, the wanderer, came in the Keystone comedies. It was there that he first detached himself from life and began to live in another world, with a specific rhythm of his own, as if the pulse-beat in him changed and was twice or half as fast as that of those who surrounded him. He created then that trajectory across the screen which is absolutely his own line of movement. No matter what the actual facts are, the curve he plots is always the same. It is of one who seems to enter from a corner of the screen, becomes entangled or involved in a force greater than himself as he advances upward and to the centre; there he spins like a marionette in a whirlpool, is flung from side to side, always in a parabola which seems centripetal until the madness of the action hurls him to refuge or compels him to flight at the opposite end of the screen. He wanders in, a stranger, an impostor, an anarchist; and passes again, buffeted, but unchanged.

◦§ For a book about popular American entertainment, the number of French words used is perhaps excessive. The one I am most inclined to defend is *Charlot* for the character Chaplin created on the screen before he began to make feature-length pictures. It is used to distinguish "the little tramp" on the screen from the citizen, tax-payer, house-owner, individual; it is an attempt to say in a single word, that Charlie Chaplin was a creative artist, that unlike many excellent and many second-rate people who played in the movies he was *not playing himself.* "Charlie" was after all, the name we called Chaplin— whereas the figure on the screen had no name until the French invented one for him. I could have used "the little tramp" or put the name "Charlie" in quotes but both seemed awkward. I did not, as a critic implied, attach an "arcane significance" to the French name, but when the same critic said that *Charlot* meant nothing more than Charlie Chaplin he was simply wrong. *Charlot* was a figure existing only on the screen and the great critical error was in confusing him with the man whose imagination brought him to life there.

The description of the typical line of movement Chaplin created for that figure seems to me accurate, but I wish I hadn't described it so exclusively in geometrical terms. Or that the terms excited the visual imagination more immediately. The high degree of Chaplin's control of his material (including himself) is proved by the fact that a diagram of his movement can be made—but it remains a diagram. ॐ

The Keystone was the time of his wildest grotesquerie (after *Tillie's Punctured Romance,* to be sure), as if he needed, for a beginning, sharply to contrast his rhythm, his gait, his gesture, *mode,* with the actual world outside. His successes in this period were confined to those films in which the world intruded with all its natural crassness upon his detached existence. There was a film in which Charlie dreamed himself back into the Stone Age and played the God of the Waters—wholly without success because he contrasted his fantasy with another fantasy in the same tempo, and could neither sink into nor stand apart from it. But in *His Night Out* the effect is perfect, and is intensified by the alternating coincidence and syncopation of rhythm in which Ben Turpin worked with him. Charlie's drunken line of march down a stairway was first followed in parallel and then in not-quite-parallel by Turpin; the degree of drunkenness was the same, then varied, then returned to identity; and the two, together, were always entirely apart from the actuality of bars and hotels and fountains and policemen which were properties in their existence. In this early day Charlie had already mastered his principles. He knew that the broad lines are funny and that the fragments—which are delicious—must "point" the main line of laughter. I recall, for example, an exquisite moment at the end of this film. Turpin is staggering down the street, dragging Charlie by the collar. Essentially the funny thing is that one drunkard should so gravely, so soberly, so obstinately take care of another and should convert himself into a policeman to do it; it is funny that they should be going nowhere, and go so doggedly. The lurching-forward body of Turpin, the singular angle formed with it by Charlie's body almost flat on the ground, added to the spectacle. And once as they went along Charlie's right hand fell to one side, and as idly as a girl plucks a water-lily from over the side of a canoe he plucked a daisy from the grass border of the path, and smelled it. The function of that gesture was to make everything that went before, and everything that came after, seem funnier; and it succeeded by creating another, incongruous image out of the picture before our eyes. The entire world, a moment earlier, had been aslant and distorted and wholly male; it righted itself suddenly and created a soft idyll of tenderness. Nearly everything of Charlie is in that moment, and I know no better way to express its elusive quality than to say that as I sat watching the film a second time, about two hours later, the repetition of the gesture came with all the effect of surprise, although I had been wondering whether he could do it so perfectly again.

This was the Charlie whom little children came to know before any other and whose name they added to their prayers. He was then popular with the people; he was soon to become universally known and admired—the Charlie of *The Bank* and of *Shoulder Arms;* and finally he became "the great artist" in *The Kid.* The second period is pure development; the third is change; and the adherents of each join with the earlier enthusiasts to instruct and alarm their idol. No doubt the middle phase is the one which is richest in memory. It includes the masterpieces *A Dog's Life, The Pawnshop, The Vagabond, Easy Street,* as well as the two I have just mentioned, and, if I am not mistaken, the *genre* pictures like *The Floorwalker, The Fireman, The Immigrant,* and the fantastic *Cure.* To name these pictures is to call to mind their special scenes, the atmosphere in which they were played: the mock heroic of *The Bank* and its parody of passion; the unbelievable scene behind the curtain in *A Dog's Life;* Charlie as policeman in *Easy Street,* which had some of the beginnings of *The Kid;* Charlie left marking time alone after the squad had marched away in the film which made camp life supportable. Compare them with the very earliest films, *The Pile Driver* and the wheel-chairman film and so on: the later ones are richer in inventiveness, the texture is more solid, the emotions grow more complex, and the interweaving of tenderness and gravity with the fun becomes infinitely more deft. In essence it is the same figure —he is still a vagrant, an outsider; only now when he becomes entangled in the lives of other people he is a bit of a crusader, too. The accidental does not occur so frequently; the progress of each film is plotted in advance; there is a definite rise and fall as in *A Dog's Life,* where the climax is in the curtain scene toward which tends the first episode of the dog and from which the flight and the rustic idyll flow gently downward. The pace in the earlier pictures was more instinctive. In *The Count* the tempo is jerky; it moves from extreme to extreme. Yet one gets the sense of the impending flight beautifully when, at the close, Charlot as the bogus count has been shown up and is fleeing pell-mell through every room in the house; the whole movement grows tense; the rate of acceleration perceptibly heightens as Charlot slides in front of a vast birthday cake, pivots on his heel, and begins to play alternate pool and golf with the frosting, making every shot count like a machine gunner barricaded in a pill-box or a bandit in a deserted cabin.

It was foreordained that the improvised kind of comedy should give way to something more calculated, and in Charlie's case it is particularly futile to cry over spilled milk because for a long time he continued to give the *effect* of impromptu; his sudden movements and his finds in the way of unsuspected sources of fun are exceptional to this day.

[1] See Appendix.

40

In *The Pawnshop* Charlie begins to sweep and catches in his broom the end of a long rope, which, instead of being swept away, keeps getting longer, actively fighting the broom. I have no way to prove it, but I am sure from the context that this is all he had originally had in mind to do with the scene. Suddenly the tape on the floor creates something in his mind, and Charlie transforms the back room of the pawnshop into a circus, with himself walking the tight rope—a graceful, nimble balancing along the thin line of tape on the floor, the quick turn and coming forward, the conventional bow, arms flung out, smiling, to receive applause at the end. Again, as ever, he has created an imaginary scene out of the materials of the actual.

"The egregious merit of Chaplin," says T. S. Eliot, "is that he has escaped in his own way from the realism of the cinema and invented a *rhythm*. Of course the unexplored opportunities of the cinema for eluding realism must be very great."

It amused me once, after seeing *The Pawnshop*, to write down exactly what had happened. Later I checked up the list, and I print it here. I believe that Chaplin is so great on the screen, his effect so complete, that few people are aware, afterward, of how much he has done. Nor can they be aware of how much of Chaplin's work is "in his own way"—even when he does something which another could have done he adds to it a touch of his own. I do not pretend that the following analysis is funny; it may be useful:

Charlot enters the pawnshop; it is evident that he is late. He compares his watch with the calendar pad hanging on the wall, and hastily begins to make up for lost time by entering the back room and going busily to work. He takes a duster out of a valise and meticulously dusts his walking-stick. Then proceeding to other objects, he fills the room with clouds of dust, and when he begins to dust the electric fan, looking at something else, the feathers are blown all over the room. He turns and sees the plucked butt of the duster—and carefully puts it away for to-morrow.

With the other assistant he takes a ladder and a bucket of water and goes out to polish the three balls and the shop sign. After some horseplay he rises to the top of the ladder and reaches over to polish the sign; the ladder sways, teeters, with Charlot on top of it. A policeman down the street looks aghast, and sways sympathetically with the ladder. Yet struggling to keep his balance, Charlot is intent on his work, and every time the ladder brings him near the sign he dabs frantically at it until he falls.

A quarrel with his fellow-worker follows. The man is caught between the rungs of the ladder, his arms imprisoned. Charlot calls a boy over to hold the other end of the ladder and begins a boxing match. Although his adversary is incapable of moving his arms, Charlot sidesteps, feints, and guards, leaping nimbly away from imaginary blows. The policeman interferes and both assistants run into the shop. By a toss of a coin Charlot is compelled to go back to fetch the bucket. He tiptoes behind the policeman, snatches the bucket, and with a wide swing and a swirling motion evades the policeman and returns. He is then caught by the boss in another fight and is discharged.

He makes a tragic appeal to be reinstated. He says he has eleven children, so high, and so high, and so high—until the fourth one is about a foot taller than himself. The boss relents only as Charlot's stricken figure is at the door. As he is pardoned, Charlot leaps upon the old boss, twining his legs around his abdomen; he is thrown off and surreptitiously kisses the old man's hand. He goes into the kitchen to help the daughter and passes dishes through the clothes wringer to dry them—passes a cup twice, as it seems not to be dry the first time. Then his hands. The jealous assistant provokes a fight; Charlot has a handful of dough and is about to throw it when the boss appears. With the same motion

42

Charlot flings the dough into the wringer, passes it through as a pie crust, seizes a pie plate, trims the crust over it, and goes out to work.

At the pawnshop counter pass a variety of human beings. Charlot is taken in by a sob story about a wedding ring; he tries to test the genuineness of goldfish by dropping acid on them. Sent to the back room, he takes his lunch out of the safe, gets into another fight, in which he is almost beating his rival to death when the girl enters. Charlot falls whimpering to the floor and is made much of. He returns to the counter and the episode of the clock begins.

A sinister figure enters, offering a clock in pawn. Charlot looks at it; then takes an auscultator and listens to its heartbeat; then taps it over crossed fingers for its pulmonary action; then taps it with a little hammer to see the quality, as with porcelain; then snaps his thumb on the bell. He takes an augur and bores a hole in it; then a can-opener, and when he has pried the lid off he smells the contents and with a disparaging gesture makes the owner smell them, too. He then does dentistry on it, with forceps; then plumbing. Finally he screws a jeweler's magnifying glass into his eye and hammers what is left in the clock, shakes out the contents, measures the mainspring from the tip of his nose to arm's length, like cloth, squirts oil on the debris to keep it quiet, and, lifting the man's hat from his head, sweeps the whole mess into it and returns it with a sad shake of the head.

A pearl-buyer has meanwhile come in and Charlot retraces his steps to the back room (carefully stepping over the buyer's hat) and begins to sweep. His broom becomes entangled with a piece of tape, which fights back and gets longer and longer. Suddenly Charlot begins to tight-rope upon it, balancing with the broom, and making a quick turn, coming forward for applause. A final quarrel with the other assistant ensues. As they are swarming round the legs of the kitchen table, the boss comes in and Charlot flees, leaps into a trunk, and is hidden. As the others enter the room, the pearl-buyer, who has stolen all the valuables, holds them up with a revolver. Charlot leaps from the trunk, fells the robber, and embraces the lovely maiden for a fade-out.

All of this takes about thirty minutes. I have put down nearly everything, for Chaplin is on the scene virtually all of the time. I am fairly certain that ninety per cent. of this film could not have been made, even badly, by anyone else. Analysis of *A Dog's Life* would give the same result: the arrival at the climax being a little more certain and the drama of the climax (the curtain scene—compared with the clock scene above) being more involved in the course of action.

⋖ In his book on Chaplin, Theodore Huff has done a sequence-by-sequence analysis of the same picture. Comparing the two, I find that in spite of all my care I had omitted a few bits. Proof of my point, that it is impossible to see everything Chaplin does, was double: Huff hadn't seen a few of the bits I recorded! ⋗

The plotting of these comedies did not destroy Charlie's inventiveness and made it possible for him to develop certain other of his characteristics. The moment the vagrant came to rest, the natural man appeared, the paradoxical creature who has the wisdom of simple souls and the incalculable strength of the weak. Charlie all through the middle period is at least half Tyl Eulenspiegl. It is another way for him to live apart from the world by assuming that the world actually means what it says, by taking every one of its conventional formulas, its polite phrases and idioms, with dreadful seriousness. He has created in Charlot a radical with an extraordinarily logical mind. Witness Charlot arriving late at the theatre and stepping on the toes of a whole row of people to his seat at the far end; the gravity of his expressions of regret is only matched by his humiliation when he dis-

44

covers that he is, after all, in the wrong row and makes his way back again and all through the next row to his proper place. It is a careful exaggeration of the social fiction that when you apologise you can do anything to anyone. The same feeling underlies the characteristic moment when Charlot is fighting and suddenly stops, takes off his hat and coat, gives them to his opponent to hold, and then promptly knocks his obliging adversary down. Revisiting once an old Charlie, I saw him do this, and a few minutes later saw the same thing in a new Harold Lloyd; all there is to know of the difference between the two men was to be learned there; for Lloyd, who is a clever fellow, made it seem a smart trick so to catch his enemy off guard, while Chaplin made the moment equal to the conventional crossing of swords or the handshake before a prize fight. Similarly, the salutation with the hat takes seriously a social convention and carries it as far as it can go. In *Pay Day* Charlot arrives late to work and attempts to mollify the furious construction-gang boss by handing him an Easter lily.

The Kid was undoubtedly a beginning in "literature" for Charlie. I realize that in admitting this I am giving the whole case away, for in the opinion of certain critics the beginning of literature is the end of creative art. This attitude is not so familiar in America, but in France you hear the Charlot of *The Kid* spoken of as "theatre," as one who has ceased to be of the film entirely. I doubt if this is just. Like the one other great artist in America (George Herriman, with whom he is eminently in sympathy), Charlie has always had the Dickens touch, a thing which in its purity we do not otherwise discover in our art. Dickens himself is mixed; only a part of him is literature, and that not the best, nor is that part essentially the one which Charlie has imported to the screen. *The Kid* had some bad things in it: the story, the halo round the head of the unmarried mother, the quarrel with the authorities; it had an unnecessary amount of realism and its tempo was uncertain, for it was neither serious film nor Keystone. Yet it possessed moments of unbelievable intensity and touches of high imagination. The scenes in and outside the doss-house were excellent and were old Charlie; the glazier's assistant was inventive and the training of Coogan to look like his foster-father was beautiful. Far above them stood the beginning of the film: Charlot, in his usual polite rags, strolling down to his club after his breakfast (it would have been a grilled bone) and, avoiding slops as Villon did, twirling his cane, taking off his fingerless gloves to reach for his cigarette case (a sardine box), and selecting from the butts one of quality, *tamping it* to shake down the excess tobacco at the tip—all of this, as Mr Herriman pointed out to me, was the creation of the society gentleman, the courageous refusal to be undermined by slums and poverty and rags. At the end of the film there was the vision of heaven: apotheosis of the long suffering of Charlot at the hands of the police, not only in *The Kid* —in a hundred films where he stood always against the authorities, always for his small independent freedom. The world in which even policemen have wings shatters, too; but something remains. The invincible Charlot, dazed by his dream, looking for wings on the actual policeman who is apparently taking him to jail, will not down. For as they start, a post comes between them, and Charlot, without the slightest effort to break away, too submissive to fight, still dodges back to walk round the post and so avoid bad luck. A moment later comes one of the highest points in Charlie's career. He is ushered into a limousine instead of a patrol wagon—it is the beginning of the happy ending. And as the motor starts he flashes at the spectators of his felicity a look of indescribable poignancy. It is frightened, it is hopeful, bewildered; it lasts a fraction of a second and is blurred by the plate glass of the car. I cannot hope to set down the quality of it, how it becomes a moment of unbearable intensity, and how one is breathless with suspense—and with adoration.

For, make no mistake, it is adoration, not less, that he deserves and has from us. He corresponds to our secret desires because he alone has passed beyond our categories, at one bound placing himself outside space and time. His escape from the world is complete and extraordinarily rapid, and what makes him more than a figure of romance is his immediate creation of another world. He has the vital energy, the composing and the functioning brain. This is what makes him æsthetically interesting, what will make him for ever a school not only of acting, but of the whole creative process. The flow of his line always corresponds to the character and tempo; there is a definite relation between the melody and the orchestration he gives it. Beyond his technique—the style of his pieces—he has composition, because he creates anything but chaos in his separate world. "You might," wrote Mr Stark Young, wise in everything but the choice of the person addressed, "you might really create in terms of the moving picture as you have already created in terms of character." As I have said, the surest way to be wrong about Charlie is to forget the Keystone.

This is precisely what Mr Stark Young would like him to do—and what Charlie may do if the intellectual nonsense about him is capable of corrupting his natural wisdom and his creative gift. Mr Young has addressed an open letter to "Dear Mr Chaplin" [1] in which he suggests that Charlie play *Liliom* and *He Who Gets Slapped* and *Peer Gynt*. (Offended as I am by these ideas, I must be fair. Mr Young does say that better than all of these, "you could do new things written by or for you, things in which you would use your full endowment, comic and otherwise . . . develop things calculated strictly for it [the screen] and for no other art, made up out of its essential quality, which is visual motion and not mere stage drama photographed. . . .") This is, of course, corruption. It means that Mr Young has either not

[1] It appeared in *The New Republic* and will probably be found in *The Flower in Drama* (Scribners).

seen the Charlie of before *The Kid* (as I suspect from the phrase about creating in terms of character) or not liked him (which I am sure about); he has failed to recognize in *The Pawnbroker* "his full endowment, comic and otherwise." It implies to me that Mr Young would prefer a "serious film" and that suggests the complete absence of a critical sense, of taste and gusto, of wisdom and gaiety, of piety and wit. "The larger field" . . . "serious efforts" . . . "a more cultured audience" . . . "the judicious"—O Lord! these are the phrases which are offered as bribes to the one man who has destroyed the world and created it in his own image!

There is a future for him as for others, and it is quite possible that the future may not be as rich and as dear as the past. I write this without having seen *The Pilgrim*, which ought to be a test case, for the two films which followed *The Kid* (*Pay Day* and *The Idle Class*) determined nothing. If the literary side conquers we shall have a great character actor and not a creator; we shall certainly not have again the image of riot and fun, the created personage, the annihilation of actuality; we may go so far as to accomplish Mr Stark Young's ideal and have a serious work of art. I hope this will not happen, because I do not believe that it is the necessary curve of Charlie's genius—it is the direction of worldly success, not in money, but in fame; it is not the curve of life at all. For the slowing-up of Charlie's physical energies and the deepening of his understanding may well restore to him his appreciation of those early monuments to laughter which are his greatest achievement. He stood then shod in absurdity, but with his feet on the earth. And he danced on the earth, an eternal figure of lightness and of the wisdom which knows that the earth was made to dance on. It was a green earth, excited with its own abundance and fruitfulness, and he possessed it entirely. For me he remains established in possession. As it spins under his feet he dances silently and with infinite grace upon it. It is as if in his whole life he had spoken only one word: "I am here *to-day"*—the beginning before time and the end without end of his wisdom and of his loveliness.

◄§ What am I, as a critic, to make of this? It is excited writing toward the end and I am brought up sharp by the word "adoration" which I wouldn't use now, the word having, even more than it used to, the foolish overtone of "adorable" (as for babies). But I still think that Chaplin was entitled to something vastly more complex than admiration, that a portion of gratitude and even something of the profound respect we call awe is his due.

I have shifted to the present tense. I cannot write as I once did, but I can express my deep feeling that Chaplin has been badly treated and that the critics of his art were stupidly affected by the enemies of his politics. When *M. Verdoux* appeared—the masterpiece of his later style, a picture before which the critics should have bowed in silent respect—some of them had the effrontery to suggest that Chaplin go back to the baggy pants and the rattan walking stick—but it was not Chaplin's youth they were trying to recapture, it was their own. He had followed a natural line of growth—a rare phenomenon in the distracting world of the movies—and they were asking him to have died twenty years ago.

Fortunately for the world, Chaplin was wiser than his critics, he outgrew his youth, he was not afraid of maturity, he escaped from his own formula, not into something unsuited to his talents, but into the full flowering of those talents which the formula was beginning to strait-jacket. One of the things for which we can without reservation thank the sound track is that it compelled Chaplin to develop all his capacities. He was resentful under this compulsion, he had never needed words (and as Élie Faure pointed out many years ago, he was the only one who never "talked," never made the motions of talking, in the silent pictures). But he had implied sound. Look-

49

ing at one of his old pictures in a projection room, without piano or orchestra, you "heard" the glissando of a harp as he slid across a dance floor and the thump of the drums, the plucking of violin strings, the spiral of woodwinds and a hundred other sounds—his movements were music.

His words were not. His decision to be his own writer was probably the right one; it eliminated the dreadful dialogue of the kind of script-writer who is not in essence a writer at all; it brought a kind of plain talk to the screen. It was flawed by the same kind of sentimental clichés one finds in his situations and gestures, by a flatness corresponding to the primitive settings and the uninspired camera-work of all his pictures. He made movies year after year as if the rest of Hollywood didn't exist, as if the cinematographer was still cranking the camera by hand in the glare of the sun, as if lighting hadn't become a special skill and the set-designer was still a carpenter. In part this can be traced to Chaplin's unique situation as the only star financing his productions with his own, not bank, money. But beyond this imposed economy, a kind of austerity operated to keep the pictures simple, to concentrate attention, not to disperse it. The language of the dialogue-movie would have been inappropriate and Chaplin seemed always to be trying to arrive at the concision and plainness of the silent-movie title, sometimes falling into its stereotyped phrases, but usually avoiding its flowery "mood" language.

As a writer and as composer of music for his films, Chaplin remains an amateur. He gains because his movies (and his alone) are the product of a single individual, as a novel is or a poem. But the theatrical arts are not novels or poems, and a powerful man can use the skill of others, as Wagner did, to carry out his intent, without doing everything himself. There was evidence in *A Woman of Paris* that Chaplin could be a great director, but all we can be sure of is that he was the best director for his own films. They would have been better, they would have contributed more to the art of the movies, if he hadn't insisted on himself as the solitary source of all the inspirations a movie requires.

Yet he created masterpieces.

One of the consequences of writing this book was that I came to know some of the people I admired and Chaplin was one of them. Our connection was professional, our meetings always had to me some of the atmosphere of an interview arranged by a press-agent, which they were not. In perhaps a dozen meetings, I can recall only one during which anything that was personal transpired. I had come West to work on a radio program and saw Chaplin at Dave Chasen's restaurant on Christmas or New Year's eve, I've forgotten which, and he asked me to dinner the next night. When I arrived he inquired about my health and (it was wartime and accommodations in hotels were difficult to get) whether I was comfortable. I reassured him on all points, but said that I didn't sleep well in Hollywood, at which he said, "Gilbert, no one sleeps well any more." I note this as the only general comment on the human condition I ever heard him make; everything else was either about his work or about his ideas which, at that time, obsessed him. For most of the evening he was protesting against the stupidity of the networks (I was working for CBS at the time) in refusing him a regular quarter-hour a week to talk to the armed forces. When I suggested that he had a better way to express what he wanted to say, he brushed me aside, as if I had asked him to do a *Shoulder Arms* again.

Professionally he was pleased that I had written about him, as he was pleased with any critical praise. He knew that I was not the first to appreciate his genius—Waldo Frank and Vachel Lindsay had long preceded me and a writer in an English weekly, whom I read in 1916, had done a remarkable study of *A Night at the Show.* I had referred with pleasure to Chaplin and with displeasure to his imitators as early as 1916, but priority in these matters is of small account. Some time after the release of *M. Verdoux,* an English actor asked Chaplin if he was pleased with what I had written about him. Chaplin replied that no one had ever written anything significant about him except the French. (Those who believe that Chaplin was was "spoiled" by the critics may take note of this.)

I am sorry my work hadn't given him greater satisfaction and I wish I knew precisely what he found in the admirable French criticism of his work that made it significant to him because that would give us a clue to what he thinks the essence of his genius is. I suspect that he cannot express that essence in words, that it must be conveyed in his work—and there are many interesting attempts in every major language to make the discovery for him. I am deterred from adding to them. But not from recording my pleasure.

The greatest performance I ever saw him give occurred on the same night as his bad-tempered attack on the networks. I had finally shifted his thoughts to the picture he was then doing, which was *Verdoux* . . . It surprised me that in view of the publicity about his private life he had chosen to do a movie about a man who murders one wife after another, but the moment he began to tell me about the picture I fell completely under his spell. It was Chaplin's habit to act out his pictures—I think it was part of his creative process—and I had seen him do it once before, when he played all the great moments of *Modern Times* after dinner at Sam Goldwyn's house. He did *Verdoux* for me at a restaurant and came to the scene of the streetwalker whom Verdoux takes to dinner, dropping poison into her wineglass. The whore tells her story, stopping now and again to reach for her glass, to lift it, to set it down again, unsipped. At the end, exhausted, she puts her hand out again for the glass. "Then I reach over," said Chaplin, "and I say 'I think there's a bit of cork in your wine' and I flick it out . . ." At this point he made a gesture, almost imperceptible, so accurate, so controlled and delicate, that I was dazzled—and it didn't seem to me that the moment came off nearly as well in the film. I had seen the creative event itself.

But, of course, we all have seen it, over and over again. The feeling I had, watching the gesture in *His Night Out,* wondering whether he could do it as well the next time, marks precisely the difference between Chaplin and all the others, of whom we know with certainty that it will be the same and will remind us that this is a repetition, whereas with him it always seems created, fresh and new and dazzling, on the spot.

His defects do not rise out of his virtues, they rise from that part of his total personality which is at war with his genius. Whenever a picture runs into a bad patch it is because Chaplin is doing something under some intellectual compulsion, which may be only the compulsion to make a picture successful at the box-office and is often the compulsion to prove a point, some intellectual concept he has defended, to prove himself right. It would give me the greatest pleasure if he proved me wrong with the picture he has made abroad. The publicity suggests that it is a criticism of those unfortunate American attitudes which exiled him. In the dispute between him and the State Department (and with that portion of the American people the State Department attitude represents) I am totally on his side. But I do not think he is his best defender. He is the best defender of others, of those deprived of defence who have to turn to him to represent them in the high courts of justice. He has pleaded their cause against the brutality of the world and I wish he were content to let others plead his. ৯৬

Say it with music

~§ The opening remark below is, fortunately, only a lead-in, not the main theme. Technology has made it meaningless. The popular song of twenty years ago is likely to lead the hit parade five years from now and sentimental parents, remembering "their song," are startled to hear it on the lips of their offspring who attach new emotions to it. One generation danced to Emil Coleman's music or stood five deep watching Eddy Duchin play and certain melodies acquired their special quality. A generation later they appear in musical film biographies or vast television tributes to composers and new records are made, new (and dubious) interpretations by eccentric soloists are added, and the old songs are popular again.

They are not always as we remembered them. When *I've Told Every Little Star*, which is pure enchantment, returned, I discovered that the words were a little different and, in fact, that my memory, having played me false, had introduced a false syncopation to adjust the melody to my wrong words. For this sort of error, we compensate by our emotional attachment. The other differences come from changes in musical style. Just as two generations ago the classics were subjected to "ragging," ragtime when it now reappears is jazzed up, and jazz in turn will be rocked if not rolled. And on top of this the incapacity of certain popular singers to keep on the pitch, the deliberate manipulation of the time to conform to a "personal" way of singing, corrupt the pureness of the originals.

This isn't anything new. The fortunate composers are those who write for the stage and, even more, for the movies. They know that in one place, at least, their music will be performed as written. They have virtually no control over the way recordings are made and, as their incomes depend to a degree on the goodwill of the most popular recording artists, they have to submit to elaboration of the simple, simplification of the complex, unpredictable variations in tempo, divergence from the key —and be grateful.

Their objective is popularity. Many song-writers are under contract to publishers of sheet-music, getting so much a year, as any other employee does. They have to turn out hits before the time for renewal comes around. There is, moreover, their "union," ASCAP. To achieve the top classification in ASCAP means a large annual income which goes on long after a composer has ceased to be active, which provides for his widow and children when he is dead. And classification is based on product, on the number of times the songs of a composer are performed. In these conditions it is not surprising that the song-writing business is as sharply focused on statistics as sponsors are on ratings. It surprised me when Irving Berlin confessed that he envied the composers of *Yes, We Have No Bananas,* although he knew perfectly well he wouldn't have taken any great pleasure in composing the song himself. He had never had a sensational runaway bestseller, zooming up to a million copies in so short a time. He was, to be sure, speaking as a publisher as well as a composer, and he faced the realities of his double business. He has since reached the position where he needs envy no one —but the pressure to produce weighs heavily on everyone in the business—to produce hits. It is surprising that so many good songs continue to be written. ॐ

The popular song is never forgotten—except in public. Great events and seven-day-wonders pass into oblivion. Hobson, who was a hero, became a prohibitionist; Aguinaldo, a good citizen; McKinley, a martyr—but *Good-by, Dolly Gray, In the Good Old Summer Time,* and *Just Break the News to Mother* are immortal in our private memories and around them crystallize the sights and sounds and smells, the very quality of the air we breathed when these songs were in their high day. A more judicious pen than mine may write about these songs without sentimentality; I cannot. For in addition to the pathos of time past, something else brings an air of gentle melancholy to "words and music." In recent years a change has come and the popular song is no longer written to be sung, but to be played. The new song that can't be sung has virtues of its own—on the whole they are virtues I prefer. But I doubt whether it will ever be, as the old song was, a clue to the social history of our time.

The popular song is so varied, so full of interest, that for a moment at least one can pretend that it isn't vulgar, detestable, the ruin of musical taste, and a symptom of degeneracy; we can pretend also that *Less Than the Dust* isn't more artistic than *Swanee.* Since the Spanish-American War the American popular song (including the foreign song popular in America) has undergone the most interesting modulations; it has expressed everything except *fin de siècle.* Out of the 'nineties persisted a characteristic song: *Ta-ra-ra-boom-de-ay,* the chorus and tune of which, woven into mysterious words about "three little niggers in a peanut shell" I must have heard at the same time as *Daisy* with its glorification of the simple life "on a bicycle built for two." Since then, for a rough generalization, we have had three types of popular song: the exotic-romantic, the sentimental, and the raggy-gay. The sentimental song we have always with us. "That sweet melody with a strong mother appeal" is advertised on the back of "Those Black Boy Blues" and Irving Berlin writes *When I Lost You* between *Alexander's*

Ragtime Band and *Some Sunny Day*. At moments it is dominant and a fake ballad, with a simple and uninteresting tune, makes *After the Ball,* by Charles K. Harris, a world wonder. Or we have a simplification of the whole history of romantic love in *Love Me and the World Is Mine.* The curious about social life in America may compare this song with *I'm Just Wild About Harry.*

Beaumarchais, who knew no jazz, makes Figaro say that what can't be said can be sung—and this applies far more to the sentimental than to the obscene. Think of the incredible, the almost unspeakable idea in the following, presumably spoken by a father to a child:

> Down in the City of Sighs and Tears,
> Down by the White Light's Glare,
> Down in the something of wasted years,
> You'll find your mamma there!

◄§ This is sheer arrogance. It is not difficult to get the text of any published song, but I refused to take the trouble to discover what "something" was in the original and I still do. As for the imagery mentioned below, it is probably derived from a rather touching story by O. Henry.

The sentimental ballads before 1920 were often about babies, separation, death. The theme of the sentimental song two generations later was the impotence of the male. The popularity of these doleful ditties is a phenomenon for social scientists to analyze. Few of them were distinguished in melody, none in words. They celebrated sadly the failure of the man to keep his woman—and in quite different terms from the earthier Negro songs of tne woman who failed to hold her man—but was going out to get herself a better one. Laments for lost love are proper in song and have been since the beginning of time, but the plaintiveness, the self-accusation, the emasculatory

58

atmosphere of the American songs of the '30s and '40s on this theme are surely exceptional. It is as if Tin Pan Alley had discovered a race of American men unknown to artists in any other field—the nearest thing to this impotent male is the bumbling father in the movies, the excellent provider who hasn't one tenth the intelligence or will-power of his wife. These songs may have become popular after the traumatic experience of the crash of 1929 and the depression that followed, the awful necessity of admitting that our whole system of society had broken down, that we were no longer the new world of endless opportunity, that another world, hostile to our own, might be coming into existence. Perhaps. But it seems to me that the American male was never—before, during, or after the crash—so committed to love or so desolate when disappointed as the song writer made him out to be.

It is, of course, possible that the song-writers of the period were the best social psychologists of them all and anticipated David Riesman by a decade, our lugubrious hero being, in fact, the alienated man, seeking for direction from the outside. A most entertaining analysis of the songs we've been singing has been made by the semanticist, S. I. Hayakawa. He contrasts the blues which "arise from the experiences of a largely agricultural and working class . . . minority with a social and cultural history different from that of the . . . majority." (The two omitted words are "Negro" and "white," Hayakawa's point being that the cultural, not the racial differences, are the major influences.) In the commercial popular song we can, he says, trace "the triple-threat semantic disorder" of Idealization, Frustration, and Demoralization. With neat quotations he lets us watch the disease develop. We begin with those songs of longing for the unknown perfect one, ("Will I ever find the girl . . . who is my ideal?") who then, to fulfil the prophecy seems to "come along"

59

("I took one look at you . . . and then my heart stood still") at which point domestic bliss is assured ("everything is rosy now"). Since it doesn't last, we get the songs of loneliness and of betrayal (where Hayakawa attributes the sentiments to women, not to men) and so into the demoralized state in which the anguished one will "never love again," but will instead "buy myself a paper doll to call my own"—that retreat into the symbolic world which the psychiatric profession "classifies as schizophrenia."

The climate of the blues is quite different. The abandoned one will sing "I'm a young woman, and I ain't done running round." There are, to be sure, popular songs more confident, more cheerful than the dolorous ones quoted, but it is hard to recall any singer who has become enormously popular by identifying himself with roaring good cheer, whereas from the time of the crooners through the criers, adolescents (of all ages) have rewarded the sad and the lonely troubadours. The song that totally satirizes the June-Moon school cannot ever be really popular, it is a tangent to the big circle of emotions and must remain so, it is to be done (as it was so beautifully done by Liza Kirk singing *I've Been Faithful to You*) on the stage or in a nightclub, it is not for the biggest sales.

It interests me to note that most of the sloppy songs I mentioned by name were actually of the pre-War-I era, and so were the satiric numbers. The age of debunking during which this book was written had little effect on our songs. One reason for this lay in the temperaments of Jerome Kern and Irving Berlin, one a spiritual descendant of the Viennese school, the other a balladeer of the big city streets. Satire did not come naturally to either of them. Gershwin combined some of the prime elements of these two dominant figures, and joined them, but the intellectual quality which is essential to satire was only half at home in him. It was entirely at home in Cole

Porter—whose most popular numbers are *Begin the Beguine* which no one attempts really to sing as it is a rhythm piece, and *Night and Day* which is sentimental in its words but so ominous in its melody that the total effect is prodigious. ❧

Or consider the pretty imagery and emotion of *I'm Tying the Leaves,* as sung by a precocious and abominable child who has been told that mother will die when the leaves begin to fall. It would be easy to say that these songs are gone never to return; but it was only two years ago that *They Needed a Songbird in Heaven—so God Took Caruso Away* ("idea suggested by George Walter Brown" to the grateful composers). I do not dare to contemplate *A Baby's Prayer at Twilight* or to wonder what constituted the *Curse of an Aching Heart;* but history has left on record the chorus of

> My Mother was a Lady
> Like yours, you will allow,
> And you may have a sister
> Who needs protection now;
> I've come to this great city
> To find a brother dear,
> And you wouldn't dare insult me, sir,
> If Jack were only here.

It was for songs like this that a masterpiece in another *genre,* the burlesque popular song, was created. I have heard *A Working Girl Was Leaving Home* credited to the brothers Smith (the boys the mother-in-law joke invented, according to George Jean Nathan, and for their sins they should have written this song) and to the late Tiny Maxwell, and to an unidentified English source. Its title and chorus at least are immortal:

(Then to him these proud words this girl did say):

> Stand back, villain; go your way!
> Here I will no longer stay.
> Although you were a marquis or an earl.
> You may tempt the upper classes
> With your villainous de-mi tasses,
> But Heaven Will Protect the Working Girl.

The cure for the sentimental song is the ironic; and irony, it happens, is not what America lives on. Even so mild an English example as *Waiting at the Church* gained its popularity chiefly from the excellent tag line:

> Can't get away
> To marry you to-day.
> My wife won't let me.

Yet appearing from time to time we had a sort of frank destruction of sentimentality in our songs. Some, like *I Picked up a Lemon in the Garden of Love,* appeal directly to the old "peaches" tradition; but we went further. In the same year as the romantic *Beautiful Garden of Roses*—it was one of the early years of the dance craze—we heard *Who Are You With To-night* (to-night? . . .) down to "Will you tell your wife in the morning, Who you are with to-night?" and the music perceptibly winked at the words. *I Love My Wife (but, Oh, You Kid!)* had little quality, but the dramatization of an old joke in *My Wife's Gone to the Country* rose to a definite gaiety in the cry of "Hooray! Hooray!" So, too, one line in the chorus of *I Wonder Who's Kissing Her Now,* a song which skilfully builds up a sentimental situation in order to tear down with two words:

> Wonder who's looking into her eyes,
> Breathing sighs, telling lies . . .

where the music pretended to make no difference between the last two phrases, except for softening, sweetening the second. Yet another in the malicious mould is *Who Paid the Rent for Mrs Rip Van Winkle (when Rip Van Winkle Went Away)*—unforgettable for the tearing upward phrase to a climax in the first *Rip* with a parallel high note on the second.

The characteristic of these songs is that they were rather like contemporary fiction in giving form to social phenomena without expressing approval or disapproval. Eternal love and fidelity go by the board with "the dreamy, peachy, creamy, Vision of pure delight," the companion who will not be mentioned to "your wife in the morning." "Tell me, Mister, Is it your sister . . ." Well, hardly.

There were, beside these realistic treatments of marriage (I continue the professorial tone) a few slightly suggestive songs, and these also were opposed to current morality, and these also were popular. One was called, I think, *Billy,* and purported to be a statement of virginal devotion: "And when I walk, I always walk with Billy . . ." and so following, to "And when I sleep, I always—dream of Bill." There were delicious implications in *Row, Row, Row,* as Al Jolson sang it; earlier still was Hattie Williams's song *Experience,* in *The Little Cherub.* The persistence of these songs is something of a miracle and the shade of difference between the permissible and the impossible is of vast importance in the success of a song. About fifteen years separate *Who Are You With To-Night?* (I quote all these songs and titles from memory, but I am fairly sure about the grammar of this one; if it was printed "whom" it was sung "who") and *He May be Your Man (but he comes to see me sometimes),* and the second song is more explicit; when Edith Wilson or Florence Mills sang the repeat chorus it shocked her audience. Essentially it is the same thing, only, fifteen years ago, the questionable stanza would have been left to the unauthorized street version.

63

The exotic romantic song in America has little to do with all of this. Before the professional glorification of our separate states began, we had the series of Indian songs of which Neil Moret's *Hiawatha* is the outstanding exemplar. The stanza is almost as hard to sing as *The Star-spangled Banner*; the chorus—it is always the chorus which makes a song—is banal, a pure rum-tum-tiddy. Yet it was more than popular, for it engendered a hundred others. *Cheyenne* and (musically) *Rainbow* are its descendants. *Hiawatha* bewilders and baffles the searcher after causes; but its badness as a song explains why the Indian song was submerged presently in the great wave of negro songs which have shown an amazing vitality, have outlived the Hawaiian exotic, and with marvelous adaptability (aided by one great natural advantage) have lived through to the present day.

The negro song is partly, but not purely, exotic. Remembering that songs are written on Forty-fifth Street in New York and put over in New York cabarets, it is easy to see how *California in September* (a dreadful song) and *Carolina* (I recall five songs embodying the name of that state; the latest is superb) are also exotic; and how *Over on the Jersey Side* and songs about Coney Island came to be written to glorify New York as a summer resort. The rustic period, again, reacts against sophistication as *In the Shade of the Old Apple Tree* reacts against the exoticism of the sheltering palm. Neither rustic nor local, however, achieves the highest success, and it is left for the Pacific to give the last setting before the shouting song of the negro and his plaintive cry are triumphant in our music.

First, however, the era of the waltz song. In earlier days America had little to do with the waltz out of comic opera and *The Merry Widow* and *My Hero* and *Beautiful Lady* and the superb melodies from *Gypsy Love* and from *Die Czardas Fürstin*, of which I forget the American name, and something from *The Arcadians* came from anywhere across the sea and captured us. The *Velia Song* and *The Girl from the Saskatchewan* were better than their corresponding waltzes; *The Chocolate Soldier* had pages of music as good as *My Hero*—many better. Only *The Dollar Princess* managed to put over its less ostentatious pieces—and that is rather amusing, since Leo Fall is held by the Viennese to be the true successor of Johann Strauss.

The mention of that great name makes it clear that the waltz song itself is a hybrid; for whatever words have been sung to *The Beautiful Blue Danube,* the music was meant to be played and for the dance; it was not meant for song. Yet the slow tempo, the softness, the gentle sentimentality of the waltz lends itself peculiarly to song—and to memory. I do not think it has anything to do with the really great things in our popular songs, but I cannot resent its success —any more than I can resent the success of another song, wholly out of our American line—*Un Peu d'Amour*. This was the last great song before the war; it held France and England and America enslaved to its amorous longing. Something more cheery and more male had to be found for the English soldier, who eventually picked up *Tipperary* (also a song of nostalgia), and for the American something snappier; but *Un Peu d'Amour* persisted during the war. To hear a soldier standing on the fire-step on a dark night, leaning his cheek against the disc of his Lewis gun, and softly humming *Un Peu d'Amour,* was to recognize that for actual millions that song and a few others like it, and not the great music to the condition of which all art aspires, were all of beauty and all of exaltation they were ever to know. The materials in this particular case were not tawdry, only equivocal. For it was a better song as *A Little Love* than in the French. The word *amour* means, but does not signify, the same thing as the word love, and *"pour t'entendre à ce moment suprême, Murmurer tout bas, tout bas: Je t'aime"* has connotations not transferred to the English. The song is a fake French and a good Anglo-Saxon piece of sentiment, precisely the counterpart of the waltz song. Like them it conquered a world.

Lehar and Monckton and Caryll and Fall and Kalman followed successes with moderate failure, and at the same time revues and American musical comedies stepped out grandly. I note three songs from this source which actually claimed all of the popular attention. The song to be sung was at its best in the Princess shows—best of all in *The Siren Song* from *Leave it to Jane*. It is Mr Kern's masterpiece, a sophisticated, tidy score with amusing and unexpected retards and pauses, with a fresh freedom of tonalities. *The Siren Song* never actually came up to *The Love Nest* in acclaim; Mr Hirsch's bid for immortality is almost contemptible in words and music and has only a single point of interest—the three notes against two in the second line of the chorus ("cozyandwarm" instead of, say, nice—and—warm). It is impermissible in a man who only a year later wrote *It's Getting Very Dark on Old Broadway.*

The third song is *Say It With Music.* Mr Berlin is as much responsible as any one for the turn from the song-to-be-sung to the song-to-be-played; yet he is so remarkable that he can reverse himself, and just as in 1915 he produced a whole revue (*Stop! Look! Listen!*) from which not one song became really popular, so, seven years later, when the singing-song had gone out, he produced a revue and gave us one more of his tributes to the art he adores. It isn't musically half as interesting as *I Love a Piano;* but it is much more singable and it has great virtues. Nothing that a jazz orchestra can do has any effect on the purity of its musical line. I wonder whether it may not be the last of the songs; for we are now full in the jazz age and darkness has set in.

66

Tearing a passion
to ragtime

❧ The reader who is at all familiar with the literature of jazz is cordially urged to skip the next two chapters entirely. They are the work of an amateur, a lover of popular music who was not (and still is not) a musicologist. The vocabulary now current in discussion of American music didn't exist at the time and the specks of theory embedded in the following pages represent what composers in the idiom of Les Six, for example, thought jazz was in the early 1920's. I happened to know some of them and also some of their American disciples and thought I was on safe theoretic ground if I followed them.

Some fifteen years after the book was published, a music critic wrote that I was the first person who had opened the world of jazz to him and then denounced me mercilessly for having misled him so completely as to the nature of that world. My major error was, clearly, in writing about the jazz that existed at the time in New York and Chicago, on records (there was no radio then)—instead of writing about the music being created in the bordellos of New Orleans, making its way up to Chicago—and totally unknown, except to its practitioners and a few of their patrons. I was, however, writing about what *was* popular, not about what should have been or would eventually become popular.

In 1925 (I think) I found a record of *The Livery Stable Blues* by The Dixieland Jass Band (so spelled) and later used it to relieve the tedium of lectures I gave, playing for contrast George Gershwin's *Stairway to Paradise*. This was my first contact with the music that eventually was to dominate the field. It came slowly into prominence, moving downtown from Harlem in New York, moving always to the center from peripheral spots in big cities.

Anyone who has read anything about jazz in the past fifteen years knows that the subject has set off more quarrels, all of them conducted with furious bad tempers, than ever raged around Wagner or Debussy or Strawinsky. Also a language has come into existence which makes the vocabulary of the classical music critic a mere primer in comparison. Program notes—such as you get on the envelope of a recording nowadays—are far more obscure than those Philip Hale used to write for the Boston Symphony and the snobbery about the right words, not to mention liking the right things, is colossal. It is time, I suspect, for someone to rescue popular music from its embattled enthusiasts. To the moderate in these matters (who proclaims himself what used to be called a square and is willing to listen to all kinds of music and to varied arguments) I recommend Marshall Stearns' *The Story of Jazz*.

In the battle between the cults, a grave injustice was done to the commercial band. The worst thing a favorite could do was to become successful—and to play a moviehouse or a nightclub. The enthusiasts were bent on keeping their finds secret and the moment a lot of people became enthusiastic, the old-timers turned upon their idol—he had "gone commercial"! There was a sort of resolute Bohemianism in this, it was cultish and arty. To be sure, Benny Goodman made changes in the composition of his band and in what he played when he moved from a small club to a movie palace, but he and his band were tremendously good in both places. And the people who had never pretended to be anything but what they were—leaders of bands for dancing at restaurants—Whiteman and Lopez and Bernie and the rest—did not deserve the contempt of the specialists. They did nothing to undermine the new music that was coming—and it is quite possible that their work, which had also been met with hostility, was necessary groundwork. Cultishness is always a symptom of insecurity and is as silly among minorities as the fear of eccentricity is among major groups.

I will not say that the thing to do about modern American music is to listen to it and stop writing about it, although this would be a blessing. I suggest that a lot of listening to the various masters, listening to what they say about their own and others' music, as well as to what they play, might correct the excesses of the fanatics. I am thinking particularly of Jelly Roll Morton's recorded interview with Alan Lomax in which he wanders from one style to another, searching for the right way for him to play what he calls "the national anthem"—namely, *The Stars and Stripes Forever*. It is like a compendium of the development of American music, without partisanship.

The violence of the partisans centers more on music to be heard than music to sing, and in this concentration they are right, because the popular song isn't at this moment particularly interesting, it is certainly not musically interesting except for the work of half a dozen men, most of them so long known in their field that they were recognized as masters in the original edition of this book. Most of them wrote musical shows of various kinds; observe them on the list of current song writers, and, except for Richard Rodgers, you have most of the people who seem to have fresh musical ideas copiously enough to be called creative. The rest manipulate half a dozen inherited styles. &

69

There is only one sense in which the word "rag" has any meaning in connexion with music, and that is not conveyed in the word "ragtime." Ragtime is not, strictly speaking, time at all; neither is *tempo rubato:* and eminently safe composers have been known to score their music *con alcuna licenza,* which leaves the delicate adjustment of time to the performer. A certain number of liberties may be taken with ragtime, and beyond this point no liberties may be taken. Within its framework, ragtime is definite enough; and you must syncopate at precisely the right, the indicated and required moment, or the effect of the syncopation is lost.

It is only when one looks at the songs that one realizes what ragtime means. For literally, the music, which has always been with us and yet arrived only yesterday, has torn to rags the sentimentality of the song which preceded it. The funeral oration for the popular song was preached in the preceding chapter. This is the coroner's inquest, with the probable verdict that the popular song was unintentionally killed by ragtime, which is in turn being slowly poisoned by jazz. A neat, unobtrusive, little man with bright eyes and an unerring capacity for understanding, appropriating, and creating strange rhythms is in the foreground, attended by negro slaves; behind him stands a rather majestic figure, pink and smooth, surrounded by devils with muted brass and saxophones. They are Irving Berlin and Paul Whiteman, and they will bear listening to. What is more, they will make listening a pleasure.

It seems strange to speak of the great George M. Cohan as a disappointment in anything he has ever tried; but looking back at the early years of the century, when it was apparent that he would be our most popular song writer as well as our most popular everything else, suddenly calls to mind that our Georgie, the Yankee Doodle Dandy, just failed to make it. Irish wit and an extraordinary aptitude for putting into simple song the most obvious of jingo sentiments were not quite enough. The situation which Cohan faced at the time was beginning to be complicated: the ballad song was becoming a bore; the substitutes for it had failed to absorb rhythms fresh enough and swift enough to please the public. And between dawn and daylight ragtime was upon us.

Enfin Berlin *vient!* How much ragtime had been sung and played before, no man may calculate; it had been heard in every minstrel show, and its musical elements were thoroughly familiar. What was needed was a crystallization, was one song which should take the whole dash and energy of ragtime and carry it to its apotheosis; with a characteristic turn of mind Berlin accomplished this in a song which had no other topic than ragtime itself. *Alexander's Ragtime Band* appeared with its bow to negro music and its introduction of *Swanee River;* it was simple and passionate and utterly unsentimental and the whole country responded to its masterful cry, *Come on and hear!* Presently *Waiting for the Robert E. Lee* is heard—a levee song and one would say that the South had already conquered; but Berlin is first of all a writer of rag and the Southern theme is dropped (the negro music remaining) while he gives the world two further dazzling rags: *The International* and *The Ragtime Violin.* Everybody's doing it was true of singing and dancing and—composing. For the day which was awakened with *Alexander's Ragtime Band* was a day of extraordinary energy and *Skeleton Rags* and *Yiddische Rags* and *Pullman Porters' Balls,* and everything that could be syncopated, and most things that could not, paid their quota to ragtime. There have been periods equally definable: the time of the waltz song, of the ballad, of jazz. What makes the first rag period important was its intense gaiety, its naïveté, its tireless curiosity about itself, its unconscious destruction of the old ballad form and the patter song. The music drove ahead; the half-understood juggling with tempo which was to become the characteristic of our music led to fresh accents, a dislocation of the beat, and to a greater freedom in the text. For half a century syncopation had existed in America, anticipating the moment when the national spirit should find in it its perfect expression; for that half century serious musicians had neglected it; they were to study it a decade later when ragtime had revealed it to them.

The early rags were made to be sung and they were sung, universally. What the departing queen of Hawaii offered in *Aloha Ohe* was swiftly integrated into the existing form and *On the Beach at Wai-ki-ki* is a rag in every respect, using material which is foreign only in appearance. (The fact that ragtime can without offense adapt the folk song of nearly every nation—and is only absurd with Puccini and Verdi's worst when it takes them seriously—indicates how essentially decent an art ragtime is.) The nostalgia which later came into Hawaiian songs does not exist in this first greatly popular song of those islands any more than it exists in the *Robert E. Lee* or in *When that Midnight Chu-chu Leaves for Alabam'*. Berlin himself was not untouched by the Hawaiian scene and in *The Hula-Hula* he wrote a song superior, in my mind, to *Wai-ki-ki*, yet never popular in the great sense. The rush and excitement of *Wai-ki-ki* aren't in *The Hula-Hula;* some one had told too much about the undulations of the dance and the sensuousness of the southern Pacific. Louis Hirsch, years later, did the same thing in *'Neath the South Sea Moon*, a respectable piece of work. But it remained for Jerome Kern, a decade and more after *Wai-ki-ki*, to make another Hawaiian song popular. This was *Ka-lu-a* (out of *Good Morning, Dearie*) and in every way it showed cleverness and intelligence. For it was not a song of Hawaii at all. It was produced in an Englishy garden, sung by women in hoopskirts surrounding Oscar Shaw in evening clothes; and it is all, all a longing for—I think it is a longing for Wai-ki-ki the song, as much as for the beach. The old romantic properties are in the words, slightly set off in mockery by the premature and internal rhymes; they are suffused with memory and the music is purely nostalgic. It was not for nothing that Mr Kern wrote *The Siren Song*.

◄§ The way a melody can be ragged so that its original sentiment completely vanishes is demonstrated by Maxine Sullivan's singing of *Annie Laurie.* "Gave me her promise true" has a sweetness if you sing it as in the original; Miss Sullivan perversely shifts the emphasis so that it comes out "gave me HER promise true," it makes no sense in the context, it is a musical hotfoot, and like everything she does, exciting. It was not this song, but *Loch Lomond,* that became a turning point in the transformation of revered sentimental classics into jazzy tunes for the professional to sing, separated from the theme of the original, musically a new creation. Many popular songs used classic or folk themes for their original emotional value. But when Miss Sullivan got through with a Scots ballad it had about the same value as *A Tisket a Tasket.*

In the paragraph below a phrase occurs which I should not use now and I haven't been too sure about leaving it in. I think it is fair to say that the words "nigger mammy" could have been used without giving offense in 1924. To use it now, in a new work, would be gratuitously insulting, but it is not insulting to say that it had been used. I hope the change in our vocabulary means that a change in feeling has occurred, because it is of small value to suppress a word and keep the thought. The substitutes for the offensive word thought up by racist Southerners seem to me abominable.

The foolish play on the name of Paul Whiteman which is also left in the book indicates, again, my ignorance of that jazz which was to come, a few years later, from the South. §►

The moment Hawaii faded out nothing was left but the South, and here the music began to drive the words with a hard hand and a high check. An observer unfamiliar with the nature of ragtime would conclude that the American people had a complex about nigger mammies and that the

73

sublimation thereof was in the popular song. The true explanation is simpler. The mother element is, of course, a sure-fire hit in the pictures and in song; but the nigger mammy enters for the same reason as cotton fields and picaninnies and Georgia—because our whole present music is derived from the negro and most composers of popular songs haven't yet discovered that the musical structure is applicable to other themes as well. (George Gershwin's *Walking Home with Angeline* in *Our Nell,* Cole Porter's *Blue Boy Blues,* about the Gainsborough painting, and Berlin's *Pack Up Your Sins and Go to the Devil* are examples of the transfer successfully accomplished, and gratifying, too. Best of all is *Limehouse Blues,* by Philip Braham, a veritable masterpiece in the *genre.)* There exist a number of natural themes—slavery, the local scene (Swanee River), the cabin, the food, and the train whereby one arrives. The genius of Tin Pan Alley has worked upon this material, and in both words and music has been amazingly imitative, uninventive, and dull. Yet the idea of taking a theme and so handling it that the slightest variation from the preceding use of the same material shall give the effect of novelty and freshness is a sound one—we know from the history of Greek drama. Alas! there was little novelty and the tradition was never firm enough to bear what they did to it. Yet they had their reward, if they can accept it vicariously, for one of them, not at the beginning and not at the end, which is not yet, took the old material and fashioned a great song. His name is George Gershwin and the song which, before the blue-jazz age, achieves pre-eminence is *Swanee.* To have heard Al Jolson sing this song is to have had one of the few great experiences which the minor arts are capable of giving; to have heard it without feeling something obscure and powerful and rich with a separate life of its own coming into being, is—I should say it is not to be alive. The verse is simple and direct, with faint foreshadowings of the subtly divided, subtly compounded elements of

74

the chorus where the name "Swanee," with a strong beat, long drawn and tender, ushers in the swift passages leading to the repetition, slow again, of the name; and the rest of the song is the proper working out of a problem in contrasting cadences, and in dynamics. After the chorus, and in another key, there is a coda, a restatement of the theme with a little more restraint, and then, surprisingly and gratefully, for the first time the introduction of the final bars of *Swanee River*. I analyze this song as if it could be taken apart and the essence of it remain; the truth is that it bears inspection and is worth inspection because it has a strongly individual quality, a definite personal touch. Mr Gershwin has progressed[1] in his technical handling of syncopation, as in *Innocent Ingénue Baby* (not primarily a song to be sung or for the dance, but to hear; it is musically the solution of a problem in pauses, and the answer is delicious); but in *Swanee* he is at his highest point, for he has taken the simple emotion of longing and let it surge through his music, he has made real what a hundred before him had falsified. He should "do it again."

Swanee was popular, but by no means as popular as *Some Sunny Day,* a song by Mr Berlin which will simply not bear analysis. I hold Mr Berlin to be still the foremost writer of popular music in spite of it. Three years and a masterly technique separate the two songs and *Some Sunny Day* is devilishly clever, but most of it isn't properly singable. It is a good dance tune; analyzed, it resolves itself into a weak treatment of *Old Black Joe* (clever Mr Berlin to take the first bar of the old *verse* for the first bar of his *chorus*) and a regrettable quotation again of *Swanee River*. The arrangement is neat, and the inversion of the first bar halfway through the chorus, when the song has dribbled into meaningless fragments, has lost all intensity and is suddenly revived and refreshed, while the words of the first bar are repeated—that sufficiently indicates the master hand. The

[1] See page 92.

75

words are among Mr Berlin's weakest and it is hard to believe that at the same moment he was revelling in the two *Music Box Revues,* in *Say It With Music* and *Pack Up Your Sins,* which are superb.

It is not entirely an accident that a consideration of the effect of ragtime on popular song begins and ends with Irving Berlin. For as surely as *Alexander's Ragtime Band* started something, *Pack Up Your Sins* is a sign that it is coming to an end. For this tremendous piece of music simply cannot be sung; it baffled the trained chorus on its first appearance, it can hardly be whistled through, and, although the words are good, they aren't known. Ragtime is now written for jazz orchestra; three phrases occupy the time of two; four, five, and even six notes the time of two or three. The words which are becoming wittier than ever are too numerous, too jostled, to be sung, and the melodic structure with arbitrarily changing beat baffles the voice and the mind as much as it intrigues the pulse and the heel. The popular song and the ragtime song are vanishing temporarily. But something terrible and wonderful has already taken their place. Already there is an indication of how they will return and—I am tired of speaking of Mr Berlin, but I can't help it—Mr Berlin has indicated how and where. His *All by Myself* is in essence a combination of the sentimental song with ragtime—so it was sung by Ethel Levey. And it is played with enthusiasm by jazz orchestras—a perceptible pleasure is ours from recognizing something entirely simple and sentimental weaving its way through those recondite harmonies.

◄§ *All by Myself* is a pleasant song, but not nearly as much an indicator toward the future as I thought it was. *Pack Up Your Sins,* on the other hand, apparently made a greater impression on me than on Berlin. I can recall only one first rate composition of his in the same style: *Let's*

Face the Music and Dance, the finale of one of the movies
with which Berlin almost revolutionized the art of the
movie musical. The fact is that Berlin apparently had to
choose between becoming a composer with an intricate
structure and remaining the balladist-troubadour. It never
was in his bent to study composition and his natural gift
for playing with rhythms was quite enough to satisfy the
demands of the stage and the screen, so that he kept on
writing music to be sung or to be danced, not to be lis-
tened to. Skilful pianists and band-leaders found enough
complexity in Berlin to make his work seem in the current, so that you never felt he lagged behind anyone. But
twenty years after my commentary, with its wrong guesses,
was written, when *Annie Get Your Gun* was produced,
Berlin had departed so little from his original inspiration
that the score seemed to me the work of a young man,
and Berlin was pleased to be told this. There isn't a style
he couldn't have imitated, successfully; on the other hand,
no one successfully imitated the style that was essentially
Berlin's.

Just after sound came in, he did a series of song-and-
dance movies on a relatively small scale, notably *Top Hat.*
These were as neat, as suffused with a simple charm, as the
Princess shows had been on the stage. And like the *Princess* shows they were engulfed in bigger, if not better,
things. Berlin went along, putting together bits and pieces
of former shows, composing new songs, making himself
a sort of national monument with his celebrations of all
the holidays in the calendar, and it was only when he returned to the stage, with *Call Me Madam,* as well as
Annie, that the spring of melody gushed again, totally
unspoiled. It has been a notable career, notable among
other things for Berlin's capacity for excluding alien ideas,
for not ever letting himself be long diverted from the
course his talents dictated—and this in a profession known

for hasty picking-up of every other man's style the moment a hit appeared. The man who wrote *This Is the Army* was the man who wrote *Yip! Yip! Yaphank!* a generation before; he had grown in skill and in range, but he had lost no essential quality and *This Is the Army, Mr. Jones* stands right beside *Oh, How I Hate to Get up in the Morning*, as fresh in every sense of the word, as lively, as totally right for the occasion. It is, in fact, one of Berlin's marked characteristics that he can seize the spirit of an event and translate it into popular song, almost as if he were our official composer—which, with *God Bless America* he very nearly became. But this is not the better side of his genius. The better side is the less monumental, the highly personal, the sentimental even, which is simple and completely unpretentious, and honest. ℰ❧

If the song returns in any way the ancient protest against its vulgarity will also return, and it is worth making up our minds about it now. The popular song takes its place between the folk song and the art song. Of these the folk song hardly exists in America to-day: *Casey Jones* and *Frankie and Johnny* are examples of what we possess and one doesn't often hear them sung along country roads or by brown-armed men at the rudder in ships that go down to the sea. The songs of the Kentucky mountains (English in provenance) and the old cowboy songs are both the object of antiquarian interest—they aren't as alive as the universal *Hail, Hail, the Gang's All Here* or *We Won't Go Home 'til Morning*. If we refuse to call our ragtime folk music, then we must face the fact that we are at a moment in history when folk songs simply do not occur. (Even the war failed to give us very much; it is interesting to note that besides *Katy* and *Mr Zip*, the songs written by the best and most expert of our composers, Berlin and Cohan, were both meant to be sung and were sung—and this took place in the midst of the change to the unsingable type.) At the opposite extreme is the art song—usually the setting and degradation of a poem written for its own sake and usually—let us say dull. The composers of art songs are about fifty paces behind the symphonists and the symphonists are nearly nowhere. The result is that we aren't in any sense *nourished* by the writers of art songs and, since we are a musical people, for better or for worse we fall back on the popular song. It is to me a question whether we would be better citizens and more noble in the sight of God if we sang *Narcissus* instead of *The Girl on the Magazine Cover*.

Once in a while something between the art and the popular song appears, and it is called *My Rosary* or *The End of a Perfect Day,* and it is unbearable. Because here you have a pretentiousness, a base desire to be above the crowd and yet to please (it is called "uplift," but it does not mean exalt) the crowd; here is the touch of "art" which makes all things false and vulgar. To be sure, these songs, too, are popular; the desire for culture is as universal as it is depressing. And these are the only popular songs which are really vulgar. I will ask no one to compare them with the real thing. Compare them with false, trivial, ridiculous imitations of the real thing—it exists in some of the occasional songs which composers are always trying and which hardly ever come off. I recall a song written about the Iroquois fire; another about Harry K. Thaw ("Just because he's a millionaire, Everybody's willing to treat him unfair"). Only the two songs about Caruso succeeded, and there never was a good one about Roosevelt. Here is one written for Jackie Coogan in *Oliver Twist:*

When the troubles came so fast you kept on smiling,
Like a sunbeam 'mid the clouds up in the sky;
Though the rest were deep in crime
You stayed spotless all the time

79

Though they flayed you
Till they made you
Weep and cry.

When your little heart was aching for a mother's tender love,
Then the Lord looked down and heard you and blessed you
    from above.
Though they tried to make you bad
You stayed good, dear little lad.
Would God I could
Be half as good
As you
Oliver Twist.

The music is just like that, too. Lower than this—much
lower, at least—the popular song never dropped. These
songs *never* become actually, universally popular because
the general taste is too high. And I cheerfully set the lowest
example beside *A Perfect Day* for comparison. One type is
not obnoxious and the other is; one is common, the other
vulgar; one is strong and foolish, the other silly and weak.
The case for the popular song may as well rest in the solution of this dilemma as anywhere.

    ⋖§   In spite of the bold ending to this chapter, I am
afraid I was on uncertain ground when I wrote it. I still
find *The End of a Perfect Day* a dreadful song, but it
comes closer than it did to being "funny without being
vulgar" because it has become a stock piece for parody.
"The touch of 'art' which makes all things false and vulgar" is permissible in argument when one doesn't define
one's terms—I know I was groping about for the one word
which would encompass the bogus and the arty, for which,
as I've said, I settled on the French phrase, *le faux bon*.
    The trouble with my argument is that I hadn't at the
time thought out the implications of what I was doing and

certainly hadn't *placed* the popular arts in relation to either the fine arts or the folk arts. With my passion for them and my willingness to separate them from the great arts, I still hankered, I'm afraid, for a respectable position in society—I was, in short, doing what I accused others of doing, I was being impressed by a sort of intellectual snobbery. If I could get the popular song to be accepted *as* the folk song of to-day (not accepted as equal to it, but as the thing itself) I would somehow have justified it. This is nonsense.

I let myself in for it because the folk-song folk had gotten to me. I wasn't in rebellion against them as I was half-consciously in rebellion against the genteel tradition. Rebellion may be a sign of youth, failure to rebel when one should is a sign of immaturity and the foregoing discussion strikes me as by all odds the most immature in the entire book. I simply hadn't taken the trouble to think things out.

I have had to, since. I have at least made some distinctions which work in my own field. In general, the works we call classic express something we believe to be *eternal* and the classics of each nation are also held to say something about the universal nature or the universal plight of humanity. The folk art of a nation is more concentrated and it expresses the experience of a people, it speaks not for eternity, but for a long-known *past*. And the popular arts in each country express the *present*.

For America, the classic and the folk arts are both imported goods. This does not make them any less important —the structure of our common law and the basic concepts of our lives are also brought over. But the circumstance that our popular arts are home-grown, without the prestige of Europe and of the past, had thrown upon them a shadow of vulgarity, as if they were the products of ignorance and intellectual bad manners. I yearned, apparently, for respectability in behalf of the waifs I had adopted. I needn't have troubled—they were soon to achieve something far better. And I would have made my point more effectively if I had been willing to take them, as I asked others to take them, for what they were. They were good enough to stand on their own native feet. ❧

Toujours jazz

   ▷ It is only fair to repeat here the warning given on page 67. The reader who has the slightest acquaintance with contemporary jazz—and in particular with the literature that has grown up around popular music today—can find the following pages of only antiquarian interest. That the music and the music-makers noted here were the subjects of controversy will seem to him preposterous. It seems preposterous to me that for a year or two after the book appeared I was frequently asked to debate the merits of jazz—on the side of the devils who were destroying "good music." And I knew nothing except what I had written here. ◃

The word jazz is already so complicated that it ought not to be subjected to any new definitions, and the thing itself so familiar that it is useless to read new meanings into it. Jazz is a type of music grown out of ragtime and still ragtime in essence; it is also a method of production and as such an orchestral development; and finally it is the symbol, or the byword, for a great many elements in the spirit of the time—as far as America is concerned it is actually our characteristic expression. This is recognized by Europeans; with a shudder by the English and with real joy by the French, who cannot, however, play it.

   ▷ They've learned since. I believe there are some very refined enthusiasts for jazz who actually prefer recordings

83

made by French bands. On this point I am likely to go very patriotic. ঌঌ

The fact that jazz is our current mode of expression, has reference to our time and the way we think and talk, is interesting; but if jazz music weren't itself good the subject would be more suitable for a sociologist than for an admirer of the gay arts. Fortunately, the music and the way it is played are both of great interest, both have qualities which cannot be despised; and the cry that jazz is the enthusiastic disorganization of music is as extravagant as the prophecy that if we do not stop "jazzing" we will go down, as a nation, into ruin. I am quite ready to uphold the contrary. If— before we have produced something better—we give up jazz we shall be sacrificing nearly all there is of gaiety and liveliness and rhythmic power in our lives. Jazz, for us, isn't a last feverish excitement, a spasm of energy before death. It is the normal development of our resources, the expected, and wonderful, arrival of America at a point of creative intensity.

ঌঌ I have spoken of my good fortune in beginning my professional life with a subject that constantly developed. It is indeed a fortunate thing, not for individuals, but for all of us, that our popular music had vitality enough to carry it through a dozen manifestations, enough to outlive its excesses and remain one of our major contributions to the arts of the entire world. It happens that this is the one of my mythical seven about which I knew least, to the development of which I contributed nothing of significance. I can, all the more, testify to a disinterested satisfaction in the progress of this music. It is, indeed, possible that our music has given the only thorough demonstration of the merits of the popular arts. It went through many phases, each one of which added something to the essentials, and the steady line was held in spite of some silly aberrations which, often enough, were not in the music, but rose from adolescent fanatics or those delayed adolescents, so familiar in connection with many popular arts, who made religions out of minor sects. Trying to look over the entire field—every acre of which I had been sure was rich in vital minerals—I can see that the great area of the movies, for instance, did not yield nearly as well as I said it would. In 1935 (that is, long after the coming of sound) H. G. Wells could still see in the movies "the possibilities of becoming the greatest art form that has ever existed." Who can see such possibilities now? The movies were indeed "the lovely art" but few who worked in it really loved it. On the other hand, I have never known a composer, arranger, or player of popular music who wasn't enamored of the art he practised. Perhaps the fundamental success of jazz can be traced to this integrity among its practitioners. ❧

Jazz is good—at least good jazz is good—and I propose to summarize some of the known reasons for holding it so. The summary will take me far from the thing one hears and dances to, from the thing itself. The analysis of jazz, musically or emotionally, is not likely to be done in the spirit of jazz itself. There isn't room on the printed page for a glissando on the trombone, for the sweet sentimental wail of the saxophone, or the sudden irruptions of the battery. Nor is there need for these—intellectually below the belt— attacks. The reason jazz is worth writing about is that it is worth listening to. I have heard it said by those who have suffered much that it is about the only native music worth listening to in America.

Strictly speaking, jazz music is a new development—something of the last two years, arriving long after jazz had begun to be played. I mean that ragtime is now so specifically written for the jazz band that it is acquiring new characteristics. Zez Confrey, Irving Berlin, Fred Fisher, and Walter

Donaldson, among others, are creating their work as jazz; the accent in each bar, for example, is marked in the text— the classic idea of the slight accent on the first note of each bar went out when ragtime came in; then ragtime created its own classic notion,—the propulsion of the accent from the first (strong) note to the second (weak). In jazz ragtime the accent can occur anywhere in the bar and is attractively unpredictable. Rhythmically—essentially—jazz is ragtime, since it is based on syncopation, and even without jazz orchestration we should have had the full employment of precise and continuous syncopation which we find in jazz now, in *Pack Up Your Sins,* for example. It is syncopation, too, which has so liberated jazz from normal polyphony, from perfect chords, that M. Darius Milhaud is led to expect from jazz a full use of polytonic and atonic harmonies; he notes that in *Kitten on the Keys* there exists already a chord of the perfect major and the perfect minor. The reason why syncopation lies behind all this is that it is fundamentally an anticipation or a suspension in one instrument (or in the bass) of what is going to happen in another (the treble); and the moment in which a note occurs prematurely or in retard is, frequently, a moment of discord on the strong beat. A dissonance sets in which may or may not be resolved later. The regular use of syncopation, therefore, destroyed the fallacy (as I hold it) of the perfect ear; and this is one reason why Americans are often readier to listen to modern music than peoples who haven't got used to dissonance in their folk and popular music.

    Ș	An apparently well-informed and respected authority tells me that the essence of rock-and-roll is accentuation in the unexpected place, strong where we expect it to be weak. It is a solemn thought that at the time I felt it necessary to defend jazz, the essential music of rock-and-roll was being sung, if not recorded, in the South. Ș€

It is not only syncopation that makes us indebted to negro music. Another element is the typical chord structure found there, the characteristic variations from the accustomed. Technically described, one of the most familiar is the subdominant seventh chord with the interval of a minor instead of a major seventh—a method of lowering the leading tone which affects so distant a piece as *A Stairway to Paradise,* where the accented syllable of Par'-adise is skilfully lowered. (By extension ragtime also uses the "diminished third.") The succession of dominant sevenths and of ninths is another characteristic, and the intrusion of tones which lie outside of our normal piano scale is common.[1] Still another attack on the perfect chord comes from the use of the instruments of the jazz band, one for which ragtime had well prepared us. The notorious slide of the trombone, now repeated in the slide of the voice, means inevitably that in its progress to the note which will make an harmonious chord, the instrument passes through discords. "Smears," as they are refreshingly called, are the deadliest enemy of the classic tradition, for the ear becomes so accustomed to discords in transition that it ceases to mind them. (We hear them, of course; the pedants are wrong to say that we will cease to appreciate the "real value" of a discord if we aren't pained by it and don't leave the hall when one is played without resolution.) In contemporary ragtime, it should be noted, the syncopation of the tonality —playing your b-flat in the bass just before it occurs in the voice, let us say—is often purely a method of warning, an indication of the direction the melody is to take.

I put the strange harmonies of jazz first, not because they are its chief characteristic, but because of the prejudice against them. The suggestion is current that they are sounds

[1] My indebtedness, and, I supppose, the indebtedness of everyone who cares at all for negro music, is apparent—to Afro-American Folksongs, by Henry Edward Krehbiel (Schirmer).

which ought never to be uttered; and with this goes an attack on the trick instruments, the motor-horns, of the battery-man. The two things have nothing in common. The instruments of the jazz band are wholly legitimate and its characteristic instrument was invented by a German, after whom it is named, in the middle of the last century, and has been used in serious music by (and since) Meyerbeer—I refer to the saxophone. There is no more legal objection to the muted trombone than to the violin *con sordino*. And the opponents of jazz bands will do well to remember that the pure and lovely D-minor symphony of César Franck was thrown out as a symphony because it used the English horn. The actual sounds produced by the jazz band are entirely legitimate. We have yet to see what use they make of them.

In Krehbiel's book the whole question of rhythm is comparatively taken for granted, as it should be. Syncopation discovered in classic music, in the Scot's snap of the Strathspey reel, in Hungarian folk music, is characteristic of three-fifths of the negro songs which Krehbiel analyzed (exactly the same proportion, by the way, as are in the interval of the ordinary *major*). But it is such a normal phenomenon that I have never found a composer to be interested in it. Krehbiel, to be sure, does refer to the "degenerate form" of syncopation which is the basis of our ragtime, and that is hopeful because it indicates that ragtime is a development—intensification, sophistication—of something normal in musical expression. The free use of syncopation has led our good composers of ragtime and jazz to discoveries in rhythm and to a mastery of complications which one finds elsewhere only in the great composers of serious music. In describing the Dahoman war dances at the Chicago World's Fair, Krehbiel says:

"Berlioz in his supremest effort with his army of drummers produced nothing to compare *in artistic interest* with

88

the harmonious drumming of these savages. The fundamental effect was a combination of double and triple time, the former kept by the singers, the latter by the drummers, but it is impossible to convey the idea of the wealth of detail achieved by the drummers by means of exchange of the rhythms, syncopation of both simultaneously, and dynamic devices."

The italics are mine. I am fully aware of the difference between savage and sophisticated, between folk music and popular music; yet I cannot help believing that this entire statement, including the Berlioz whom I greatly admire, could be applied to Paul Whiteman playing *Pack Up Your Sins* or his incredible mingling of *A Stairway to Paradise* with a sort of *Beale Street Blues*.

Freedom with rhythm is audible—should I say palpable? —everywhere. *Stumbling* (Zez Confrey) is in effect a waltz played against a more rapid counter-rhythm, and is interesting also for its fixed groups of uneven notes—triplets with the first note held or omitted for a time, and then with the third note omitted. A similar effect with other means occurs in the treatment of three notes in *Innocent Ingénue Baby*, by George Gershwin, where the same note falls under a different beat with a delightful sense of surprise and uncertainty. Mr Hooker's words are equally tricky, for it isn't "Innocent-Ingénue-Baby" at all; it is Innocent Ingénue (*baby*). In *By and By* Gershwin has shifted an accent from the first to the second simply by giving the second the time-value usually given to the first, a fresh, delightful treatment of a sentimental expression. The variety of method is vastly interesting. Louis Hirsch, whom I rank fairly low as a composer for jazz, has done perfectly one obvious, necessary thing: stopped syncopating in the middle of a piece of ragtime. In the phrase "shake and shimmy everywhere" in *It's Getting Very Dark on Old Broadway,* he presents the whole-tone scale descending in two bars of full unsyncopated quarter-notes. In the works of Zez Confrey (they are issued with a snobbish tasty cover, rather like the works of Claude Debussy) the syncopation and the exploitation of concurrent, apparently irreconcilable rhythms is first exasperating and eventually exciting. They are specifically piano pieces and require a brilliant proficiency to render them.

It is a little difficult, unless one has the piano score, to determine what part is the work of the composer, what of the jazz orchestra. You can only be fairly certain that whatever melody occurs is the composer's, and that rhythmically he is followed with some fidelity. All you need to do is to listen to the violin, piano, or whatever instrument it is which holds the beat, to realize what the composer has given. Harmonization is often, and orchestration nearly always, left to other hands. Mr Berlin makes a habit now of giving credit to his chief collaborator, and he deserves it.[1]

Mr Berlin's masterpieces (June, 1923, but who shall say?) in jazz are *Everybody Step* and *Pack Up Your Sins.* I have written so much about him in connexion with song and shows that I can say little more. I see no letting down of his energy, none in his inventiveness. He is, oddly, one of the simplest of our composers. A good way to estimate his capacity is to play the more sentimental songs (*I'm Gonna Pin My Medal on the Girl I Left Behind, Someone Else May Be There While I'm Gone, All by Myself*) in slow time and then in fast. The amazing way they hold together in each tempo, the way in which the sentiment, the flow of the melody, disengages itself in the slow, and then the rhythm, the beat takes first place in the fast time, is exceptional. You cannot do the same with his own *Some Sunny Day,* nor with *Chicago* or *Carolina in the Morning.* Berlin's work is

[1] It has been clairvoyantly pointed out to me by another composer that Berlin's preëminence in ragtime and jazz may be traced to his solitary devotion to melody and rhythm; in the jazz sense there remains something always pure in his work. This supports the suggestion made in the next paragraph.

musically interesting, and that means it has a chance to survive. I have no such confidence in *Dardanella* or *Chicago*. The famous unmelodic four notes occur in the latter as in *Pack Up Your Sins* (the source is the same, but we need not go into that); the working out is vastly inferior. Fred Fisher's work is sledge hammer in comparison with Berlin's, and lacks Berlin's humour. Of that quality Walter Donaldson has some, and Gershwin much. Donaldson wrote Al Jolson's *Mammy* (I can't remember which, but I'm afraid I didn't like it), and a song I count heavily on: *Carolina in the Morning*. This song is, incidentally, a startling example of how jazz is improving the lyrics, for the majority of jazz songs are not meant primarily for singing, so the balladists take liberties, and not being held to a definite end-rhyme give us "strolling with your girlie when the dew is pearly early in the morning."[1] The music is clean, rapid, and audacious. It carries the introduction (of the chorus) almost to the point of exhaustion, suspending the resolution of its phrases until the last possible moment, and then lets go, with a vast relief on the long, somewhat yodelly note. Confrey has done the same thing in *Kitten on the Keys* where one bar is repeated five times with successive tightening of interest.

❧ I expected to be surprised in re-reading this book, but did not expect to read that I didn't like Jolson's *Mammy* song. As a word of warning, this does not refer to Gershwin's *Swanee* which is a Mammy-song of the first order of merit. Considerable ransacking of my memory and the memories of others fails to identify the Donaldson *Mammy*. ❧

[1] Internal, off-beat rhyme occurred as long ago as *Waiting for the Robert E. Lee*. But de Sylva has used it intelligently, but not expertly enough in *Where is the Man of My Dreams?* and Brian Hooker and William Le Baron make it a great factor in their highly sophisticated lyrics. So also Cole Porter.

Two composers are possible successors to Berlin if he ever chooses to stop. I omit Jerome Kern—a consideration of musical style will indicate why. I am sure of Gershwin and would be more sure of Cole Porter if his astonishing lyrics did not so dazzle me as to make me distrust my estimate of his music. Gershwin is in Berlin's tradition; he has almost all the older man's qualities as a composer (not as a lyrics writer; nor has he Berlin's sense of a song on the stage). That is to say, Gershwin is capable of everything, from *Swanee* to *A Stairway to Paradise*. His sentiment is gentler than Berlin's, his "attack" more delicate. Delicacy, even dreaminess, is a quality he alone brings into jazz music. And his sense of variation in rhythm, of an oddly placed accent, of emphasis and colour, is impeccable. He isn't of the stage, yet, so he lacks Berlin's occasional bright hardness; he never has Berlin's smartness; and with a greater musical knowledge he seems possessed of an insatiable interest and curiosity. I feel I can bank on him.

◆§ In 1926, Ring Lardner published a story called *Rhythm*. In his biography of Lardner, Donald Elder describes it: "about a popular composer who was nearly ruined by being taken seriously by intellectuals." Quite correctly sensing an implication in the story, Elder says, "It is amusing if not entirely convincing; and it is a clue to his own attitude about writers of any kind. If that attitude served as a defense, it was also genuine enough. For himself he chose to remain a popular writer in whatever field he worked."

Before this story was published, Ring Lardner and I had exchanged the letters for publicity quoted on page 128 and had become friendly—we never saw one another frequently enough to become friends, and I'm not sure that we would have, in any case, but he was aware of my great admiration professionally and of my great liking,

92

and as I saw him either with the Fitzgeralds or other close friends of his, our relation was always warm. I assumed then, and he knew it and said nothing to the contrary, that *Rhythm* was a fanciful story about someone like George Gershwin who might have been ruined by someone like me. Most critics of Lardner think it a story of relatively little merit and when I included it in *The Portable Ring Lardner* I did so on a confessed personal basis.

But the story, in a trifling way, brings up a point that was often made: the "intellectual's" appreciation of the popular artist might make him, in turn, try to win the favor of the intellectuals and fatally deprive him of the common touch. It is, as every thoughtful person knows, a preposterous idea, running counter to all the known facts among which the most deplorable is that the critics do not have nearly enough influence on the popular arts.

Gershwin was not only hailed by the critics, he was positively "taken up" by the *café society* which was just then coming into being. An intense, enormously self-centered, handsome and utterly likable person, he might easily have been spoiled by his quick success. I see no indication in his work that he was deflected for a moment from his natural direction. The only phrase in all I wrote of him that he picked out for comment was "insatiable interest and curiosity". How did I guess that, he asked me, and I could only answer that even then he seemed to me to be trying half a dozen styles in order to discover the one exactly right for him.

He found it and it carried him into the theatre and eventually into opera, but the push came originally from within the popular arts, from Paul Whiteman who wanted to "elevate" jazz and thought the right way was to give a concert at Aeolian Hall. Gershwin had already appeared at Aeolian Hall, as accompanist to Eve Gauthier in a group of his own songs. Miss Gauthier was not trying to

93

elevate anything, she sang songs in all styles, she liked Gershwin's, so she put them on her program—and it gave me great pleasure to be the middleman in bringing the composer and the singer together. For Aeolian Hall, Whiteman wanted something special and commissioned works by Victor Herbert as well as by Gershwin. The *Rhapsody in Blue* was an immense success.

It was clear that Gershwin had committed a crime, but the nature of the crime (rape or theft) was not determined, nor was there any agreement as to the victim. Was Gershwin merely a traitor to his class (the Tin Pan Alleyists) or had he violated the sacred shrines of music? He had departed from the sacred 32-bars, he had gotten himself orchestrated, there weren't any words to the thing. On the other hand, he had had the effrontery to borrow a designation from Liszt—and it wasn't (you know) really a Rhapsody at all, it didn't follow the form exactly. Besides, there was that schmaltzy passage!

The two-faced snobbery of the entire argument made it silly. Gershwin had certain natural gifts and they were developing naturally. He had some agreeable things to say and he said them in the tones that came to him. It is true he was learning a larger vocabulary, he was studying music because he loved music, he was impressed by the grandeur of the great composers—he was also young. He was too young to inflict harm on the classics and young enough not to be harmed by them. He went on his way, which was Broadway for part of the road, and he took other paths at times and some led to dead ends, for him. The *Concerto* was probably one of these; *Porgy and Bess* was not. No enthusiast for grand opera myself, I took pleasure only in the arias of *Porgy* and found the staging insufferably arty. It seemed to me that the style of opera had been imposed on the materials, it did not grow out of them. But if Gershwin had been "corrupted" it was by the lovers of opera, not by me. &

Banking on Porter is dangerous because essentially he is much more sophisticated in general attitude of mind than any of the others, and although he has written ragtime and patter songs and jazz of exceptional goodness, he has one quality which may bar him forever from the highest place—I mean that he is essentially a parodist. I know of no one else with such a sense for musical styles. A blues, a 1910 rag, a Savoy operetta serio-comic love song, a mother song—he writes them all with a perfect feeling for their musical nature, and almost always with satiric intention, with a touch of parody. It is only the most sophisticated form which is germane to him; in highly complex jazzing he is so much at home, his curiosity is so engaged, he feels the problem so much, that the element of parody diminishes. Yet *The Blue Boy Blues,* almost as intricate a thing as Berlin ever wrote, with a melody overlaid on a running syncopated comment, has a slight touch of parody in the very excess of its skill. Jazz has always mocked itself a little; it is possible that it will divide and follow two strains—the negro and the intellectual. In the second case Porter will be one of its leaders and Whiteman will be his orchestra. The song *Soon,* for example, is a deliberate annihilation of the Southern negro sentiment carefully done by playing Harlem jazz, with a Harlem theme, mercilessly burlesquing the *clichés* of the Southern song—the Swanee-Mammy element—in favour of a Harlem alley. Porter's parody is almost too facile; *Soon* is an exasperatingly good piece of jazz in itself. He is a tireless experimenter, and the fact that in 1923 others are doing things he tried in 1919, makes me wonder whether his excessive intelligence and sophistication may not be pointing a way which steadier and essentially more *native* jazz writers will presently follow. Native, I mean, to jazz; taking it more seriously. Whether any of them could compose such a ballet as Porter did for the Ballet Suédois is another question.

The other way is still open—the way of Sissle and Blake,

of Creamer and Layton, of A. Harrington Gibbs. The last is a name unknown to me ten days before the moment of writing; I do not know if it represents a Southern negro or a Welshman. But—if he has composed anything, if *Runnin'* *Wild* isn't a direct transcript of a negro devil-tune—he is in the school of the negro composers and he has accomplished wonders already. For *Runnin' Wild* is a masterpiece in its *genre*. Note the cleverness of the execution: the melody is virtually without accompaniment; it consists of groups of three notes, the interval of time being simple, and the interval of pitch in the group or between two successive groups, is quite conventional. Once three groups of three notes are played in succession; toward the end the group is twice lengthened to four notes; the orchestra is heard after each group has been sung, giving an unnerving effect of alternating sound and silence. But there is something more: There is the complete evocation of the two negro spirits—the darky (South, slave) and the buck (Harlem); the negro and the nigger. It ends with a shout which is lyrical and ecstatic at once, wild and free. It is an enchantingly gay piece, it expresses its title—one sees our own Gilda Grey stepping out in it bravely; it is, in a way, a summary of the feeling of negro music which *Shuffle Along* and its followers restored to prominence.

More must be said of the negro side of jazz than I can say here. Its technical interest hasn't yet been discussed by anyone sufficiently expert and sufficiently enthusiastic at the same time. In words and music the negro side expresses something which underlies a great deal of America—our independence, our carelessness, our frankness, and gaiety. In each of these the negro is more intense than we are, and we surpass him when we combine a more varied and more intelligent life with his instinctive qualities. *Aggravatin'* *Papa* (don't you try to two-time me) isn't exactly the American response to a suspected infidelity, yet it is humanly sound, and is only a little more simple and savage than we

96

are. The superb *I'm Just Wild about Harry* is, actually, closer to the American feeling of 1922 than "I always dream of Bill"; as expression it is more honest than, say, *Beautiful Garden of Roses;* and *He May be Your Man* is simply a letting down of our reticences, a frankness beyond us.

I shift between the two teams, Sissle and Blake, Creamer and Layton, uncertain which has most to give. Sissle and Blake wrote *Shuffle Along;* the others accomplished the intricate, puzzling rhythm of *Sweet Angelina,* one or two other songs in *Strut Miss Lizzie,* and *Come Along, I'm through with Worrying.* Of this song a special word can be said. It is based on *Swing Low, Sweet Chariot,* and imposes on that melody a negro theme (the shiftlessness and assurance of "bound to live until I die") and a musical structure similar to that applied to the same original by Anton Dvorak in the *New World Symphony.* I am only a moderate admirer of this work; I am not trying to put *Come Along* into the same category, for its value is wholly independent of its comparative merits; nor am I claiming that jazz is equal to or greater or less than symphonic music. But I do feel that the treatment of a negro melody, by negroes, to make a popular and beautiful song for Americans ought not to be always neglected, always despised. I say also that our serious composers have missed so much in not seeing what the ragtime composers have done, that (like Lady Bracknell) they ought to be exposed to comment on the platform.

&§ One of the most exciting manifestations of the music neglected at that time was the funeral music of the New Orleans bands. It has been made available in an unlikely place, a segment of *Cinerama Holiday,* with Papa Celestin leading the players through the streets of the city, away from the cemetery. The music begins as a dirge and slowly modulates into the triumphant declaration of *The Saints Go Marching In.* &∾

If they cannot hear the almost unearthly cry of the *Beale Street Blues* I can only be sorry for them; the whole of Handy's work is melodically of the greatest interest and is to me so versatile, so changing, in quality, that I am incapable of suggesting its elements. Observed in the works of others, the blues retain some of this elusive nature—they are equivocal between simplicity, sadness, irony, and something approaching frenzy. The original negro spiritual has had more respect, but the elements have been sparsely used, and one fancies that even in looking at these our serious composers have felt the presence of a regrettable vulgarity in syncopation and in the melodic line. *Jesus Heal' de Sick* is negro from the Bahamas; its syncopation, its cry, "Bow low!" are repeated in any number of others; the spirituals themselves were often made out of the common songs in which common feeling rose to intense and poetic expression —as in *Round About de Mountain,* a funeral song with the Resurrection in a magnificent phrase, "An she'll rise in His arms." The only place we have these things left, whether you call the present version debased or sophisticated, gain or loss, is in ragtime, in jazz. I do *not* think that the negro (in African plastic or in American rag) is our salvation. But he has kept alive things without which our lives would be perceptibly meaner, paler, and nearer to atrophy and decay.

I say the negro is not our salvation because with all my feeling for what he instinctively offers, for his desirable indifference to our set of conventions about emotional decency, I am on the side of civilization. To anyone who inherits several thousand centuries of civilization, none of the things the negro offers can matter unless they are apprehended by the mind as well as by the body and the spirit. The beat of the tom-tom affects the feet and the pulse, I am sure; in *Emperor Jones* the throbbing of the drum affected our minds and our sensibilities at once. There will always exist wayward, instinctive, and primitive geniuses who will affect us directly, without the interposition of the intellect;

98

but if the process of civilization continues (will it? I am not so sure, nor entirely convinced that it should) the greatest art is likely to be that in which an uncorrupted sensibility is *worked* by a creative intelligence. So far in their music the negroes have given their response to the world with an exceptional naïveté, a directness of expression which has interested *our* minds as well as touched our emotions; they have shown comparatively little evidence of the functioning of *their* intelligence. *Runnin' Wild,* whether it be transposed or transcribed, is singularly instinctive, and instinctively one recognizes it and makes it the musical motif of a gay night. But one falls back on *Pack Up Your Sins* and *Soon* as more interesting pieces of music even if one can whistle only the first two bars. (I pass the question of falling farther back, to the music of high seriousness, which is another matter; it is quite possible, however, that the *Sacre du Printemps* of Strawinsky, to choose an example not unaffected by the jazz age, will outlive the marble monument of the Music Box.)

꿔 This is central to the argument of the entire book and it is a pity that, in the next pages, it becomes unnecessarily involved in racial distinctions.

Let me dispose of these first. It was possible, in a more friendly era, to make "a little joke" about Whiteman's name. Some fifteen years later, this passage was unearthed as proof—not of my ignorance of the best Negro music, but of a prejudice against it, with implications of grosser prejudice still. By that time I knew several of the great Negroes in music, Paul Robeson, Fats Waller, Taylor Gordon, and others. I can't be sure with which of these I discussed the supposedly offensive wording, but I know that they went far to reassure me. The simple fact is that the qualities of Negro music exploited at the time were the anti-intellectual ones, and this happened over and over again in the years that followed. It is also true that neither

I nor, so far as I know, anyone else, perceived at that time the discipline, which is half-instinctive and half-intellectual, that is required in the great improvisations of jazz players. I still think it is fair to say that when a composer counts on virtuosi to make more of his music than he writes down, he is not doing the same kind of work as the composer who goes through the "fundamental brain work" of writing out precisely what, in the end, he wants us to hear. I put it as a difference, without saying one is better than the other, without attempting to say which method will give us greater satisfactions in the long run. I am, however, an intellectual, and my prejudices probably show.

It is not my business now to defend, or apologize for, the lapses in judgment and the imperfect memory betrayed by these pages. I was writing about things that were highly popular at the time, trying to uncover neglected merits in them, to justify their popularity. I was not trying to say what should be popular.

It is, however, no pleasure to me to become aware now that at the time I wrote about Whiteman's band, Bix Biederbecke was playing in it. I must have heard him— and his name does not occur in these pages. I hope I was alluding to him when I speak of those elements in the Whiteman band which gave the feeling of the wild and free, the qualities of fervour combined with accuracy, which persisted in spite of the "mechanically perfect organization" of his band which, I recognized, paid for its perfection by losing some of the qualities of the best Negro groups. ॐ

Nowhere is the failure of the negro to exploit his gifts more obvious than in the use he has made of the jazz orchestra; for although nearly every negro jazz band is better than nearly every white band, no negro band has yet come up to the level of the best white ones, and the leader of the best of all, by a little joke, is called Whiteman. The negro's instinctive feeling for colourful instruments in the band is marked; he was probably the one to see what could be done with the equivocal voice of the saxophone—a reed in brass, partaking of the qualities of two choirs in the orchestra at once. He saw that it could imitate the voice, and in the person of Miss Florence Mills saw that the voice could equally imitate the saxophone. The shakes, thrills, vibratos, smears, and slides are natural to him, although they produce tones outside the scale, because he has never been tutored into a feeling for perfect tones, as white men have; and he uses these with a great joy in the surprise they give, in the way they adorn or destroy a melody; he is given also to letting instruments follow their own bent, because he has a faultless sense of rhythm and he always comes out right in the end. But this is only the beginning of the jazz band— for its perfection we go afield.

We go farther than Ted Lewis, whom Mr Walter Haviland calls a genius. M Darius Milhaud has told me that the jazz band at the Hotel Brunswick in Boston is one of the best he heard in America, and stranger things have happened. The best of the negro bands (although he is dead, I make exception for that superb 369th Hell-fighters Infantry Band as it was conducted by the lamented Jim Europe) are probably in the neighborhood of 140th street and Lenox avenue in New York and in the negro district of Chicago. Many hotels and night clubs in New York have good jazz bands; I limit myself to three which are representative, and, by their frequent appearances in vaudeville, are familiar. Ted Lewis is one of the three; Vincent Lopez and Paul Whiteman are the others. There is a popular band led by Barney Bernie (as I recall the name, perhaps incorrectly) which is an imitation Ted Lewis, and not a good one. Lewis must be prepared for imitators, for he does with notorious success something that had as well not be done at all. He is totally, but brilliantly, wrong in the use of his materials, for he is doing what he cannot do—*i.e.,* trying to make a negro jazz orchestra. It is a good band; like Europe's, it omits strings; it is quite the noisiest of the orchestras, as that of Lopez is the quietest, and Lewis uses its (and his) talents for the perpetration of a series of musical travesties, jokes, and puns, and games. I quote a eulogy by Mr Haviland:[1]

For instance, there is his travesty of the marriage ceremony. To the jazzed tune of the good old classic "Wedding March" Lewis puts a snowy, flower-decked bridal veil on the sleek, pomaded head of the trombone player. He puts it on crooked, with a scornful flip of his slender, malicious hands. Then he leads forward the hardest-looking saxaphone player, and pretends to marry "Ham" and "Eggs"—and incidentally draws the correct conclusion as to marriage as it exists in America to-day. Perfect satire in less than three minutes.

Well, this is extraordinarily tedious and would be hissed off the stage if it were not for the actual skill Lewis has in effecting amusing orchestra combinations. His own violence, his exaggeration of the tempermental conductor, his nasal voice and lean figure in excessively odd black clothes, his pontificating over the orchestra, his announcement that he is going to murder music—all indicate a lack of appreciation of the medium. He may be a good vaudeville stunt, but he is not a great jazz leader. Again Mr Haviland:

It is not music. It has the form of music, but he has filled it with energy instead of spirituality. What is the difference? You'll understand if you hear his jazz band. It interprets the American life of to-day; its hard surface, its scorn of tradition, its repudiation of form, its astonishing sophistication—and most important, its mechanical, rather than spiritual civilization.

[1] In "The Spice of Variety," which he conducts for *Saucy Stories.*

And again no. Lewis may have a perfectly trained orchestra, but the *sense* of control which one absolutely requires he does not give. He has violence, not energy, and he cannot interpret those qualities which Mr Haviland so justly discovers as being of our contemporary life because he isn't hard and scornful and sophisticated himself—he is merely callous to some beauties and afraid of others, and by dint of being in revolt against a serene and classic beauty pays it unconscious tribute. (I fear also that Lewis imagines the "Wedding March" classic in more senses than one.) It may be noted also that the tone of travesty is not correct for contemporary America; we require neither that nor irony. Parody, rising to satire, is our indicated medium—Mr Dooley, not *Ulysses*.

The orchestra of Vincent Lopez I take as an example of the good, workmanlike, competent, inventive, adequate band. It plays at the Hotel Pennsylvania and in vaudeville, and although Lopez lacks the ingenuity of Lewis in sound, he has a greater sense of the capacities of jazz, and instead of doing a jazz wedding he takes the entire score of "that infernal nonsense, *Pinafore*," cuts it to five characteristic fragments, and jazzes it—shall I say mercilessly or reverently? Because he likes Sullivan and he likes jazz. And the inevitable occurs; *Pinafore* is good and stands the treatment; jazz is good and loses nothing by this odd application. The orchestra has verve and, not being dominated by an excessive personality, has humour and character of its own. I trust these moderate words will not conceal a vast admiration.

Jim Europe seemed to have a constructive intelligence and, had he lived, I am sure he would have been an even greater conductor than Whiteman. To-day I know of no second to Whiteman in the complete exploitation of jazz. It is a real perfection of the instrument, a mechanically perfect organization which pays for its perfection by losing much of the element of surprise; little is left to hazard and there are no accidents. Whiteman has been clever enough to preserve the sense of impromptu and his principal band —that of the Palais Royal in New York—is so much under control (his and its own) that it can make the slightest variation count for more than all the running away from the beat which is common *chez* Lewis. Like Karl Muck and Jim Europe, Whiteman is a bit of a *kapellmeister;* his beat is regular or entirely absent; he never plays the music with his hand, or designs the contours of a melody, or otherwise *acts.* I know that people miss these things; I would miss them gladly a thousand times for what Whiteman gives in return. I mean that a sudden bellow or a groan or an improvised cluck is all very well; but the real surprise is constructive, the real thrill is in such a moment as the middle of Whiteman's performance of *A Stairway to Paradise* when a genuine Blues occurs. That is real intelligence and the rest—is nowhere. The sleek, dull, rather portly figure stands before his orchestra, sidewise, almost somnolent, and listens. A look of the eye, a twitch of the knee, are his semaphoric signals. Occasionally he picks up a violin and plays a few bars; but the work has been done before and he is there only to know that the results are perfect. And all the time the band is producing music with fervour and accuracy, hard and sensitive at once. All the free, the instinctive, the wild in negro jazz which could be integrated into his music, he has kept; he has added to it, has worked his material, until it runs sweetly in his dynamo, without grinding or scraping. It becomes the machine which conceals machinery. He has arrived at one high point of jazz—the highest until new material in the music is provided for him.

The title of this essay is provoked by that of the best and bitterest attack launched against the ragtime age—Clive Bell's *Plus de Jazz.* (In *Since Cézanne.*) "No more jazz," said Mr Bell in 1921, and, "Jazz is dying." Recalling that Mr Bell is at some pains to dissociate from the movement the greatest of living painters, Picasso; that he concedes to it a great composer, Strawinsky, and T. S. Eliot, whom he calls "about the best of our living poets," James Joyce whom he wofully underestimates, Virginia Woolf, Cendrars, Picabia, Cocteau, and the musicians of *les six,*—remembering the degree of discrimination and justice which these concessions require, I quote some of the more bitter things about jazz because it would be shirking not to indicate where the answer may lie:

Appropriately it (the jazz movement) took its name from music—the art that is always behind the times. . . . Impudence is its essence—impudence in quite natural and legitimate revolt against nobility and beauty: impudence which finds its technical equivalent in syncopation: impudence which rags. . . . After impudence comes the determination to surprise: you shall not be gradually moved to the depths, you shall be given such a start as makes you jigger all over. . . .

. . . Its fears and dislikes—for instance, its horror of the noble and the beautiful are childish; and so is its way of expressing them. Not by irony and sarcasm, but by jeers and grimaces, does Jazz mark its antipathies. Irony and wit are for grown-ups. Jazz dislikes them as much as it dislikes nobility and beauty. They are the products of the cultivated intellect and Jazz cannot away with intellect or culture. . . . Nobility, beauty, and intellectual subtlety are alike ruled out. . . .

. . . And, of course, it was delightful for those who sat drinking their cocktails and listening to nigger bands, to be told that, besides being the jolliest people on earth, they were the most sensitive and critically gifted. They . . . were the possessors of natural, uncorrupted taste. . . . Their instinct might be trusted: so, no more classical concerts and music lessons. . . .

The encouragement given to fatuous ignorance to swell with admiration of its own incompetence is perhaps what has turned most violently so many intelligent and sensitive people against Jazz. They see that it encourages thousands of the stupid and vulgar to fancy that they can understand art, and hundreds of the conceited to imagine that they can create it. . . .

It is understood that Mr Bell is discussing the whole of the jazz movement, not ragtime music alone. I do not wish to go into the other arts, except to say that if he is jazz, then Mr Joyce's sense of form, his tremendous intellectual grasp of his æsthetic problem, and his solution of that problem, are far more proof than is required of the case for jazz. Similarly for Mr Eliot. It is not exactly horror of the noble that underlies Mr Joyce's travesty of English prose style, nor is it to Mr Eliot that the reproach about irony and wit is to be made. In music it is of course not impudence, but emphasis (distortion or transposition of emphasis) which finds its technical equivalent in syncopation, for syncopation is a method of rendering an emotion, not an emotion in itself. (Listen to Strawinsky.) Surprise, yes; but in the jazz of Lewis and not in that of Whiteman, which does not jeer or grimace, which has wit and structure—*i.e.*, employs the intellect. Nobility—no. But under what compulsion are we always to be noble? The cocktail drinkers may have been told a lot of nonsense about their position as arbiters of the arts; precisely the same nonsense is taught in our schools and preached by belated æsthetes to people whose claims are not a whit better—since it doesn't matter what their admirers think of themselves—it is what jazz and Rostand and Michelangelo are in themselves that matters. I have used the word art throughout this book in connexion with jazz and jazzy things; if anyone imagines that the word is belittled thereby and can no longer be adequate to the dignity of Leonardo or Shakespeare, I am sorry. I do not think I have given encouragement to "fatuous ignorance" by praising simple and unpretentious things at the expense of the fake and the *faux bon*. I have suggested that people do what they please about the gay arts, about jazz; that they do it with discrimination and without worrying whether it is noble or not, or good form or intellectually right. I am fairly certain that if they are ever actually to see Picasso it will be

106

because they have acquired the habit of seeing—something, anything—without *arrière-pensée*, because they will know what the pleasure is that a work of art can give, even if it be jazz art. Here is Mr Bell's conclusion, with most of which I agree:

Even to understand art a man must make a great intellectual effort. One thing is not as good as another; so artists and amateurs must learn to choose. No easy matter, that: discrimination of this sort being something altogether different from telling a Manhattan from a Martini. To select as an artist or discriminate as a critic are needed feeling and intellect and—most distressing of all—study. However, unless I mistake, the effort will be made. The age of easy acceptance of the first thing that comes is closing. Thought rather than spirits is required, quality rather than colour, knowledge rather than irreticence, intellect rather than singularity, wit rather than romps, precision rather than surprise, dignity rather than impudence, and lucidity above all things: *plus de Jazz.*

It is not so written, but it sounds like "Above all things, no more jazz!" A critic who would have hated jazz as bitterly as Mr Bell does, wrote once, alluding to a painter of the second rank:

But, besides those great men, there is a certain number of artists who have a distinct faculty of their own, by which they convey to us a peculiar quality of pleasure which we cannot get elsewhere; and these, too, have their place in general culture, and must be interpreted to it by those who have felt their charm strongly, and are often the objects of a special diligence and a consideration wholly affectionate, just because there is not about them the stress of a great name and authority.

—and beside the great arts there is a certain number of lesser arts which have also a pleasure to give; and if we savour it strongly and honestly we shall lose none of our delight in the others. But if we fear and hate *them,* how shall we go into the Presence?

~§ The quotation from Walter Pater was not identified because it appeared on the title page of the first edition. For the second I substituted the lines from Havelock Ellis which are also the epigraph of the last chapter: "For there are many arts, not among those we conventionally call 'fine', which seem to me fundamental for living."

It is interesting to note that in the 1950's an English critic was saying much the same thing as Bell had said. The intellectual tendency to see no difference between the popular arts and the great ones (precisely opposite to their attitude in the 1920's) was ascribed by Denis Brogan to "egalitarian nationalism . . . asserting or implying that here is something fresh, new, admirable in the most popular success that gives them a claim on our attention . . . It is smart, for the smart, to make . . . Gershwin equal Richard Strauss." And conceding that "the affection of the eggheads (then known as highbrows) for 'the seven lively arts' had a good deal of justification when Gilbert Seldes launched the phrase and the crusade," he contrasts the movies and jazz with "the last vapid runnings of the not very strong New England brew . . ." It was better to plug *The Garrick Gaieties* than read the works of the epigoni of Emerson or Howells." But such nonsense to-day, Mr Brogan holds, "is much more like a *trahison de clercs.*"

I was never able to move Clive Bell far from his position. When, reviewing this book, he called George Herriman "genial, in the French as well as the English sense of the word," he had gone as far as he could. But I could never take Bell's dislike of jazz, or of anything contemporary, seriously. We became great friends through our mutual association with *The Dial,* and the quality I most enjoyed in him was his spontaneous interest in anything that offered itself—an interest which didn't preclude criti-

108

cal thinking, to be sure, but did exclude prejudice. In his review he granted the practitioners of the lively arts a sense of style, finding the same quality also in a great cricketer, but he was adamant on nobility. It was not the position to be expected from one of the Bloomsbury gang which was more marked by a questing eye for anything new and was devoted to the belittling style of Lytton Strachey when there was a chance to deflate the accepted nobility of people and of ideas. (Bell has just published an attractive study of his friends, entitled, quite properly, "Old Friends.")

"Even to understand art a man must make a great intellectual effort," he says. The implication is that when no such effort is needed, the object contemplated has no valid title to the name of art. But Bell seems also to say that nothing can be created in any of the forms he calls jazz which will require intellectual effort—and this is precisely the sort of dogmatism against which I was directing myself. ❧

Mr Dooley,
meet Mr Lardner

✑ This may not be the first appreciation of Lardner as an artist, but it is almost certainly among the last ever written about Mr Dooley. The odd thing is that I wasn't aware of doing anything at all out of the way in considering Lardner as a great writer, but I did feel I was restoring to currency a great and neglected body of work, the commentaries of Finley Peter Dunne in the Dooley series. I knew, as the text indicates, that the dialect in which the conversations were written would operate against them, but I thought there was a chance. I was wrong. Van Wyck Brooks may have been premature, but his epitaph stands: Mr Dooley is forgotten.

What saved Lardner from the same fate was not a more interesting temperament alone, but the fact that he was a hard-working, disciplined artist in fiction, whereas Dunne worked only in the field of running commentary on passing events. Lardner's daily journalism was sometimes tremendously funny and he was never better than when he had set pieces to do—a sporting event lasting several days or a political convention. He gave himself a theme and worked it thoroughly. But as I discovered when I edited his occasional pieces and then the collection in the Viking Portable series, the really memorable things are the stories and the fantasies.

I would have done a better report on Lardner if I hadn't been so intent on drawing the parallel between his work and Mr Dooley. This led me to stress a single element: satire; and to underestimate other qualities. Mencken had, of course, recognized Lardner's mastery of the vernacular, but neither he nor I had discovered the singular merit of Lardner's slang, that the turns of speech and the distortions and errors were extraordinarily accurate mirrors of what went on in the *minds* of his characters. It is not so much the compression of satire that makes a word like "he—ll" so exactly right—it is what the word tells us about the man who thought he was doing the right thing by spelling the word that way. Lardner was, in short, a creative writer with clear perceptions into the characters he wanted to render—unlettered men and women whom, as an artist, he never made the mistake of holding in contempt. They were simple folk, but he rendered them completely. He gave them their necessary dimensions. I am thinking particularly of the stories he wrote after *You Know Me Al*. It's a minor consolation to my pride that none of these was published in book form at the time this piece about Lardner was written. But I had read them and, in the case of *The Golden Honeymoon,* knew their quality well enough. ❧

One of the most illuminating things Van Wyck Brooks ever said, about himself, was that Mr Dooley is already forgotten. It was particularly illuminating because Mr Brooks was in England when he made that statement, and it was some time before 1914—and it happens that it was in England, in 1917 that I was made to understand how living Mr Dooley is, how relevant to affairs and situations of the moment, and how much English men and women consider him as one of the better items in the heritage of Americans. The writer of *The Ordeal of Mark Twain* is an invaluable critic for America; yet one wishes that he, too, could see Mr Dooley's place in our literature; one still hopes that he will begin to enjoy Ring Lardner.

The juxtaposition of these two names would be reasonable even if both of them did not write in slang, for one is the greatest of our retired satirists and the other has every chance (if not every intention) of becoming the greatest of our active ones. I should like to say at once that I am not addressing an open letter to Dear Mr Lardner, bidding him, while there is yet time, to think on higher things. I do not want him to forswear for a moment his hold on the popular imagination, nor to write for a more judicious *clientèle*. I am satisfied to have Mr Lardner amuse me; if the strain of satire in him is an accident and he prefers to go on with his slang humour—I can always read Mr Dooley or Dean Swift. But if the growing vein of satire in all of Lardner's work is what I think it is, he has much to learn from Mr Dooley. I shall presently come to Mr Dooley and indicate what it is Lardner can learn in those beautiful pages; the main thing is that he is probably the only man in America with the capacity of learning the lesson of the master, and happily he can learn it without ceasing for a moment to live in his own world. I do not wish to force upon him the ordeal of being worried about.

There may have been a time when Mr Lardner gave cause for worry. Perhaps when *You Know Me Al* had run as long as it needed to run, one might have feared that Mr Lardner, having discovered the American language as his medium, simply didn't know what to do with it. If his humour was going to depend for ever on "1-sided" and "4-taste" and odd misspellings, it might cease to be funny. It was necessary, in short, that Mr Lardner should have something personal to say. He has answered the question of his future by showing the beginnings of a first-rate satirist, continuing the tradition of Mark Twain and Mr Dooley. And

113

having these tentatives in mind we can begin to look back and wonder whether he wasn't always something of a satirist, unconsciously.

The dates may confound my argument, so I will omit them; substantially Lardner began writing the letters of a busher just when the more serious magazines were exploiting the intellectual idea of "inside baseball." Those were the days—and they must have been funny, we feel *circa* 1923 when the bought and sold world's series and the letters of the fishing pitcher and suchlike scandal are in our memories, carefully tucked away because the honour of the national game is safe in the hands of a dictator—those were the days when the manager of a baseball team was regarded as a combination of a captain of finance (later events rather justified that assumption) a Freud, and an unborn Einstein. A fine body of college graduates, clean-living, sport-loving, well-read boys were the players; and a sport-loving, game-for-the-game's sake body of men the enthusiasts. Hughie Fullerton and Paul Elmer More might be seen any day in the same column, and John J. McGraw, who allowed himself to be called Muggsy to show what a good democrat he was, lunched daily at the President's table. Into this pretentious parade Mr Lardner injected the busher—and baseball has never recovered. The busher was simply a roughneck and a fool, a braggart and a liar; he was on occasions a good ball player, and he seemed to be inflated with the hot air which had been written about him. He pricked the bubble, and I do not wonder that Heywood Broun, despairing of making interesting his accounts of a recent world's series, publicly prayed to God to change places with him for duration. Nothing short of divine power could save them.

◄§ Baseball survived Lardner's contempt, but it seems to me that the sentimentality of the sports writers was exposed and deflated for good by Lardner and, after Lard-

ner, by events. Grantland Rice was the best of the senti-
mentalists—the worst were as bad as the radio-TV report-
ers are to-day. ॐ

It is a long time since the days of the busher and when
Lardner returned to baseball it was clear that the subject
interested him in no degree, and that he had changed much
as a writer. It is not necessary to belittle the earlier work;
only to note that in 1922 the Lardner touch was much more
deft, that the language was both richer and more accurate,
and that he was continually writing parodies, sometimes of
a phrase, often of a whole style. Three or four of the reports
he wrote for the New York *American* were jewels—and, although they had little to do with baseball, they must have
been written in the few hours which intervene between the
end of a game and the moment of going to press. The
whole series of articles ought to be reprinted; I am limited
to snatches from two of them. The first set the theme: that
Lardner had promised his wife a fur coat from his winnings
—he had bet on the Yankees. The headline was

Rings' Mrs.
Outa Luck
On Fur Coat

and then followed:

Well friends you can imagine my surprise and horror when
I found out to-night that the impression had got around some
way another that as soon as this serious was over I was plan-
ing to buy a expensive fur coat for my Mrs. and put a lot of
money into same and buy a coat that would probably run up
into hundreds and hundreds of dollars.
Well I did not mean to give no such kind of a impression
and I certainly hope that my little article was not read that way
by everybody a specially around my little home because in the
first place I am not a sucker enough to invest hundreds and

hundreds of dollars in a garment which the chances are that the Mrs. will not wear it more than a couple times all winter, as the way it looks now we are libel to have the most openest winter in history, and if women folks should walk along the st. in expensive fur coats in the kind of weather which it looks like we are going to have, why, they would only be laughed at and any way I believe a couple can have a whole lot better time in winter staying home and reading a good book or maybe have a few friends in to play bridge.

Further and more, I met a man at supper last night that has been in the fur business all his life and ain't did nothing you might say only deal in furs and this man says that they are a great many furs in this world which is reasonable priced that has got as much warmth in them as high price furs and looks a great deal better.

For inst. he says that a man is a sucker to invest thousands and thousands of dollars in expensive furs like Erminie, mule-skin, squirrel skin and Kerensky when for a hundred dollars, or not even that much, why a man can buy a owl skin or horse skin or weasel skin garment that looks like big dough and practically prostrates people with the heat when they wear them.

So I hope my readers will put a quietus on the silly rumour that I am planning to plunge in the fur market. I will see that my Mrs. is dressed in as warm a style as she has been accustomed to but neither her or I is the kind that likes to make a big show and go up and down Fifth ave. sweltering in a $700 hog-skin garment in order so as people will turn around and gap at us. Live and let live is my slocum.

These reports are reprinted in full in *The Portable Ring Lardner*. In editing Lardner I found little of interest preceding *You Know Me Al,* but Donald Elder has brought together earlier work which indicates that there was no sudden explosion of talent in Lardner—his skill and his essential attitudes developed slowly and in a straight line. Elder wrote an excellent biography of Lardner which is also a generously documented study of his work.

If this were not funny its secondary qualities would not be worth noting. The single sentence which makes up the second paragraph is a miracle of condensation, for it contains the whole mind and character of the individual created behind it (it is not Ring Lardner, obviously) and at the same time it is a miracle of the ear, for the rhythm and intonation of the American spoken language is perfectly caught and held in it. What is the use of *Babbitt* in five hundred pages if we have Lardner in five hundred words? The fur episode was continued two days later, the Yankees continuing to lose and three kittens—"three members of what is sometimes referred to as the feline tribe"—out at Mr Lardner's "heavily mortgaged home in Great Neck . . . is practically doomed you might say . . ." because Mr Lardner has met a man "who has did nothing all his life but sell and wear fur coats" and who assured him that catskin garments no bigger than a guest towel were all the rage and had been seen on "some of the best-dressed women in New York strolling up and down Tenth avenue. . . ."

"These 3 little members of the feline tribe is the cutest and best behaved kitties in all catdom, their conduct having always been above reproaches outside of a tendency on the part of Ringer to bite strangers' knuckles. Nowhere on Long Island is there a more loveable trio of grimalkins, and how it pierces my old heart to think that some day next week these 3 little fellows must be shot down like a dog so as their fur can be fashioned into a warm winter coat for she who their antics has so often caused to screech with laughter."

The annihilation of the whole Black Beauty-Beautiful Joe style of writing in the last sentence is complete, and is accomplished with the retention of Lardner's own peculiarities. It may shock Mr Lardner to know that he has done in little what Mr Joyce has done on the grand scale in *Ulysses*.

It shocked other people, too. I suppose I intended this. The implication of the sentence as it stands is parallel to the earlier one concerning *Babbitt*. I really meant that there are great passages, and occasionally a few sentences, in *Ulysses* which are devastating parodies of the sentimental style, and was thinking specifically of the scene on the beach in which Cissy Caffrey's mind is revealed to us in a parody of the family-magazine serial.

My underestimation of Lardner in what follows deserves rebuke. The work I do not even mention by name is a masterly series of sketches, *The Big Town,* loosely connected so as to appear as a novel. It is in one of these that Lardner's perfect sentence appears. The writer is describing a summer hotel—as a man would describe it whose women-folk have made him stay there—and says, "the hotel has all the modern conveniences, but the barber is also the valet so a man can't look their best at the same time." The only basic defence of grammar is that it enables us to express ourselves accurately—and here is a totally wrong sentence which still says exactly what is in the speaker's mind.

Scott Fitzgerald wrote a touching and in many ways misguided piece about Lardner after his death in which he made much more of the constriction of Lardner's interests than I do. He said Lardner's life was bounded by the baseball diamond, which simply isn't true. The narrator of *The Big Town* might as well be the Busher of *You Know Me Al,* but his wife and sister-in-law and the odd assortment of characters and caricatures they meet are shrewdly observed human beings and Lardner's stories about the theatrical and musical worlds bring in still another group. More important, Lardner did not remain in a state of adolescent worship of his dumb athletes, he matured in insight as he matured in capacity to render his insights. He remained limited and he repeated himself toward the end of his life, because he lost interest in everything. Elder's book, wisely avoiding psychoanalysis, as Lardner avoided it, does not throw much light on the underlying causes of Lardner's withdrawal into solitude and drinking and finally into the death he seemed not to find unwelcome.

Lardner's relations with the intellectuals is another matter. A first-draft of this essay appeared in *Vanity Fair* and Lardner wrote me a note of thanks in which he said "some of it was over my head, but those who should know tell me it was all a boost." This was—and was meant to be taken as—nonsense. There was very little he didn't understand and he knew that I knew this. But it was easier for him to pretend to be the character he had created, the good-hearted ignoramus. He was, as Sherwood Anderson said, "sticking to the gang." Why he had to do this, I cannot say. Elder believes that Lardner was leery of the influence of intellectuals on popular artists and that *Rhythm,* as I have noted, represents a genuine feeling, a fear that sweetness might be corrupted by the cold miasma of the intellect. Before he died, Lardner had a vast critical acclaim and a collection of his stories was sent out by a book club. It didn't affect him in the slightest degree. He still wanted to do revue sketches and songs. I had the feeling that he had, in the last years of his life, passed beyond the capacity to be pleased by anything in the way of critical acclaim. It was only another item in a large account which added up to Nothing. &

Indeed I feel that there must be hidden parody in the earlier writings of Mr Lardner, too, because he is so clean in handling it now. Satire in detail he had—there is a dictionary of it in his one word "he-ll." Elsewhere, in a series later than *You Know Me Al* he has described a half-fatuous, half-hardheaded roughneck dragging his silly and scheming wife and sister-in-law through the hotels and apartments of the backwash of society, and the story grew more and more sardonic, more and more entertaining; little of the aimless, sickly, trivial life of the merely prosperous escaped him. Unlike Mr Dooley, his chief concerns were private ones; it is only recently that he has touched upon public affairs. For a long time his only "universal" was baseball—a form of entertainment which now bores him exceedingly. He is also bored, I gather from an interview in the New York *Globe*, with the sort of fiction he has been writing, and amuses himself with writing plays. But as a satirist he is turning slowly towards matters of pith, and the question of his ultimate rank depends on this: Can he, as he broadens out, retain the swift, destructive, and tremendously funny turn of phrase, the hard and resistant mind, the gaiety of spirit which have made him a humorist? Can he, in short, learn from Mr Dooley and remain Mr Lardner? For many reasons I think he can.

Between the busher and these newspaper reports Mr Lardner has written much; among his ephemera, even, there are many pages not to be lost. I shall return to them after drawing a long course with Mr Dooley as my centre, for it is one of the significant things about Mr Dooley that you must always keep him in your eye when you are scanning the horizon for an American satirist.

Mr Dooley was a satirist of the highest order and an excellent humorist. The combination is interesting. Psycho-analysts may determine at a later date that the reason he wrote in dialect was that he was afraid to attack the American people directly; I prefer to believe that the good sense of his creator (Finley Peter Dunne, to be sure; but one always thinks of Martin Dooley in his independent existence) saw that a benevolent humour was the correct medium for a satire adequate to America. And that is America's good fortune. Read the criticism of American warfare and politics as developed in the satire of Mr Dooley and compare it with the satire of French politics and warfare as expressed in the irony of Anatole France; without measuring the quality of

120

the one by the other, think only that each is *adequate* to the subject. Less than the bitterness of *Penguin Island* and the *Histoire contemporaine* would not have served for France; more than the laughter of Dooley would have been disproportionate and unmanly for us.

Satire is like parody in admitting the integrity of the subject; it is a pruning knife applied for the good of the tree; and irony is a dagger with corrosive poison at the tip. Satire is proper to America because essentially the satirist believes that life is all right, and that only the extravagances and frailties of American life, at the moment of writing, need correction or are subject to mockery. The Frenchman, in a highly organized society, which he takes to be not only the best expression of life, but life itself, turns to irony as his natural mode when he is confronted with the ineluctable vision of its evil.

The danger is, to be sure, that our satirists remain superficial. When the thing is done roughly, without much humour, with no rich sense of the vastness and variety of the comic carnival, we get little more than the eternal "wise crack"; and the wise crack is no more entertaining in misspelled English than it is in capital letters, no more in pidgin than in Yiddish. I do not mean that George Ade and Wallace Irwin and Bill Nye and Montague Glass haven't each a special quality which makes for amusement; I do mean that they lack the great general qualities of knowing and understanding which create humour. An illustration will do more than any defining to make the difference clear. The Japanese Schoolboy used to begin his letters, "To Hon. Editor" and Ring Lardner is, I suppose, the only man in America who can begin, "Well, friends . . ."

Ambrose Bierce is generally supposed to have had this quality; certainly he had intelligence and wrote respectable English with a cold pen. His *Dictionary* does not impress me as the work of a spirit naturally ironical. Ade wrote satirically a long time ago; once in a while something occurs in the *Fables* to justify the acclaim of which F. P. A. is the curator. There is much more in Artemus Ward, whose glory is kept alive, worthily, by the sardonic leader-writer of *The Freeman,* Mr Albert Jay Nock. As language neither Ade nor Ward approaches in interest the studies of Mark Twain in *Life on the Mississippi,* nor those of Dooley and Lardner. The difference between Bill Nye and Ward on one side and Montague Glass and Lardner on the other, is that the former did not use an actually viable language or dialect, but used distortions of English for a specific effect. (I am far from suggesting that Ward did not use American notably, nor that his language is the better part of his work; he was a real satirist.) It is my guess that in the beginning the misspelled words signified that the speaker was the hard sensible common man with none of "your" refinements. Juvenal and Johnson may have been superior to the thing attacked; it pleased the democratic American to pretend to be beneath it. The literary success of the dialects is another matter, which anyone who believes that ours is still an Anglo-Saxon country will do well to consider. Montague Glass is particularly interesting in this respect. He impresses me as being neither a wise nor a foolish man, but a smart one. What gave him his vogue was his conformity with the norm of business acuteness and his use of a highly complex private racial idiom, which expresses a highly complex integrated almost secret racial life; he transferred, almost transliterated it into recognizable, at least understandable English, with such a climax as "I wish I were dead, God forbid!" which was recognized by the populace as a part of American life ten years before Mr Henry Ford bought the Protocols. The racial dialect is also exploited, but not with so reliable an ear, by Hugh Wiley in his negro stories; it is possible that the stories of Octavus Roy Cohen are more accurate (they are not so entertaining); but the life they represent is, in any case, too near to America to be surprising to us.

I am convinced that nearly all of Mr Dooley and nearly all of the later Lardner would stand without dialect. It is not an odd-looking word that impresses most in Mr Dooley's masterpieces about the Dreyfus case. "The witness will confine himself to forgeries" is English as Swift would have written it, and is neither better nor worse than, "How th' divvle can they perjure thimsilves if they ain't sworn?" or " 'Let us proceed,' says th' impartial an' fair-minded judge, 'to th' thrile iv th' haynious monsther Cap Dhry-fuss' he says. Up jumps Zola, an' says he in Frinch: 'Jackuse,' he says, which is a hell of a mane thing to say to anny man. An' they thrun him out. 'Judge' says th' attorney f'r th' difinse, 'an' gintlemen iv' th' jury' he says. 'Ye're a liar,' says th' judge. 'Cap, ye're guilty, an' ye know it,' he says. . . . 'Let us pro-ceed to hearin' th' tisti-mony,' he says . . . Be this time Zola has come back; an' he jumps up, an', says he, 'Jackuse,' he says. An' they thrun him out."

It is no wonder that this passage was reprinted by the New York *Evening Post* after the expulsion of the Socialists from Albany. Nearly everything serious in Dooley has the same relevance, and one reads about war experts and "disqualifying the enemy" (in relation to the Spanish-American and Boer Wars) with a slightly dizzying sensation that this man has said everything that needed to be said twenty years in advance of his time. We needed him badly during the war, but a comic song about him had somehow withdrawn his name from the rank of great literature and we had to do with sad second-bests. There isn't a chance in the world that he will be forgotten, because he is recognized in England and we shall some day reimport his reputation. For he has the great advantage of being at the same time a humorist and a social historian, an every-day philosopher and the *homme moyen sensuel*.

His qualities are so immediate that analyzing them appears superfluous. He gets his effects by distortion, not by exaggeration. When he told Mr Roosevelt to call the next edition of his book *Alone in Cubia* he extracted an essence from it, rather than inflated it. His adversatives are surprising and devastating. He conceives a Blood-is-thicker-than-Water speech in these terms (from the English to the American): "Foolish and frivolous people, cheap but thruehearted and insincere cousins. . . . Ye ar-re savage but inthrestin'." Sometimes he leaves out the "but": "They was followed be th' gin'rals iv th' Fr-rinch ar-rmy, stalwart, fearless men, with coarse, disagreeable faces." His unexpectedness goes farther; he once said that left alone General Shafter could have taken "Sandago" without losing an ounce.

I do not wish to write a literary essay about Mr Dooley, and having mentioned Swift I have little to say. I must admit that the Irish of Mr Dooley is stage-Irish; what makes it acceptable is that it is entirely Dooley-Irish, and whatever the spelling, whatever the oddities of words, the intonation is always right. For of course it is possible to write a dialect without imitation of sound, and to do it effectively and honestly. Sherwood Anderson has done it in *I Want to Know Why* and in *I'm a Fool;* Lardner has done it in *The Golden Honeymoon;* and the amiable efforts of Mr John V. A. Weaver are ineffective because in nine out of ten cases he is setting slang words, well observed and accurately recorded, to the rhythm of literary English. Mr Dooley's rhythm is always that of the estimable, easy-going barkeeper who is speaking.

The eminence of Lardner as user of the American language was, as I have said, observed early by H. L. Mencken. There was, in Lardner's time a writer about baseball who used slang, Charles E. Van Loan, and there were probably people who thought the two men were doing the same thing. The difference was that Lardner put down what people thought, he didn't translate what they should have thought into wrong words. And he had not only a remarkable ear for the vulgar pronunciation of words, but an inner ear for the cadence of speech, for that special quality which makes each one of us sing what we say to a specific tune, with a rhythm of its own. Listeners to recent campaign speeches can compare the staccato delivery of Adlai Stevenson, throwing out groups of three or four words, pausing, ending often with a single word after the pause, and the legato of Eisenhower's delivery. The contour of one nation's speech differs from the contour of another and within a nation, as we know from comparing Midwest and South, for instance, there are minor variations.

As for the primary ear, Lardner was almost pedantic in his distinctions. Here is a comment he made on Weaver, whom many people took to be an authentic reporter: "For the most part this organ (pure American) has served Mr. Weaver well. But I think that on occasion it consciously or unconsciously plays him false. It has told him, for example, that we say *everythin'* and *anythin'*. We don't. We say *somethin'* and *nothin'*, but we say *anything* and *everything*. There appears to be somethin' about the *y* near the middle of both these words that impels us to acknowledge the *g* on the end of them. Mr. Weaver's ear has also give or gave (not gi'n) him a bum hunch on *thing* itself. It has told him to make it *thin'*. But it's a real effort to drop the *g* off this little word and, as a rule, our language is not looking for trouble. His ear has gone wrong on the American for *fellow, kind of,* and *sort of*. Only on the stage or in 'comic strips' do we use *feller, kinder,* and *sorter*. *Kinda* and *sorta* are what us common fellas say. "And how about the lines, 'Now that I'm sure he never won't come back' and 'You don't know how to dream and never won't'? *Never will* and *won't never* are American. *Never won't* ain't . . .

"We say 'He come up to me in the club,' but we also

say, 'He come up to I and Charley in the club.' Charley's presence in the club seems, for 'some reason another' to alter my case . . .

"My theory on this particular point is that when the common American citizen, whom we will call Joe, was in his last year in school . . . the teacher asked him how many boys there were in his family. He replied, 'Just Frank and me.' 'Just Frank and I,' corrected the teacher, And the correction got Joe all balled up." (From a review in *The Bookman*, 1921, quoted in *Ring Lardner*, by Donald Elder.) ॐ

One looks back with a certain envy to the time when a barkeeper could talk about the world. Our present social situation is disjected, and the period before the war seems incredibly calm and halcyon. It seems to us that then America was settling into the character it had made for itself in the Civil War, a time of consolidation and certainty. A minor passion for social justice seems to have been the only great force hostile to that sense of security and self-satisfaction without which no civilization can become sophisticated and refined. It was pre-eminently the time when a satirist could exist. Mr Dooley is the proof that he did. He understood his America, as in his time, and without bitterness he makes it live again.

Ten years from now, if we settle down, Mr Lardner may have another such opportunity. For the moment he is driven to the surface; he has no *point d'appui* for his attack; in a bewildering and unsure civilization, he is himself unsure. It is possible that he will become so accustomed to shallow waters that he will never venture into deep; I should be sorry, because he has qualities too precious to be wasted. He is developing a strain of wild imagination, of something approaching fantasy. And his occasional pieces of fiction are far beyond the average of stories written in America. *The Golden Honeymoon* (which Mr Edward J. O'Brien had the

126

acumen to put in his collection of the best stories of 1922) is almost a masterpiece; it has a sort of artistic wisdom, is without tricks, and is beautifully written. He has also written a burlesque which failed drearily with the 49-ers and a sketch, *The Bull Pen,* in which the busher reappeared, which was a moderate success in the Ziegfeld Follies. This piece and *The Golden Honeymoon* show a fresh tendency on Lardner's part to understate; they are actually quiet, as if he were tired of noisiness. I do not think he is tired of anything. In an interview recently he said, "Some philosopher once said that if you want a thing badly when you're young you're likely to get too much of it before you're old; *I hope to God he knew what he was talking about.*" He is afraid of nothing; one fancies he doesn't care for too many things.

He grew weary, a little while ago, of the literary diaries published from week to week by the highbrows, these records "of who they seen and talked to and what they done since the last time we heard from them" and so he wrote his own for the New York Sunday *American.* Among the items chronicled were:

"When I got home Sousa was there and we played some Brahms and Grieg with me at the piano and him at one end of a cornet. 'How well you play, Lardy,' was Sousa's remark. Brahms called up in the evening and him and his wife come over and played rummy. . . ." (This is grotesque, but he knows his subject.) "Had breakfast with Mayor Hylan and Senator Lodge. . . . Went home and played some Rubinstein on the black keys. . . . President Harding called up long distants to say hello. The Mrs talked to him as I was playing with the cat. . . . Took a ride on the Long Island R.R. to study human nature. . . ." And so on. It is a little better than verbal parody, is it not, Lardy?

Mr Lardner pretends still to feel some of the he-man's contempt for letters, suggesting at the same time the fatheaded pride of a real-estate broker who has had a patriotic poem printed in the local paper. He is, as Sherwood Anderson says, "sticking to the gang." But he is wise and witty and he has few compunctions about being vulgar. It is his most precious asset. For in America the fear of vulgarity is the beginning of deadness. Abase! (if I may quote Mr Dooley).

⋖§ Lardner's first major collection, *How to Write Short Stories*, was published in the same month as this book. By arrangement, we wrote letters to one another, for publicity purposes, and Lardner published them in his column. His letter to me, an epitome of all his stylistic tricks, follows:

Dear Gilbert (as I have learned to think of you):—

Just recd. notice from the Harper boys that you have got out a book nicknamed the 7 Lively Arts and listen Gilbert, here is the kind of sucker they thought I was. They said I could buy a regular copy of the book for $4.00 and no hundreds dollars, but they was also getting out a special autographed edition of 300 copies with each copy numbered, with uncut edges, Javanese batik sides and a natural linen back, which the price of it was $10.00 or only $6.00 more than a regular copy. Well of course we can't have no Javanese batik in the house on acct. of the children, but irregardless of that, why what do they think I am, paying $6.00 for your signature which I already seen it 100 times and did not think it was such a he—ll of a spectacle, and besides which the next time you drop in at what I laughingly call my home, I will give you $.50 worth of drinks and then haul out my $4.00 copy of your book in front of the Great Neck smart set and say Gil old boy will you put your name in front of this and you will say yes or run the wrist of getting bood off Long Island. That is how I will get a autographed copy of your book and save $5.50 and as far as the 300 numbered copies is concerned, why we ain't got so many books we half to have any of them numbered. We can still call them all by name.

Personly, whenever I get a letter from some gal in Detroit or somewheres asking for my autograph and I think they can't get along without it, why I send it to them for nothing and sometimes half to use my own stamps. That is the difference between you and I, Gilbert and here is another difference, I will be paying $4.00 for a copy of your book, but when my book, "How to Write Short Stories," comes out you will get a free copy because you are a critic and I am just a man about Great Neck. And further and more my autograph is right on the cover of each and every copy of my book and it don't cost no $10.00 or nowheres near that amt. As to which book is worth the most money I will leave that to clean living right thinking American citizens to decide and no matter what their decision is I will still think they are the fairest minded jury in the world or else a bunch of ½ witted, degenerate mormons.

Ring W. Lardner

This was, as I have said, written for publicity purposes. But Lardner was always punctilious. The last lines had read ". . . I will either think they are. . . . or a bunch . . ." The corrections in the typed letter were made by Lardner before signing it—and they make the sentence say exactly, instead of approximately, what he intended it to say. ক

A tribute to
Florenz Ziegfeld

The incurable romanticist, George Jean Nathan, was the first to speak boldly in print and establish the rule of the silver-limbed, implacable Aphrodite in the theatre of Florenz Ziegfeld; and the equally incurable realist, Heywood Broun, has discovered that it isn't so. Mr Nathan, obsessed by the idea that the world in general, and America in particular, goes to any extreme to conceal its interest in sex, really did a service to humanity by pointing out that there *were* beautiful girls in revues and that these girls constituted one of the main reasons for the attendance of men at the performances. Mr Broun, sensing a lack of abandon and frenzy in the modern bacchanale, says, simply, that it isn't so, and implies that anyone who could get a thrill out of that—! Like the king in that story of Hans Christian Andersen, of which Mr Broun is inordinately fond, the girls haven't any clothes on; and this little child, noticing the fact, is dreadfully disappointed.

Now Mr Ziegfeld is, in the opinion of those who work for him, a genius, and can well afford to say, "A plague on both your houses," for he has built up what he himself calls a national institution, glorifying, not degrading, the American girl (*pauvre petite*). He can afford to look with complacency upon undergraduates charging upon his theatre in the anticipation of unholy delights, and forced to bear the

131

clownings of Eddie Cantor or the wise sayings of Will Rogers; then he can turn to Dr John Roach Straton who, having heard from Mr Broun that the Follies are chaste, approaches to see some monstrosity of a classic ballet and hears the vast decent sensuality of a jazz number instead.

Mr Ziegfeld has lived through so much—through the period when it was believed indecent to be undressed and through the manlier period when nudity was contrasted with nakedness (it is the basis of a sort of Y. M. C. A. æsthetics that the nude is always pure) and through the long period, 1911-15, when the reviewers discovered the superior attractiveness of the stockinged leg; art in the shape of Joseph Urban has left a permanent mark upon him, and he has trafficked in strange seas for numbers and devices; what was vulgar and what was delicate, boresome and thrilling, have all passed through his hands; he has sent genius whistling down the wind to the vaudeville stage and built up new successes with secondary material; the storehouses are littered with the gaudy monuments of his imitators. And all the time the secret of his success has been staring Broadway in the face.

It is well to speak of Mr Ziegfeld's success because in the last few years several things have happened to the revue; for almost as long as I remember the Ziegfeld Follies, I remember the Winter Garden opposition, the Passing Show, its exact antithesis.[1] But lately there have arrived at least two productions which give every guaranty of permanence, in addition to some others which may turn out to be equally sure of survival. I mean the Music Box Revue and the Greenwich Village Follies. The Music Box is only in its third year; its chiefs assets are one of the most agreeable theatres in New York, assuring a reputation on the road, and first call on the

[1] Since writing this I am informed that the Winter Garden has changed, at least structurally. But even if the type of show at that house also changes, *The Passing Show* as a type will be seen elsewhere, so I leave what I have written. In 1913 or 1914 Mr H. K. Moderwell wrote of the worst show in years, "They call it *The Passing Show*. Let it pass." Apparently they did.

still unsatisfied talents of Mr Irving Berlin. The Greenwich Village Follies, even if it lose its present director, John Murray Anderson, will continue to be successful for one of the strangest reasons in the world—its reputation for being "artistic." The Winter Garden, the two Follies, and the Music Box, are the four points of the compass in this truly magnetic field. When the needle points due north, I usually find Mr Ziegfeld fairly snug under the Pole Star.

There are, if you count the chorus individually, about a hundred reasons for seeing a revue; there is only one reason for thinking about it, and that is that at one point, and only one point, the revue touches upon art. The revue as a production manifests the same impatience with half measures, with boggling, with the good enough and the nearly successful, which every great artist feels, or pretends to feel, in regard to his own work. It shows a mania for perfection; it aspires to be precise and definite, it corresponds to those *de luxe* railway trains which are always exactly on time, to the millions of spare parts that always fit, to the ease of commerce when there is a fixed price; jazz or symphony may sound from the orchestra pit, but underneath is the real tone of the revue, the steady, incorruptible purr of the dynamo. And with the possible exception of architecture, *via* the back door of construction, the revue is the most notable place in which this great American dislike of bungling, the real pleasure in a thing perfectly done, apply even vaguely to the arts.

If you can bring into focus, simultaneously, a good revue and a production of grand opera at the Metropolitan Opera House, the superiority of the lesser art is striking. Like the revue, grand opera is composed of elements drawn from many sources; like the revue, success depends on the fusion of these elements into a new unit, through the highest skill in production. And this sort of perfection the Metropolitan not only never achieves—it is actually absolved in advance from the necessity of attempting it. I am aware that it has the highest-paid singers, the best orchestra, some of the best conductors, dancers and stage hands, and the worst scenery in the world, in addition to an exceptionally astute impresario; but the production of these elements is so haphazard and clumsy that if any revue-producer hit as low a level in his work, he would be stoned off Broadway. Yet the Metropolitan is considered a great institution and complacently permitted to run at a loss, because its material is ART.

The same thing is true in other fields—in producing serious plays, in writing great novels, we will stand for a second-rateness we would not for a moment abide in the construction of a bridge or the making of an omelette, or the production of a revue. And because in a revue the bunk doesn't carry, the revue is one of the few places you can go with the assurance that the thing, however tawdry in itself, will be well done. If it is tawdry, it is so in keeping with the taste of its patrons, and without pretense; whereas in the major arts—no matter how magnificent the masquerade of Art may be—the taste of a production is usually several notches below the taste of the patrons.

The good revue pleases the eye, the ear, and the pulse; the very good revue does this *so well that it pleases the mind*. It operates in that equivocal zone where a thing does not have to be funny—it need only sound funny; nor be beautiful if it can for a fleeting moment appear beautiful. It does not have to send them away laughing or even whistling; all it needs to do is to keep the perceptions of the audience fully engaged all the time, and the evaporation of its pleasures will bring the audience back again and again.

⌐§ Revues have almost ceased to exist in the American theatre. One reason is that they are as costly as a "book show," which can be sold to the movies, whereas a topical revue can only sell a few of its less timely numbers. It is probable, also, that the temper of the times is not hospitable even to the slight irreverence of the revue. The two landmarks after Ziegfeld are special cases. *Of Thee I*

134

Sing was a revue in spirit, with a book so well constructed, a point of view so shrewd and refreshing, that the show won the Pulitzer prize for drama—it was a political satire with the structural elements of a revue built in. The other, *Pins and Needles,* was straight revue—of the early depression years! It satirized even itself with *Sing Me a Song of Social Significance* and in size and feel was like several revues which came out of the West, shoestring productions compared to those discussed here, but bright and attractive. The style for small revues had been set earlier, by the *Garrick Gaieties* to which the young Rodgers and Hart contributed and by several delectable *Little Shows.*

None of these, with the exception of *Of Thee I Sing,* was nearly as well made as a Ziegfeld Follies—all had what the Follies sacrificed, spontaneity and a lot of good humor. ஒ

The secret I have alluded to is how to create the atmosphere of seeming—and Mr Ziegfeld knows the secret in every detail. In brief, he makes everything appear perfect by a consummate smoothness of production. Undoubtedly ten or fifteen other people help in this—I use Mr Ziegfeld's name because in the end he is responsible for the kind of show put out in his name and because the smoothness I refer to goes far beyond the mechanism of the stage or skill in directing a chorus. It is not the smoothness of a connecting rod running in oil, but of a batter where all the ingredients are so promptly introduced and so thoroughly integrated that in the end a man may stand up and say, This is a Show. Everyone with a grain of sense knows that Mr Urban can make all the sets for a production and Mr Berlin write all the music; Mr Ziegfeld has the added grain to see that if he's going to have a great variety of things and people, he had better divide his *décor* and his music among many different talents.

There have been funnier revues and revues more pleasing

to the eye and revues with far better popular music; nowhere have all the necessary ingredients appeared to such a high average of advantage. Mr Anderson could barely keep Bert Savoy within the bounds of a revue; the Music Box collapses entirely as a revue at a few dance steps by Bobby Clark. But Ziegfeld as early as 1910 was able to throw together Harry Watson (Young Kid Battling Dugan, nowadays, in vaudeville), Fannie Brice, Anna Held, Bert Williams, and Lillian Lorraine and, as if to prove that he was none the less producing a revue, bring down his curtain on a set-piece of "Our American Colleges." And twelve years later, with Will Rogers and Gilda Grey and Victor Herbert and Ring Lardner, he is still producing a revue and brings both curtains down on his chorus—once *en masse* and the second time undressing for the street in silhouette.

I cannot estimate the amount of satisfaction which since those early days Mr Ziegfeld has provided. My own memories do not go back to the actual productions in which Anna Held figured; I recall only the virtuous indignation of elderly people and my own mixed feelings of curiosity and disgust when I overheard reports of the goings-on. But from the time I begin to remember them until to-day there has always been a peculiar quality of pleasure in the Ziegfeld shows, and the uninterrupted supply of things pleasant to see and entertaining to hear, has been admirable. Mr Ziegfeld has never been actually courageous; his novelties are never more audacious than, say, radiolite costumes or an Urban backdrop. He is apparently pledged to the tedious set-pieces which are supposed to be artistic—the Ben Ali Haggin effects, the Fan in Many Lands or the ballet of A Night in Statuary Hall with the discobolus coming to life and the arms of the Venus de Milo miraculously restored. There are years, too, in which Mr Ziegfeld, discovering new talent, follows but one vein and leaves his shows so much in one tone that a slight depression sets in. Mr Edmund Wilson, in the *Dial* repeats the plaint of Mr Heywood Broun in the *World*—that the Follies are frigid—the girls are all straight, the ballet becomes a drill, the very laughs are organized and mechanical. Well, it happens to be the function of the Ziegfeld Follies to be Apollonic, not Dionysian; the leap and the cry of the bacchanale give way to the song and dance, and when we want the true frenzy we have to go elsewhere. I doubt whether even the success of the negro shows will frighten Ziegfeld into mingling with his other elements some that will be riotous and wild; the best they can do will be to prevent Ziegfeld from growing too utterly "refined." He tends at this moment to quiet fun of the Lardner type and the occasional horseplay with which he accentuates this murmur, this smile, is usually unsuccessful. I am, myself, more moved by broader strokes than his, but I recognize that Ziegfeld, and not the producers of *Shuffle Along,* is in the main current of our development—that we tend to a mechanically perfect society in which we will either master the machine or be enslaved by it. And the only way to master it—since we cannot escape—will be by understanding it in every detail. That is exactly Mr Ziegfeld's present preoccupation. I dissent, however, from the suggestion that the physical loveliness of the Ziegfeld chorus has ceased to be seductive. Some, as Mr Lardner once said—some like 'em cold, and there are at least five other choruses which affect me as pleasurably. But for those that like the Ziegfeld-type chorus, which has always a deal of stateliness and a haughty air of being damned well bred, Mr Ziegfeld's production of the wares is perfect. He has simply moved his chorus one step backward in order to make them appear slightly inaccessible and so a little more desirable. His attack is indirect, but it is no less certain.

In the back of the mind there always remains the idea that a revue ought to be a revue of something, and as far as I know, George M. Cohan is the last of those who have tried to accomplish that. Weber and Fields presented burlesque; Mr Cohan's efforts are not lost in that dim perspective, and they seem superior, for he wove his amazingly expert parodies of

137

current successes into a new creation, a veritable review. The high spirits and sophistication of the Cohan revues have not frequently been equalled on our stage, for the whole of Cohan's talents were poured into them without reserve. The parodies and satire were merciless and spared not even himself; for he took the old jibe about his Yankee-Doodleism and wrote apropos of a show of his which had failed: "Go, get a Flag, For you need it, you need it, you know you need it!" He took off *Common Clay* in swift and expert patter; he destroyed the "song hit" with *Down by the Erie* ten years earlier and ten times better than the Forty-niners did; he advertised himself and ridiculed his own self-advertisement; he was the principal actor and he played fair with Willie Collier and Charles Winninger and Louise Dresser. Throughout he was the high point of Cohanism, of that shrewd, cocksure, arrogant, wise, and witty man who was the true expression of the America of Remember the Maine!, the McKinley elections, the Yellow Kid, and *Coon! Coon! Coon!* He was always smart, always versatile. To this day he is smart enough to produce *Mary* and *Little Nelly Kelly,* knowing that the old stuff goes biggest and that even in the midst of his own sophistication he can capture vaster audiences with his own simplicity. This is an abdication of his proper function, to be sure. The man who had so much to do with the great-American-drama (I allude to *Seven Keys to Baldpate* and the description "great-American" is deliberate) and who could take any trash (*A Prince There Was*) and make it go, through the indefatigable energy and the cleverness of his own acting, and who could fight the world with his preposterous *Tavern*—this man had no right to give up doing what he did so well. I care nothing for the famous nasalities of George M. Cohan; after the Four Cohans I saw him first as actor, so I do not mourn for his dancing days. But I know that with only a fraction of Berlin's gifts as a composer, he had something which even Berlin lacks: the complete sense of the boards. His revues would have been desirable additions to each theatrical season

138

if they had done no more than produce himself. His hard sense, his unimaginative but not unsympathetic response to everything that took place on the street and at the bar and on the stage made him a prince of reviewers—he was not without malice and he was wholly without philosophy. Perhaps that is why his revues were wonderfully gay. Why they ever stopped I cannot tell; when they stopped, strangely enough, they left the field to the Winter Garden. I make no claim that the revues at this house are always pleasing; people apparently still exist who are enthusiasts for Valeska Surratt. But I do claim that they are always revues, even if they are sometimes to be weighed by avoirdupois and not by critical standard.

    €§ I did not mourn for Cohan's dancing days, he did, and out of nostalgia wrote his best piece for the theatre, *The Song and Dance Man*. Like most of his later work, it had a note of resentment. Cohan couldn't change and didn't like public taste to change. But this play was all fondness for the past and in it Cohan, for once, wrote brilliantly in the vernacular, without strain, almost without slang. ¢~

The annihilation of all the vast and silly posturing which went on a few years ago under the name of *The Jest* was accomplished in a perfect burlesque by Blanche Ring and Charles Winninger (the latter played Leo Ditrichstein in one of the Cohan revues) and if *The Sheik* never reached the stage it is possibly because Eddie Cantor burlesqued it in advance on a bicycle and with a time clock for the women of the harem. What has held the Winter Garden down (except, of course, when Al Jolson there inhabited) is the lack of good music; for the humour has always been broad and the slap-stick merry. The shows there always seem to be hankering a little for the additional vulgarity of out-and-out burlesque, but the Rath Brothers were as much at home there as the Avon Comedy Four; if my head were at stake I could not recall a single thing there which could be called exquisite, but I swear that as the show girls shuffled precariously up and down the runway I did at times fancy I heard the stamping of a goatish foot behind the scenes, and if I didn't like the sound, I was in the minority. The Winter Garden has always been, in part, a direct assault on the senses and the method of art is always indirect; Mr Ziegfeld knows this and always manages to bathe his scenes in a cool virginal light, to the intensification of pleasure for the connoisseurs.

The difference between these two shows can be measured by watching one figure pass across the stage of each. Last year at the Winter Garden Conchita Piquer sang a *malagueña*. (You can discover all you need to know about the *malagueña* in Mr Santayana's Soliloquies; to us it is the perfect exotic, as strange to our ears as Chinese song—stranger because it remains recognizably Occidental, yet seems to be based on no intervals known to our scales, and its rhythm is capricious and uncertain). She sang it "wildly well," with a pert assured air of superiority. Yet she cast flowers into the audience as she did so, and the background and the massing of the chorus behind her were all out of key and prevented the song from being what at the Ziegfeld Follies it inevitably must have been, exquisite.

At the Follies passes Gilda Grey, a performer of limited talents gifted with unutterable intensity. Against a flaring background in which all the signs of all of Broadway are crowded together, she sings a commentary on the negro invasion—*It's Getting Very Dark on Old Broadway*—the scene fades and radiolite picks out the white dresses of the chorus, the hands and faces recede into undistinguishable black. And while the chorus sings Miss Grey's voice rises in a deep and shuddering ecstasy to cry out the two words, "Getting darker!" To disengage that cry, to insure its repercussion, went all the skill of production in everything that preceded and in everything that followed. It was exciting, but it was also exquisite, and that is exactly what the Winter Garden could not have done.

Neither of the two Music Box revues has reached that height, because in neither has production kept pace with Berlin's music. It is part of the technique of the revue to have "stunts" and Berlin, being *capable du tout,* last year set a dining menu to music. Yet nothing was added when lobster and mayonnaise and celery appeared in the flesh; even worse, this year something precious is lost when one of Berlin's veritable masterpieces, *Pack Up Your Sins and Go to the Devil,* is produced with an endless number of trapdoors and hoists and all the other mechanics of the stage. The first of the two revues flourished on humour—Willie Collier and Sam Bernard were inexpressibly funny—and on Berlin's *Say It With Music;* so long as it stayed in New York the appearance in person of Mr Berlin, explaining to the well-remembered tunes how he wrote each of his masterpieces of ragtime, added much.

The tone of this revue was the tone of the building itself— varying from the cool and well-proportioned exterior to the comfortable, a little lavish interior. Florence Moore was as outrageous as ever, and at least as active; she is the most tireless person on the stage and to me the most tiring, for her vitality affects me as a cyclone in which I am quite unnecessarily involved. All the more surprising, then, was her shift from horseplay to burlesque in the house-hunting scene with Sam Bernard, at the end of which the children were shot by their despairing parents to remove the one obstacle between them and the perfect apartment. In an earlier scene Collier had had his chance—the one in which Bernard tried to explain his difficulties and to read a letter. All of Bernard's stutterings and flounderings in the English vocabulary availed nothing against Collier's imperturbable indifference. Collier has always had a divine spark—it was visible even in *The Hottentot*— and in that scene it glowed beautifully. The show was, to be sure, held in the matrix of Berlin's score, and was as much held *down* as up to that level—I mean it was not spoiled by the intrusion of alien theatrical elements. Since then a new hydraulic system has apparently been added to the equipment of the stage, and Hassard Short, confusing the dynamics of the theatre with mere hoisting power, moves everything that can be moved except the audience. The elements are all there, but they are produced as if it were a benefit, not a revue.

John Murray Anderson's is the hardest case to be sure about. A year ago he "struck a new note in revues"—by producing one without a scintilla of interest in any of its proceedings. Nothing quite so lackadaisical and dull has ever had such a success. Yet he had long before established a repute for being artistic—and, as far as I can judge, it was by the exploitation of millions of yards of draperies in place of the usual canvas scenery. It was a sound notion, and in the first of these productions, *What's in a Name?* there was a pretty air of the semi-professional, a challenging suggestion of improvisation, as if the chorus and principals weren't sure from moment to moment what the *régisseur* might suggest for them to do next.

He has always presented some of the loveliest and some of the ugliest costumes in New York; and now that draperies are no longer his only resource, he falls back upon transformations in scenery, or makes a painted backdrop of the Moonlight Sonata come to life, with music, to the astonishment of the multitude.

In short, it would appear that Mr Anderson is introducing into the revue precisely that element of artistic bunk which has long been the property of the bogus arts. I resent it, and resent it the more because he doesn't need it. In his recent show there were elements beyond words to praise; the singing of Yvonne George was superb and superbly arranged; the Widow Brown song, sung and *danced* by Bert Savoy, had a quality of tenderness which all the sentimental songs in the Ziegfeld Follies try vainly to transmit; the two little tumblers, Fortunello and Cirillino, are by name and manner of the

142

commedia dell'arte and John Hazzard's song about Alaska, with slides by Walter Hoban, is the stuff that Forty-niners are made of.

It was in this show that the Herriman-Carpenter ballet of Krazy Kat was tried and dismissed, and the fault here is the fault of Mr Anderson throughout. Again it was attempted with an artistic dancer, when everyone who has intelligence of Krazy knows that it should be done by an American stunt dancer until the time when Mr Chaplin finds time to do it. Krazy Kat is exquisite and funny—and whether Mr Carpenter lets him remain so or not, it is clear that Mr Anderson wanted him to be artistic at all cost. So with his whole production; he has sacrificed fun all the way down the line; one is pleased, much more than amused, and the gigantic revelry, the broad levity of Bert Savoy stand apart from the show like a stranger. It is the one revue in which the mass dancing entirely fails to remain in the memory, and I am convinced that if Miss Brice hadn't, in the Ziegfeld Follies, made *Mon Homme* a popular hit, Miss George's far more fiery and varied and more generally interesting rendition of it would leave it cold in the ears of the audiences. For Mr Anderson has so far learned only to put over separate things, and until you put the whole thing over the individual things gain but half their victories.

That completes the circle to Mr Ziegfeld, and, since it is a question of putting it over, associates with him another man who on at least one occasion has done as well, Mr Charles Dillingham. If you omit the one man shows as practised by Ed Wynn, Frank Tinney and Al Jolson, and the nondescripts of Hitchcock, and pass over *Stop! Look! Listen!* as varying too far from the revue type, there remains *Watch Your Step* as another high spot in production, with the dancing of the Castles, the humours of that very great comedian, Harry Kelly, and of Tinney, the scenery and costumes by Robert McQuinn and Helen Dryden, and the whole story of contemporary dancing in Mr Berlin's music. Except for Harry Kelly, every item was bettered in *Stop! Look! Listen!*, but in spite of the presence of Gaby Deslys, it was not a revue—whereas *Watch Your Step* almost consciously set out to proclaim itself superior in fineness and slickness to the Follies and almost succeeded.

I am trying to sketch the main *types* of revue, not to write a history of the revue; it is to be hoped that someone sufficiently sentimental can be found to do the job. Whether in a history the drunken scene of Leon Errol in the subway would figure largely, I do not know; I am not even sure that the scene in the Grand Central while it was building, with Bert Williams as the porter, would be noted; quite possibly the memory of Lillian Lorraine on the swings—to me merely a bearable necessity—and Frank Carter singing, (1918) *I'm Going to Pin My Medal on the Girl I Left Behind,* will seem more important than Ina Claire's mimicry of Frances Starr's *Marie-Odile.* It is possible that the injection of real humour, like Lardner's, may make the set scenes like Laceland or the History of Shoes through the Ages or Our Colleges more and more dispensable. I do not know. I feel fairly certain only of this: that the relative importance of the workers in the field is measured by their mastery of the art of production far more than by their skill in picking individuals and stunts. I am also convinced that those who have arrived at this perfection in an effort to give America pleasure have done more for us than those who haven't got half way in trying to give us art.

The Darktown strutters
on Broadway

Anyone so minded can write an entirely false history of American civilization by setting down in parallel columns the vogues and rages which have overtaken us and Europe at the same time. The highly patriotic, but a bit undergraduate, habit of slanging your own country is always more effective if the facts about any other country are a little obscure, and, thanks to the cable and the efficacy of transatlantic mails, we now know virtually everything that isn't so, and virtually nothing that is important, about Europe. So it is quite possible for a critic to say that in literature the taste of Europe is far beyond ours, on the ground that Harold Bell Wright is the typical American author and Conrad and Anatole France and Tolstoi the typical European. I mean that this is possible if a critic has never heard of the work of Nat Gould and William Le Queux in England, for instance.

The latest of these false parallels would be this: that while Europe was going in for the primitive sculpture of the African negro, America devoted itself and its theatres to musical shows composed and produced by the nonprimitive negroes of Harlem, New York.[1] The wail of the saxophone in *Shuffle*

[1] This review appeared in *Vanity Fair* sometime in the summer of 1922. I allow it to stand with nothing more than verbal corrections in spite of my dislike of books which collect articles expressly written for magazine publication, because I feel that the negro show is extraordinarily transient

Along had not yet died in my ears when a Serious Critic made moan in his journal that the authors of that piece were truckling to the white man's sense of superiority by exhibiting their own flesh and blood as a pack of cheats and scoundrels. What had impressed me as a fairly awkward mechanism for introducing songs and dances was by him taken as a libel on a race; and forgetting the picaresque romance from the *Odyssey* to *Get-Rich-Quick-Wallingford,* forgetting that all peoples seem to take an abundant pleasure in exposing themselves as delightful rogues, he wept over this degradation. At about that time Mr Clive Bell, marking a reaction from the extreme vogue of African plastic, still ranked the sculptures produced by savage and semicivilized negroes as only a little below those of the two or three great periods of artistic production. Again it would seem that Europe had, in its effete way, stolen a march on us.

In effect the coloured shows were entertaining and interesting to think about, whether they were good or bad, and most of them were pretty bad. As shows, that is. As shows in a country which really knowns how to produce soul-satisfying eye-and-ear entertainment. They had certain attractive qualities, and if they were in essence second rate, they were at least dynamic, while the first-rate thing in Europe was static. While Europe remained calm after the war we, hysterically, went in for an enormous increase of pace in the active arts of the theatre. I do not know whether we are altogether the losers, and leave the question to others. I do know that for a

and that a transient criticism of it is adequate. The permanent qualities are touched on elsewhere; especially in the essay entitled "Toujours Jazz." Since this was written there have been other negro shows, and I have heard that one was beter than *Shuffle Along.* What has interested me more is the report that there is a "nigger show by white men" which is standing them up every night. This verifies a prediction made below—that the negro show would have an effect on the white man's. I am not at all sure that there will not continue to be negro shows for a long time—why in Heaven's name shouldn't there be? They have their qualities and their great virtues. It is only in relation to the sophisticated Broadway piece that I find them lacking; and have perhaps not been fair enough to them.

146

moment these pieces seem to have overshadowed our (can I say?) native revues.

Of course, in America no one cares for revues except the unenlightened millions who pay to see them, so there is no one to rise and make lamentation over this state of affairs. For years we have laboured to perfect our revues—and the shuffling feet of a barbarian summon up an evil djinn to banish them. The serene smoothness of manœuvre which Mr Wayburn prepares for Mr Ziegfeld shrinks from the boards before the haphazard leaping of unstudied numbers; the sweet gravity of the dancers is forgotten for the barbarous rhythm of any half dozen darkies with a sense of syncopation innate in them. Lavishness from Joseph Urban precariously maintains itself against the smudged back-drop and the over-all; and over the prostrate and flowerlike and seductive beauty of the chorus-girl, there steps and struts, magnificently struts, the high-yaller!

The comparatively sober truth is that negro cabaret in the theatre is only a diversion, a necessary and healthful variation from our norm. It has qualities seldom exquisite and always arresting; and these qualities, having slowly vanished from the revue, have found themselves again in burlesque and in these exotics. And I think it highly probable that their only lasting effect will be to restore certain highly desirable things to revue and musical comedy. If there is any doubt of their goodness, another contrast will prove the point.

The one claim never made for the negro shows is that they are artistic. Set beside them, then, a professedly artistic revue, the *Pinwheel,* compounded of native and exotic effects. It had two or three interesting or exciting numbers; but the whole effect was one of dreariness. The pall of art was upon it; it died nightly. And *Shuffle Along,* without art, but with tremendous vitality, not only lived through the night, but dragged provincial New Yorkers to a midnight show as well. Facing the other way, one beholds a straight fake, the untimely efforts of Messrs McIntyre and Heath, who served

147

only to remind us that in time since overpast the real nigger show, as practised by Williams and Walker, existed, and that what we are seeing now is actually a continuation thereof, brought down from Harlem to Broadway.

Now it was fairly obvious that *Shuffle Along* had been conceived as an entertainment for negroes; that is why it remained solid when it took Broadway, to the intense surprise of its producers. It was, in short, an exotic for us, but it wasn't an exotic for themselves. Its honesty was its success, and its honesty put a certain stamp upon its successors. In all of them there is visible a regrettable tendency to imitate, at moments, the worst features of our usual musical comedy. But the major portion of each show is native, and so good.

They have all of them an appearance of unpremeditated violence which distinguishes them from the calculated and beautiful effects of Mr Ziegfeld or Mr John Murray Anderson. It goes much beyond the celebrated (and by this time faked) appearance of "enjoying themselves." They may never forgive me for it, but I really do not care whether the actors and actresses who amuse me are having a good time themselves. The theatre, for them, is a place for *producing*, not for *enjoying* sensations and effects; so the one thing I wish them is that when they are good they may have the purely moral pleasure of being good. It is the method that counts, and in the negro shows the method has been always the maximum pressure in song and dance, and the minimum of subtlety in the conversations and patter songs. The exceptions are not notable.

The songs and dances must be scored *fff*, a *stretto*, and after that those diverging lines which indicate *crescendo;* the lines of violence never again approach each other in these numbers, and one has to wait for the appearance of a fairly silly sentimental song for a moment of quiet. The strange people who direct these shows and the responsive animals who sing and dance have with some success controverted the notion that it is in contrasts that the intelligent man has his greatest pleasure. One feels that the show is a continuous wild cry and an

148

uninterrupted joyous rage, that the *élan vital* is inexhaustible and unbridled and enormously good.

The most skilful individual player has been Florence Mills; merely to watch her walk out upon the stage, with her long, free stride and her superb, shameless swing, is an æsthetic pleasure; she is a school and exemplar of carriage and deportment; two other actors I have seen so take a stage; Cohan by stage instinct, Marie Tempest by a cultivated genius. Florence Mills is almost the definition of the romantic *"une force qui va,"* but she remains an original, with little or nothing to give beyond her presence, her instinctive grace, and her baffling, seductive voice. Without that endowment, a small one in comparison with, say, Gilda Grey's, almost all the others give nothing but energy, and the trouble there is that if you have nothing but energy to give, you must give more than you can afford. The wild cry is a little too piercing at times, the postures and the pattings and the leapings all a little beyond the necessary measure. It remains simple; but simplicity, even if it isn't usually vulgar, can be a bit rough.

In the past few years the line of development of most of our revues and musical shows has been clearly marked; the bad old days were slowly forgotten and whatever was suggestive had to become subtle; and gradually, as the surface polish grew brighter, the suggestive humours underneath were forgotten; our revues became denatured in more senses than one. There is one *risqué* moment in the whole of a recent *Follies,* and that is one more than usual. The twittering about love and a kiss goes on; but the Great Reality of Sex is (quite properly, I am sure) forgotten. And in an encore stanza of *He May Be Your Man, But He comes to See Me—Sometimes,* as sung at the Plantation, the whole conventionalized fabric of our popular love songs was flung aside and the gay reality exposed. This amorous frankness is part of a simple realism— a sophisticated realism couldn't occur in a musical show, unless in the manner of Offenbach's *La Belle Hélène.* It is a fitting counterpart to the exaggerated postures, the slightly lubricious gestures and movements, of the dance. Another simplicity, and a very good one, is in such a song as that about a dog from Tennessee in *Oh, Joy*—a song which with that one quality, and against indifferent music and unexceptional words, broke up the show.

Behind the frankness and the violence and the simplicity there is found the most important factor of all—the music. And behind that stands a figure exceedingly attractive and, in its tragedy, almost moving, that of the late Jim Europe. Of the music itself—of jazz and the use of spirituals and the whole question of our national music—this is clearly not the place to write. One wishes to mention a name or two: Shelton Brooks, least *habile* of pseudo-Balieffs, wrote long ago *The Darktown Strutters' Ball,* which ought not to be forgotten; Creamer and Layton composed all of *Strut, Miss Lizzie,* and therein appeared *Sweet Angeline,* as complex a piece of syncopation as Mr Berlin ever composed. What portion of *Shuffle Along* was composed by Noble Sissle and Eubie Blake I do not know, but Sissle in action and Blake at the piano were wholly satisfying and expert. And all of these composers, and all of the jazz bands who play for them, have the ineffable advantage of being assured, in advance, of dancers who in fancy or straight dancing have the essential feelings for rhythm and broken rhythm in their bones.

And that interior response to syncopation Jim Europe had to the highest possible degree. He had been, before the war, the band leader at the Castles'; I am told by one who knows of such matters that his actual vogue was passing when the war came. He returned with the 369th U. S. Infantry "Hell-Fighters" Band and for a few Sunday nights in March, 1919, he packed the old Manhattan Opera House to the doors.

Say that what he played had nothing to do with music; say that to mention the name of a conductor in the same breath with his name is an atrocity of taste—I cannot help

150

believing that Jim Europe had the essential quality of music in him, and that, in his field, however far from any other it may have been, he was as great as Karl Muck in his. He did have contrast; it was out of the contracting stresses of a regular beat and a divergent that he created his effects. The hand kept perfect time, and his right knee, with a sharp and subtle little motion, stressed the acceleration or retard of the syncope. His dynamics were beautiful because he knew the value of noise and knew how to produce it and how to make it effective; he knew how to keep perfectly a running commentary of wit over the masses of his sound; and the ease and smoothness of his own performance as conductor had all the qualities of greatness. He rebuked a drummer in his band for some infraction of discipline and was killed.

Whatever the negro show has to give to the perfected Broadway production has its sources fairly deep in the negro consciousness, and I put Jim Europe forth as its symbol because in him nearly all that is most precious came to the surface. He seemed sensitive to the ecstasy and pathos of the spirituals as he was to the ecstasy and joy of jazz. He was, as conductor, vigorous and unaffected and clean. In *Shuffle Along*, Messrs Sissle and Blake paid honour to his memory, but the unacknowledged debt of the others is greater. I am inclined to think that, if sterility does not set in for the more notable Broadway product, it will be because something of what Jim Europe had to give has been quintessentialized by his successors and adopted.

◄§ I do not take much pleasure in the fact that my predictions about Negro revues was fulfilled. They were economically impracticable, although they cost far less than a Follies show, because they seldom became reverberating hits that filled big theatres. They could afford to play to a half-empty house, but the owner of the house wanted it full.

At the same time, the development of very big night clubs, many of which employed Negro entertainers and choruses, made the theatre-show superfluous. Many of them had been expanded Harlem nightclub productions with some perfunctory imitations of Winter Garden numbers added. They were better in their earlier state.

Two names in the foregoing affect me. *The Darktown Strutters' Ball* was easily as good as I thought it and is constantly played today. And Florence Mills, who died very young, is, after all these years, a great person in the memory of all who ever saw her. A European composer, seeing her offstage, said to me, "this is the first aristocrat I've seen in America" and called attention to the fragile wrists and ankles, the delicacy of her entire form, the enlightened gaiety of her expression. When she sang, the whole of her person was engaged, so that even if I cannot remember her voice, I am still under the spell of her singing. When she died the whole of Harlem and a great part of the rest of New York attended the funeral services. 𝒢

Plan for a
lyric theatre in America

I am going to establish a lyric theatre in America. Not an art theatre and not a temple of the drama, and not an experimental theatre. A lyric theatre where there will always be Mozart and Jerome Kern and Gilbert-and-Sullivan and Lehar—and NEVER by any chance Puccini or the Ring or Ibsen. I shall avoid the good things and the bad alike in the serious forms; I shall have Russian Ballets and American ballets. The chief thing is that it will be a theatre devoted to *all* the forms of light musical entertainment and to nothing else. My theatre will put an end to those disheartening revivals (or resurrections) of popular musical shows because the shows will be kept alive, just as "grand" operas are kept alive by appearing in a repertory. Into the repertory I shall incorporate—as soon as their independent existence is at an end—such successes as *The Night Boat* and such failures as *The Land of Joy*. There will never be a chance for *fashion* to destroy things essentially good. I shall produce new pieces, too; and if they are good they will run along with frequent presentations until they are absorbed in the general scheme. And I think I shall have pastiches frequently—of revues and topical productions which aren't, as entireties, capable of continuing.

That is the abridgement of a scheme, and I say I shall do it in the hope that someone else, even if it be the Messrs

153

Shubert, will do it instead. Because I like musical comedy and it annoys me that I can hear *Un bel di* (which I want never to hear again) fifteen times a season, and cannot hear *The Sun Shines Brighter* or *The Ragtime Melodrama* ever again. And I know that our present type of musical comedy is so good, so vigorous and snappy, that it tends to kill off its predecessors; a repertory is the only thing; and the usual objections to repertory will fail here, because in this case the devotees of musical shows will know in advance that. "it is going to be a good show." I don't know whether the bill should change every day or every week; I feel certain that there ought to be half a dozen centres across the continent, and two or three touring companies. Further details I cannot give now. I shall try to find some means, however, of distinguishing between the second-act finale of *The Mottled Mask* ("On to the ball at the palace of Prince Gregory") from the second-act finale of *The Madcap in Motley* ("On to the ball at the palace of Prince Gregory"). It is not part of my scheme to keep bad shows alive.

The rare entertainment such a theatre will afford can be guessed if you look for a moment at the changes in musical shows since 1900. We were then coming out of the Gilbert and Sullivan tradition and (after a great vogue of extravaganza) coming into the Viennese mode. It is the fashion now, especially in France, to belittle the Viennese operetta, to call its waltz song heavy and its structure a bore. Possibly these things are true; but Vienna has been the home of operetta for over a century and has done well by itself most of the time. Illumination of this predominant influence you can get by going to the Redoutensaal and hearing a performance of *The Marriage of Figaro,* and within the next few days hearing *Die Fledermaus* and whatever new piece Lehar or Fall or Oscar Straus has composed. For what one seldom knows from its loftier production is that *Figaro* is in essence and detail a musical comedy and that almost all we know of the form stems from the combination effected there by a great composer, a fine dramatist, and an exceptionally skilful librettist.[1] The imperial ballroom with its tapestried walls, its small stage on which only conventionalized scenery can be set, its divided stairway coming down on the stage, is a setting admirably contrived to give the whole loveliness of operetta. The last scene is in the garden of the count: six boxed trees and moonlight create the effect. And at the last moment, the happy ending, the electric lights are thrown on, the vast crystal chandelier lighting up over the garden, and the event recedes into its real, its secondary framework, as entertainment. One recognizes it for what it is—the gay and exquisite counterpart of grand opera, from which neither the Savoy nor the Viennese operetta ever departed. Musically the Viennese type corresponds more clearly to Italian, the Gilbert and Sullivan to French opera. The absurd conventions of production are taken bodily from the older and more respected type. The same thing is as obviously true in Cimarosa's *Marriage Secret* as it is in *The Chocolate Soldier*—the latter being, except for a weaker libretto, a perfect parallel to *Figaro*. (And nearly as worthy of the perpetual life which is apparently to be denied it.)

It is still unnecessary to describe the Viennese operetta in detail, for immediately after the war it came again into vogue and one or two excellent examples—*The Last Waltz* was one of them—re-established some of its ancient prestige. It is at bottom produced *for the music*. In one the music may be chiefly sung, in another danced. Everything else— *décor*, story, humorous episodes—is secondary. Recently an effort has been made to change this. Oscar Straus' *Törichte Jungfrau* at the *Grossesschauspielhaus* (Reinhardt's catacombs in Berlin) was all production—and nearly all dreadful. Lehar's latest, *Das Gelbe Jacke* (not, however, our

---

[1] For da Ponte's share in the work, cf. Edgar Istel: Das Libretto, which analyzes the changes made in Beaumarchais' play.

Yellow Jacket) is entirely in the pure Viennese mode, and the Vienna production (February, 1923) indicates how Viennese operetta is improved in transit to our shores. For our production of musical comedy is almost equal to our production of revue, which is incontestably the finest in the world. With their emphasis on music the Viennese shows naturally centre about the famous waltz-song; and one good waltz has been able to make a show a success. Rudolf Friml made a success of *High Jinks* with a fox-trot.

The English type as we know it, including Caryll and Monckton and Rubens, has had for thirty years the Savoy tradition. This requires a plot of more frivolity than the Viennese, and lyrics of greater humour. The successes have been moderate—"I've got a motto" is no masterpiece. The degree of fun has been higher and the seductiveness of the music less. It was perfectly natural that (with *Adele* to help them on) a combination of virtues should take place in America in the beautiful *Princess Shows* of Comstock and Gest, where the talents of P. G. Wodehouse, Guy Bolton, and Jerome Kern, stage-managed perfectly by Robert Milton, produced a fresh and attractive type of musical show which for five years progressed in popularity—but had few imitators—and suddenly seemed to disappear. It was, in fact, transformed into something else, something good. But one should look at the original closely to discern its exceptional virtues.

Each of the Princess shows had a reasonable, but not serious, plot. The advantage of a plot isn't, as one often hears, that it gives the appearance of reality to the piece, for who should expect that? There is no reason why a musical comedy should not be wholly preposterous, dramatically or psychologically, provided, like *Iolanthe,* it has a logic of its own. No. The advantage is that when there is a definitely perceptible structure everything else arrives with greater intensity of effect. The best of the Princess shows

156

had the weakest plot, for *Leave It to Jane* was based on Ade's *College Widow,* which has no great quality. Since songs and dances had to take up much time, this plot was gratifyingly reduced to a few essential lines and played without sentiment. The result was a rush of action in which everything found place. The later pieces were on librettos by Guy Bolton, suggesting French farces, and full of neat arrangements. None of them was stupid. They all gave place for Mr Wodehouse's exceptional talents as a lyric-writer. He is as an English humorist superior to most, and as a master of complicated, original, amusing rhymes is the best man in the business. A special quality of making fun is discernible in all his lyrics, and he does good parodies, like *When It's Nesting Time in Flatbush.* The Princess type made rather a fetish of simplicity (I quote from memory):

> Although the thing that's smart is
> To stay out all night on parties,
> I'll be sitting, with my knitting,
> In the good old-fashioned way,

and of sentiment:

> The breeze in the trees brings a scent of orange blossoms
>   And the skies turn soft and blue,
> When there's no one around except the girl you love
>   And the girl you love loves you,

which was often not amorous and rose to as fine a thing as *The Siren Song:*

> Come to us, we've waited so long for you,
> Every day we make a new song for you;
>   Come, come, to us, we love you so.
> Leave behind the world and its fretting
> And we will give you rest and forgetting,
>   So sang the sirens ages and ages ago.

There was also patter as in the Cleopatra song:

> And when she tired, as girls will do,
>   Of Bill or Jack or Jim,
> The time had come, his friends all knew,
>   To say good-by to him.
> She would not stand by any means
> Regretful, stormy, farewell scenes,
> To such low stuff she would not stoop
> So she just put poison in the soup.
>
> When out with Cleopatterer
> Men always made their wills;
> They knew they had no time to waste.
> When the gumbo had that funny taste
> They'd take her hand and squeeze it
>   And murmur, "Oh, you kid!"
> But they none of 'em liked to start to feed
>   Till Cleopatterer did.

and in each of these types Wodehouse was faultless.

Fortunately for him and for us these songs were set to a music which in addition to being delightful let the words appear, and occasionally was so fluent, so inevitable, that it made the words seem even simpler and more conversational than they are. Jerome Kern composed nearly all of the Princess shows and the collected scores are impressive. He is the most erudite of our simple composers and he manipulates material with inordinate skill. He can adapt German folksong (*Freut euch das Leben* underlies *Phoebe Snow*); he didn't do so well by *Kingdom Comin'*, which was botched and cut; he also understands Sullivan. But his best work, *The Siren Song, The Little Ships, The Sun Shines Brighter,* have a melodious line, a structure, and a general tidiness of execution which are all their own. *The Siren Song* corresponds exactly to the Viennese waltz, but both the words and the music are impersonal; they are a gentle hymn to seduction, with humour. Scattered between languorous rhythms are bursts of gaiety, like a handful of pebbles thrown against a window—which doesn't open—for the song ends in a tender melancholy. It is a real achievement. Compare the lines I have quoted above with "Come, come, I love you only," from *The Chocolate Soldier*—phrases you would expect to arrive at the same musical conclusion. The crash of *"Oh, Hero Mine!"* in the second is good drama, saved from being too obvious by being sung to the coward Sergius and not to the protagonist Bluntschli. But in comparison the gentle ending of *The Siren Song* is, as song, superior: "So sang the Sirens, ages and ages ago"—and you take it or leave it. The music, at least, is not forcing your hand.

The Princess shows never had any great stars; instead, they had the one quality which always makes for success—*esprit de corps*. In each the company was aware of the nature and quality of the piece it was playing, and it worked in variations of that genial and sophisticated atmosphere. It was simply against the tone of the Princess shows to be dull; and I, who like nearly all musical shows, found in them my greatest delight.

They passed into something else because they were exquisitely proportioned on a small scale—the scale, by the way of *The Beggar's Opera*, which they resembled—and the whole tendency of the time was toward elaboration. They involved small choruses, little eccentric dancing, and required no humorist *hors de texte*. I count it a triumph for Mr Dillingham, as well as for the others concerned, that they have been able to preserve so much of the Princess in some of the Globe productions. The best of these, I think, is *Good-morning, Dearie*. It has an adequate plot; it has room for Harland Dixon, a fine dancer; for Ada Lewis, an expert broad comedienne; for Maurice and his partner, whose name I don't remember; for a large dancing chorus and for stunts; better still it did little to hinder Jerome

Kern. It was here that he took the most famous of waltzes and implicated it masterfully in a blues; and here that all the seductiveness and gaiety of the Princess music returned with *Ka-lu-a* and *Didn't You Believe?* There were a few faults in the production; the *décor* lacked freshness, although it didn't actually offend; the Chinese scene was hackneyed. But on the whole it is the best musical comedy I have seen since the Princess shows.

What forced us to be elaborate was not the memory of the Viennese type, but the growing complexity of revue, always cutting into musical comedy. It should be noted that *Around the Map* (which I hold the best musical comedy —not operetta—I saw before the Princess shows) first brought Joseph Urban into the field, taking him from the Boston Opera House and pushing him on the way to Ziegfeld, where he was tardily recognized by the Metropolitan for whom he has made *Oberon! Around the Map* had some twenty scenes, it dealt with a trip around the world in search of safety socks, and was all gay (with Else Alder), all good music (Caryll) and only the beginning of elaboration. But Mr Berlin's two shows and a host of others indicated that to survive musical comedy would have to appear lavish. Comparatively simple shows still occur—*Tangerine* was one; but we seem to be in for something fairly elaborate —in music as in the Le-Baron-Kreisler pieces, in *décor* as in the Shubert-Century productions, in stars and stunts as in Dillingham's.

I do not pretend to cover the ground, and to name the names, in this sketch; not even to characterize all the types. I don't know what to say about *Mary,* in which George M. Cohan worked a chorus into a state of frantic energy and Louis Hirsch provided *The Love Nest;* nor of twenty other individual successes. One composer remains whose work is often so good, whose case is so illuminating, that he must be considered. That is Victor Herbert. It should be said at once that even long after his early successes he composed a

160

fine musical comedy, *The Only Girl*. The difficulty about Mr Herbert is that he has succumbed to the American habit of thinking that grand opera is great opera. I have heard him at one of his *premières* speaking from the conductor's dais to assure the audience that the present piece was in the high line of operetta, that more pieces like it would put an end to the vulgarity of musical shows. The regrettable fact was that *The Madcap Duchess* put an end to nothing but itself; I recall the name, that Ann Swinburne was in it, and that it had a good patter song; the rest was doleful. Whereas two weeks later in the same house I heard *The Lady of the Slipper,* in which Mr Herbert, setting out to write an ordinary simple musical show, was a thoroughly competent composer, full of ingenuity and interest and taste and invention. If he had only taken his eyes off the Metropolitan Opera House he would probably have been the best of the lot to-day. He suffers—although he is vastly respected —because he failed in respect to the fine art of the musical show.

The wonderful thing about that art is that it is made up of varied elements which are fused into something greater than themselves. There is a song and dance by Julia Sanderson, who is not a great artist; or the sudden apparition of a little man pursued in a harem, bounding upon a scarlet pouffe six feet in diameter and nuzzling like a dog— Jimmy Barton, in fact, who is one; and the rambling story told by Percival Knight in *The Quaker Girl* or the drunken scene by Clifton Crawford in *The Peasant Girl;* there is *In the Night,* from *The Queen of the Movies* or Johnny Dooley falling out of the clerk's desk in *Listen, Lester;* there is Donald Brian, the perpetual *jeune premier,* or the amazing Spanish song in *Apple Blossoms,* or a setting designed by Norman-Bel Geddes or costumes by Helen Dryden or the *Sandman* song from *The Dollar Princess,* or the entrance of the Bulgarians in *The Chocolate Soldier* or the wickedly expert prosody of Brian Hooker. What is it takes all of these and composes them into something beautiful and entertaining? Skill in production is part of it, but not all, for the same elements: colour, light, sound, movement, can be combined into other forms which lack that particular air of urbanity, of well-being, of rich contentment and interest which is the special atmosphere of musical shows. I can only find a word and say that the secret resides in it—high spirits. For a musical comedy, even a sentimental one, must be high-spirited in execution—that was the lesson of an unsentimental one, *The Beggar's Opera;* and at the same time there must be some courage, some defiance of nature and sound sense, a feeling for fantasy which means that the life of the spirit is high, even when the life of the body is in chains. It is for this freedom of the spirit, released by music as always and diverted by all the other elements in them, that these shows are cherished. It is, naturally, as a counter-attack on solemnity that I am going to found my theatre.

◄§ Once every five years or so a plan for just such a theatre is broached and nothing ever comes of it. Perhaps it was feasible when I wrote out my plan—which I never intended, myself, to put into action. By now, the cost of producing musicals has had an effect on the kind of musicals we get: they have to be elaborate, they have to be smash hits, they have to be supported by the "expense-account" set. The nearest thing we have to a musical repertory theatre occurs in out-of-the-way places during the summer.

Yet it seems to me that the materials for this kind of theatre, including the essential one which is a genuine public liking for the type, are at hand. By 1960, let us say, *My Fair Lady* will have left Broadway and five national companies, no doubt, will cease to operate. Even *Oklahoma!* came to an end. By that time wholly new audiences in New York and in a hundred other places will be ready to see the show and to see *Oklahoma!* which will stand reviving, no matter what happens to the movie. To be sure, *My Fair Lady* will have appeared in television and perhaps as a movie also, but the distinguishing mark of a musical is that it is seen again and again with undiminished satisfaction. Some of those mentioned in the preceding pages I saw as often as five times in a single month (I was working on a newspaper at the time). Since a good musical show is not a medium for ideas (no matter how many ideas it uses) it has nothing in it to grow stale and its base-element, the music, is precisely what we actively want to hear over and over again. Moreover, a continuing lyric theatre would re-do its shows, bringing fresh ideas of production, new dances, and fresh faces as well as the remembered elements.

However, the times are against me and much that is delightful in the theatre is lost. Revivals seldom are successful. The most conspicuous exception in our time was *Pal Joey* which was a near-failure when it was first offered, a great success fifteen years later. Many of the New York critics seemed to apologize for their obtuseness in failing to see its virtues the first time round and gave it a warm welcome the second time. I was lucky in having admired it from the start. It has now vanished again. If my theatre were in operation, it would never be absent long. &

The one-man show

&§ I was not trying to make book on posterity when I
wrote this, but it is gratifying to note that three of the
men concerned here went on to later careers and are even
better known than they were at a time when I imagined
them at the height of their powers. (Radio, movies with
sound, and television were still to come—and gave new
professional life to men of varied talent.)

A strange thing has happened to star-billing in our time.
When I wrote this, the star was the person who did most
for the show in which he appeared. Nowadays, in television, it is the man who does least. You have not only the
self-effacing Ed Sullivan who has a great deal to do with
the character of the variety program he introduces, you
have second-order stars, male and female, of Hollywood
who merely announce the name of a weekly play and say
a few empty words about it and become such important
"personalities," to the sponsor, that often the program is
renamed to include the star's name. This is popularity
not by talent, but by exposure. The people I deal with
here were prodigious in talent, they appeared once every
year or so in a show—and deserved their success. &»

When all the other grave æsthetic questions about the stage
are answered, some profound theorist may explain the existence of the one-man show. Since I am not a materialist,
I cannot concede the obvious solution—that a man finds

enough money to produce himself in a Broadway show—
because there is something attractive and mysterious about
this type of entertainment which the explanation fails to
explain.

The theory of the one-man show is apparently that there
are individuals so endowed, so versatile, and so beloved,
that no other vehicle will suffice to let them do their work.
Conversely, that they are of such quality that *they* suffice for
the strange entertainment with which they are surrounded
and that nothing else matters provided they are long and
frequent on the stage. Six men and two women are in the
first roster of the one-man show: Fred Stone, Ed Wynn,
Raymond Hitchcock, Eddie Cantor, Frank Tinney, and Al
Jolson; below them, leading the women, Elsie Janis and
Nora Bayes. And omitting Jolson because he is so great that
he cannot be put in any company, the greatest one-man show
was one in which none of these appeared—it was one in
which even the man himself didn't appear. It was a show
in which one man succeeded where all of these, this time
not excluding Jolson, had failed: for he made the whole
production *his kind* of show—and the others have never
quite managed to do more than make themselves.

The chief example of this failure is Hitchcock, whose
series lapses ever so often, leaving him stranded on the bleak
shore of a *Pin Wheel Revue*—an artistic, an intellectual,
an incredibly stupid production which Hitchy manfully
tried first to save and then to abandon. There were in the
better Hitchy shows other first-rate people: one who mas-
queraded as Joseph Cook and was none other than Joe Cook
the Humorist out of vaudeville and out of his element; Ray
Dooley was with Hitchy, I believe, and there were always
good dancers. Hitchy kept on the stage a long time, as *conférencier* and as participant, and his amiable drollery was
always at the same level—just enough. He never quite concealed the strain of making a production *go;* one always
wanted to be much more amused, and Hitchy never got

166

beyond the episode of the Captain of the Fire Brigade or trying to buy the middle two-cent stamp in a sheet of a hundred. A series of vaudeville sketches doesn't make a one-man show, even if he plays in all of them; and the moment Hitchcock was off, *Hitchy-koo* went to pieces, some good and some bad, and all trying a little too hard to be something else.

Eddie Cantor and Al Jolson appear in the two different Winter Garden types of show—the Jolson and the Winter Garden *in impuris naturalibus*. Jolson infuses something both gay and broad into his pieces; even the recurrence of Lawrence D'Orsay cannot win back the original Winter Garden atmosphere and even the disappearance of Kitty Doner cannot diminish Jolson's private quality. Of the straight Winter Garden shows, the 1922 with Eddie Cantor was the best in ten years, made so by Cantor and made by him, in spite of the billing, into a one-man show. The nervous energy of Cantor isn't sufficient to animate the active, but indifferent choruses of the Shuberts. One thing, however, he can do superbly—the lamb led to the slaughter. It is best when he chooses to play the timid, Ghetto-bred, pale-faced Jewish lad, seduced by glory or the prospects of pay into competing with athletes and bruisers. One thing he cannot do and should learn not to try—the blackface song and comedy of his master, Jolson. The scenes of violence vary; that of the osteopath was an exploitation of meaningless brutality; I cared for nothing after Eddie's frightened entrance, "Are you the Ostermoor?" But the aviation examination and the application for the police force were excellent pieces of construction, holding sympathy all the way through and keeping on the safe side of nausea. Both of these were before the Winter Garden days and the Winter Garden exploit was better than either. He played here a cutter in a hand-me-down clothing store and it was his function to leap into the breach whenever a customer showed the slightest tendency to leave without buying a

167

suit. The victim was obsessed by some idea of having "a belt in the back" and was forced into sailor suits and fancy costume and was generally made miserable. Eddie's terrific rushes from the wings, his appeals to God to strike him dead "on the spot" if the suit now being tried on wasn't the best suit in the world, his helplessness and his, "Well, kill me, so kill me," as apology when his partner revealed the damning fact that that happened to be the man's old suit—all of this was worth the whole of the Potash-Perlmutter cycle. And the whole-heartedness of Cantor's violence—essentially the bullying of a coward who has at last discovered some one weaker than himself, was faultless. He sings well the slightly suggestive songs like *After the Ball* (new version), and his three broken dance steps with the sawing motion of his gloved hands create an image exceedingly precise and palpable. There is in him just enough for the one-man show, but so far it has been limited by his tendency to imitate and by failure to develop his own sources of strength. Even in *Kid Boots* he just fails to make the grade.

◄§ There was a silly feud between the admirers of Cantor and of Jolson and I was ranged with the Jolsonites, so that I may underestimate Cantor here. There seems to be no form of entertainment he cannot encompass to the satisfaction of a great many people. To my taste there is none in which he is the unquestioned best of the batch. The spasmodic energy which I saw in him from the beginning has had to be slightly checked with the passing of time, but the will behind it is still there. The dynamics are impressive. But no amount of critical analysis will do any good. I fall back on the human privilege (not to be abused by critics) of having a blind spot. ε»

The one-man show *requires* its leader to leave nothing in himself unexploited—there is too much for him to do and he must take everything on himself—the requirements are

168

exactly opposite to those of the vaudeville act where the actor must work in the briefest compass, with the utmost concentration, and get his effects in the shortest time. Frank Tinney's success in vaudeville marks the limitations of his success in his shows—for he imposed on vaudeville that languid easy-going manner of his and was just enough out of vaudeville tempo (he is very deceptive in this) to appear to be a novelty there. In essence he isn't a good one-man, for his line is limited and his humour and his good-humour (in which he is matched only by Ed Wynn) are not capable of the strain of a long winter's evening entertainment. Tinney was excellent in a quarrel scene with Bernard Granville (in a Ziegfeld *Follies,* I think) the two pacing in opposite directions, the width of the stage between them, always from footlights to backdrop and never crossing the stage; he was disputatious and entertaining on the negative of the proposition that the Erie railroad (pronounced for reasons of his own, Ee-righ) is a very expensive railroad; his appearance in *Watch Your Step* was almost perfect. (Consult Mr A. Woollcott's *Shouts and Murmurs* for everything about Tinney; Mr Woollcott's descriptions are accurate and evocative and he errs only in his estimate of Tinney's quality.) Tinney has everything except the excess of vitality, the surcharge of genius. He has method nearly to perfection and it is a wholly original, ingratiating, and, up to a certain point, adaptable method. What he has done is to destroy the "good joke," for all of Tinney's jokes are bad ones and he gets his effect by fumbling about with them, by lengthening the preliminaries, by false starts, erasures, corrections—until his arrival at the point relieves the suspense. I have heard him take at least ten minutes to put over: "Lend me a dollar for a week, old man.—Who is the weak old man?" and not a moment was superfluous. He is expert at kidding the audience, and as he is never in character he never steps out. There isn't quite enough of him, that is all.

There is enough of Fred Stone for versatility and not

enough for specific personal appeal. As acrobat, dancer, ventriloquist, and cut-up Stone is easily in the lead; but the unnamable quality is lacking. See him climbing up an arbour to meet his Juliet in the balcony; he is discovered, hangs head downward in peril of his life, seizes a potted flower and with it begins to dust the vines—it is Chaplinesque in conception and beautifully executed. See him on the slack rope continually on the point of falling off and continually recovering and seeming to hang on by his boot toe; or in *The Lady of the Slipper* making a beautiful series of leaps from chair to divan, from divan to table, to a triumphant exit through the unsuspected scenery; or in another quality recall the famous "Very good, Eddie," of *Chin-Chin.* He is incredible; one wouldn't miss him for worlds; yet it is always what he does and not himself that constitutes the attraction. I wonder whether I do not wrong him altogether by classing him with the one-men, for it was always something more than Montgomery and Stone in the days of *The Red Mill* and Stone does not exaggerate himself on the stage. His command of attributes is greater than that of any other player; he does everything with a beautiful, errorless accuracy—and the pleasure of seeing things *exactly right,* all the time, is not to be underestimated.

It is Ed Wynn's pleasure to make everything seem utterly haphazard. Wynn is a surd in the theatre—there is always something left unresolved in reducing him to the lowest term, and he is incommensurable because there are no standards for him and no similars. I prefer to see him wandering through a good revue, changing hats, worrying about a "rewolwer" in the first scene and stopping dead in the twentieth to declare that it wasn't a "rewolwer" at all, but a pistol. When he came to put on a one-man show he preserved the best part of this incoherence. He made it his business to appear before a drop curtain and explain in an amazing vocabulary and with painstaking gravity exactly what was to occur in the next scene. He affects to be awkward (to quote him, I might go so far as to call him uncouth. . . . I think I *will* call him uncouth. . . . He is uncouth); his gestures are florid and wide, his earnestness makes all things vivid. Each of these explanations involves a bad pun and none, of course, has anything to do with the scene that actually follows. Like Jolson and Cantor, he takes the stage at a given moment and entertains. His famous inventions seemed to be the crudest form of humour—a typewriter carriage for eating corn on the cob, a burning candle to set in one's ears in order to wake up in time— yet sheer ebullition carried them high into the field of "nice, clean fun." Wynn's words come tumbling out of him, agglutinated, chaotic, disorderly; he is abashed by his own occasional temerity, he is timid and covers it with brashness —and all of this is a carefully created personage; it is *not* Ed Wynn. He has found a little odd corner of life which no one else cultivates; it is a sort of rusticity in the face of *simple* things; he is a perpetual immigrant obsessed by hats and shoes and words and small ideas, instead of bothering about skyscrapers. The deepness of his zanylike appreciation of every-day things is the secret of his capacity for making them startling and funny. His one fault is the show with which he surrounds himself.

⤢ Ed Wynn's later career is a sentimentalist's dream. He went into eclipse as so many others did and surprised most of us, perhaps including himself, by a sensational comeback in the days before television had the transcontinental coaxial cable. His shows were done in Hollywood and were among the few seen in the faulty kinescope of those days in the East. He was one of the very first well-grounded showmen to appear, you knew at once that you were being entertained by a great professional. The remorseless turn of the wheel discarded him again, but not for long. He returned as a straight actor and again won every heart. That is his special quality. ⤣

I have never seen Elsie Janis better than she was in *The Lady of the Slipper*—with the exception of Gaby Deslys I have never seen any woman comparable to Miss Janis in that piece, and in it she had qualities which ought to have made her appearance in an individual show a much greater success than it actually turned out to be. For, except a voice, Miss Janis has everything. She is a beautiful dancer and her legs are handsomer than Mistinguett's, and she is the finest mimic I have ever seen on the stage, several shades ahead of Ina Claire. An exceptional intelligence operates in the creation of these caricatures, for they are all created by seizing upon vital characteristics of tone, gesture, tempo of movement, spirit; and the arrangement of her hair and the contortions of her face are only guide-signs to the accomplished act. She is herself of an abounding grace, a suppleness of body and of mind, and the measure of her skill is the exact degree in which her grace and simplicity are transformed into harshness or angularity or sophistication as she passes one after another of our stage personalities before her mirror. This year I saw her in a Paris music-hall take off Mistinguett and Max Dearly. She presented them singing *Give Me Moonlight* in their own imagined versions and her throaty "Give me a gas light" for the creator of *Mon Homme* was superb. She offered to sing it, at the end, as she herself ought to sing it—and danced it without uttering a sound. It reminded one of Irene Castle in *Watch Your Step*. For an exact calculation of her capacities and a sensible, modest intention to stay within them and to exploit them to the limit are parts of Elsie Janis's intelligence. To be sure, it isn't her intelligence—it is her loveliness and her talent that endear her to us. But it is grateful, for once in a way, to find a talent so great, a loveliness so irresistible, joined to an intelligence which sets all in motion and spoils nothing.

I suspect that in spite of the best of the one-man shows there is something wrong with the idea—perhaps because

172

the environment requires more than any man has yet been able to give. And the one perfect example is, as I have suggested, proof of this. Because *Stop! Look! Listen!* which was only a moderate success on Broadway and involved the talents of Gaby Deslys, Doyle and Dixon, Harry Fox, Tempest and Sunshine, the beautiful Justine Johnston, Helen Barnes, Helen Dryden as costumer and Robert McQuinn as scenic designer, a beautiful chorus and an excellent producer, was actually the one-man show of Irving Berlin. For once a complete and varied show expressed the spirit of one man to perfection. In that piece, Berlin wrote two of his masterpieces and about four other superb songs; and, more than that, suffused the entire production with the gay spirit of his music. There occurred *The Ragtime Melodrama* danced by Doyle and Dixon—only the Common Clay scene from the Cohan revue ever approached it, and Doyle and Dixon never danced better (unless, possibly, a quarter of an hour earlier in *The Hula-Hula*); there was *The Girl on the Magazine Cover,* perfectly set and costumed, a really good sentimental song with its quaint introduction of *Lohengrin* (not the *Wedding March*); there was *When I Get Back to the U.S.A.* sung against a chorus of *My Country, 'Tis of Thee*; there was Gaby's wicked *Take Off a Little Bit* and Harry Fox's *Press-Agent Song*—and finally the second of Berlin's three great tributes to his art: *I Love a Piano,* which, like the mother of Louis Napoleon, he wrote for six pianos and in which everything in syncopation up to that time was epitomized and carried to a perfect conclusion. Whatever was gay, light, colourful, whatever was accurate, assured, confident, and good-humoured, was in this miraculous production. I saw it twelve times in two weeks— lured partly, I must confess, by the hope that Harry Pilcer would break at least a leg in his fall down the golden stairs. He never did; in spite of which, seeing it again, months later, it still seemed to me the apotheosis of pure show. I think I could reconstruct every moment of it, including the useless plot and Justine Johnston's ankles; it seems a pity that all of it, the ephemeral and the permanent, should have already passed from the stage. It was a beginning in ragtime operetta which Mr Berlin has never followed up; his inexhaustible talents have been diverted into other things; he is now a maker of revues. Yet when he saw *The Beggar's Opera,* Mr Berlin felt something plucking at his sleeve, reminding him that it was his job, and his alone, to create the comparable type for America.

At that moment he thought back to *Stop! Look! Listen!*— but he had already begun to build the Music Box—and we must wait patiently for what time will bring as a real successor to his one-man show. At any rate, we have had it. We know, now, what it can amount to—and it is enough. Enough, at any rate, to put the veritable one-man show fairly definitely out of the running.

The dæmonic
in the American theatre

One man on the American stage, and one woman, are possessed—Al Jolson and Fanny Brice. Their dæmons are not of the same order, but together they represent all we have of the Great God Pan, and we ought to be grateful for it. For in addition to being more or less a Christian country, America is a Protestant community and a business organization—and none of these units is peculiarly prolific in the creation of dæmonic individuals. We can bring forth Roosevelts—dynamic creatures, to be sure; but the fury and the exultation of Jolson is a hundred times higher in voltage than that of Roosevelt; we can produce courageous and adventurous women who shoot lions or manage construction gangs and remain pale beside the extraordinary "cutting loose" of Fanny Brice.

To say that each of these two is possessed by a dæmon is a mediæval and perfectly sound way of expressing their intensity of action. It does not prove anything—not even that they are geniuses of a fairly high rank, which in my opinion they are. I use the word possessed because it connotes a quality lacking elsewhere on the stage, and to be found only at moments in other aspects of American life—in religious mania, in good jazz bands, in a rare outbreak of mob violence. The particular intensity I mean is exactly what you do not see at a baseball game, but may at a prize fight, nor in the productions of David Belasco, nor at a political convention; you may see it on the Stock Exchange and you can see it, canalized and disciplined, but still intense, in our skyscraper architecture. It was visible at moments in the old Russian Ballet.

In Jolson there is always one thing you can be sure of: that whatever he does he does at the highest possible pressure. I do not mean that one gets the sense of his effort, for his work is at times the easiest seeming, the most effortless in the world. Only he never saves up—for the next scene, or the next week, or the next show. His generosity is extravagant; he flings into a comic song or three-minute impersonation so much energy, violence, so much of the *totality* of one human being, that you feel it would suffice for a hundred others. In the days when the runway was planked down the centre of every good theatre in America, this galvanic little figure, leaping and shouting—yet always essentially dancing and singing—upon it was the concentration of our national health and gaiety. In *Row, Row, Row* he would bounce up on the runway, propel himself by imaginary oars over the heads of the audience, draw equally imaginary slivers from the seat of his trousers, and infuse into the song something wild and roaring and insanely funny. The very phonograph record of his famous *Toreador* song is full of vitality. Even in later days when the programme announces simply "Al Jolson" (about 10.15 P.M. in each of his reviews) he appears and sings and talks to the audience and dances off—and when he has done more than any other ten men, he returns and, blandly announcing that "You ain't heard nothing yet," proceeds to do twice as much again. He is the great master of the one-man show because he gives so much while he is on that the audience remains content while he is off—and his electrical energy almost always develops activity in those about him.

If it were necessary, a plea could be made for violence

176

per se in the American theatre, because everything tends to prettify and restrain, and the energy of the theatre is dying out. But Jolson, who lacks discipline almost entirely, has other qualities besides violence. He has an excellent baritone voice, a good ear for dialect, a nimble presence, and a distinct sense of character. Of course it would be impossible not to recognize him the moment he appears on the stage; of course he is always Jolson—but he is also always Gus and always Inbad the Porter, and always Bombo. He has created a way of being for the characters he takes on; they live specifically in the mad world of the Jolson show; their wit and their bathos are singularly creditable characteristics of themselves—not of Jolson. You may recall a scene—I think the show was called *Dancing Around*—in which a lady knocks at the door of a house. From within comes the voice of Jolson singing, "You made me love you, I didn't wanna do it, I didn't wanna do it"—the voice approaches, dwindles away, resumes—it is a swift characterization of the lazy servant coming to open the door and ready to insult callers, since the master is out. Suddenly the black face leaps through the doorway and cries out, "We don' want no ice," and is gone. Or Jolson as the black slave of Columbus, reproached by his master for a long absence. His lips begin to quiver, his chin to tremble; the tears are approaching, when his human independence softly asserts itself and he wails, "We all have our *moments*." It is quite true, for Jolson's technique is the exploitation of these moments; he has himself said that he is the greatest master of hokum in the business, and in the theatre the art of hokum is to make each second count for itself, to save any moment from dulness by the happy intervention of a slap on the back, or by jumping out of character and back again, or any other trick. For there is no question of legitimacy here —everything is right if it makes 'em laugh.

He does more than make 'em laugh; he gives them what I am convinced is a genuine emotional effect ranging from the thrill to the shock. I remember coming home after eighteen months in Europe, during the war, and stepping from the boat to one of the first nights of *Sinbad*. The spectacle of Jolson's vitality had the same quality as the impression I got from the New York sky line—one had forgotten that there still existed in the world a force so boundless, an exaltation so high, and that anyone could still storm Heaven with laughter and cheers. He sang on that occasion *'N Everything* and *Swanee*. I have suggested elsewhere that hearing him sing *Swanee* is what book reviewers and young girls loosely call an experience. I know what Jolson does with false sentiment; here he was dealing with something which by the grace of George Gershwin came true, and there was no necessity for putting anything over. In the absurd black-face which is so little negroid that it goes well with diversions in Yiddish accents, Jolson created image after image of longing, and his existence through the song was wholly in *its* rhythm. Five years later I heard Jolson in a second-rate show, before an audience listless or hostile, sing this out-dated and forgotten song, and create again, for each of us seated before him, the same image—and saw also the tremendous leap in vitality and happiness which took possession of the audience as he sang it. It was marvelous. In the first weeks of *Sinbad* he sang the words of *'N Everything* as they are printed. Gradually (I saw the show in many phases) he interpolated, improvised, always with his absolute sense of rhythmic effect; until at the end it was a series of amorous cries and shouts of triumph to Eros. I have heard him sing also the absurd song about "It isn't raining rain, It's raining violets" and remarked him modulating that from sentimentality into a conscious bathos, with his gloved fingers flittering together and his voice rising to absurd *fortissimi* and the general air of kidding the piece.

He does not generally kid his Mammy songs—as why should he who sings them better than anyone else? He cannot underplay anything, he lacks restraint, and he leans on the second-rate sentiment of these songs until they are forced to render up the little that is real in them. I dislike them and dislike his doing them—as I dislike Bell Baker singing *Elie, Elie!* But it is quite possible that my discomfort at these exhibitions is proof of their quality. They and a few very cheap jokes and a few sly remarks about sexual perversions are Jolson's only faults. They are few. For a man who has, year after year, established an intimate relation with no less than a million people, every twelvemonth, he is singularly uncorrupted. That relation is the thing which sets him so far above all the other one-man-show stars. Eddie Cantor gives at times the effect of being as energetic; Wynn is always and Tinney sometimes funnier. But no one else, except Miss Brice, so holds an audience in the hollow of the hand. The hand is steady; the audience never moves. And on the great nights when everything is right, Jolson is driven by a power beyond himself. One sees that he knows what he is doing, but one sees that he doesn't half realize the power and intensity with which he is doing it. In those moments I cannot help thinking of him as a genius.

Quite to that point Fanny Brice hasn't reached. She hasn't, to begin with, the physical vitality of Jolson. But she has a more delicate mind and a richer humour—qualities which generally destroy vitality altogether, and which only enrich hers. She is first a great farceur; and in her songs she is exactly in the tradition of Yvette Guilbert, without the range, so far as we know, which enabled Mme Guilbert to create the whole of mediæval France for us in ten lines of a song. The quality, however, is the same, and Fanny's evocations are as vivid and as poignant as Yvette's—they require from us exactly the same tribute of admiration. She has grown in power since she sang and made immortal, *I Should Worry*. Hear her now creating the tragedy of *Second-Hand Rose* or of the one Florodora Baby who—"five little dumbells got married for money, And I got married for love. . . ." These things are done with two-thirds of Yvette

Guilbert's material missing, for there are no accessories and, although the words (some of the best are by Blanche Merrill) are good, the music isn't always distinguished. And the effects are irreproachable. Give Fanny a song she can get her teeth into, *Mon Homme,* and the result is less certain, but not less interesting. This was one of a series of realistic songs for Mistinguett, who sang it very much as Yvonne George did when she appeared in America. Miss Brice took it *lento affetuoso;* since the precise character of the song had changed a bit from its rather more outspoken French original. Miss Brice suppressed Fanny altogether in this song—she was being, I fear, "a serious artist"; but she is of such an extraordinary talent that she can do even this. Yvonne George sang it better simply because the figure she evoked as Mon Homme was exactly the fake apache about whom it was written, and not the "my feller" who lurked behind Miss Brice. It was amusing to learn that without a Yiddish accent and without those immense rushes of drollery, without the enormous gawkishness of her other impersonations, Miss Brice could put a song over. But I am for Fanny against Miss Brice and to Fanny I return.

Fanny is one of the few people who "make fun." She creates that peculiar quality of entertainment which is wholly light-hearted and everything else is added unto her. Of this special quality nothing can be said; one either sees it or doesn't, savours it or not. Fanny arrives on the scene with an indescribable gesture—after seeing it twenty times I believe that it consists of a feminine salute, touching the forehead and then flinging out her arm to the topmost gallery. There is magic in it, establishing her character at once —the magic must reside in her incredible elbow. She hasn't so much to give as Jolson, but she gives it with the same generosity, there are no reserves, and it is all for fun. Her Yiddish Squow (how else can I spell that amazing effect?) and her Heiland Lassie are examples—there isn't an *arrière-pensée* in them. "The Chiff is after me . . . he says I appil

180

to him . . . he likes my type . . ." it is the complete give away of herself and she doesn't care.

And this carelessness goes through her other exceptional qualities of caricature and satire. For the first there is the famous Vamp, in which she plays the crucial scene of all the vampire stories, preluding it with the first four lines of the poem Mr Kipling failed to throw into the wastepaper basket, and fatuously adding, "I can't get over it"—after which point everything is flung into another plane—the hollow laughter, the haughty gesture, the pretended compassion, that famous defense of the vampire which here, however, ends with the magnificent line, "I may be a bad woman, but I'm awful good company." In this brief episode she does three things at once: recites a parody, imitates the moving-picture vamp, and creates through these another, truly comic character. For satire it is Fanny's special quality that with the utmost economy of means she always creates the original in the very process of destroying it, as in two numbers which are exquisite, her present opening song in vaudeville with its reiterations of Victor Herbert's *Kiss Me Again,* and her Spring Dance. The first is pressed far into burlesque, but before she gets there it has fatally destroyed the whole tedious business of polite and sentimental concert-room vocalism; and the second (Fanny in ballet, with her amazingly angular parody of five-position dancing) puts an end forever to that great obsession of ours, classical interpretative dancing.

Fanny's refinement of technique is far beyond Jolson's; her effects are broad enough, but her methods are all delicate. The frenzy which takes hold of her is as real as his. With him she has the supreme pleasure of knowing that she can do no wrong—and her spirits mount and intensify with every moment on the stage. She creates rapidly and her characterizations have an exceptional roundness and fulness; when the dæmon attends she is superb.

It is noteworthy that these two stars bring something to

America which America lacks and loves—they are, I suppose, two of our most popular entertainers—and that both are racially out of the dominant caste. Possibly this accounts for their fine carelessness about our superstitions of politeness and gentility. The medium in which they work requires more decency and less frankness than usually exist in our private lives; but within these bounds Jolson and Brice go farther, go with more contempt for artificial notions of propriety, than anyone else. Jolson has re-created an ancient type, the scalawag servant with his surface dulness and hidden cleverness, a creation as real as Sganarelle. And Fanny has torn through all the conventions and cried out that gaiety still exists. They are parallel lines surcharged with vital energy. I should like to see that fourth-dimensional show in which they will meet.

◄§ So far as I know, they never did on the stage, perhaps they were on a program together in radio.

Jolson's career was extraordinary in many ways and perhaps most in the effect his career had on the movies. It was his "You ain't heard nothin' yet" in *The Jazz Singer* that announced the coming of speech to the movies in 1927* and it was the movie in which Larry Parks played

---

* It is only natural that such an historic occasion should become the subject of legend and a source of disputation among historians. The legend is that Al Jolson, on the spur of the moment interpolated the words, "Say (or Hey) Mom, listen to this." But the English author of *The Miracle of the Movies*, Leslie Wood, took the trouble to examine a print (at the Museum of Modern Art in New York) and reports that these words occur in the seventh reel. In the second, Jolson is being applauded for his singing of *Dirty Hands, Dirty Face,* and then says to his audience at Coffee Dan's Cafe: "Wait a minute . . . wait a minute. You ain't heard nothing yet." As the line was followed by others, it could not have been a sudden impromptu. Bosley Crowther in *The Lion Roars,* says: ". . . Then Jolson made up in blackface, said, "You ain't heard nothin' yet, folks . . ." and began bellowing *Mammy,* a maudlin song."

The significance of the occasion is that here we had completely synchronized *speech*. Songs had been heard before, but they didn't have the sensational effect of common speech.

Jolson that started a new cycle of pictures built around players and composers—few of which had the merit of the forerunner. A word should be said in thanks to Sidney Skolsky who was convinced of the possibilities in a story of Jolson's career even without Jolson and perhaps the most spectacular demonstration of the qualities I called "dæmonic" was the sense of exuberant life which came off the screen when he was almost perfectly rendered by someone else.

As I write this, the news comes that Baby Snooks, the abominable and adorable brat created by Fannie Brice will be revived for a television show. This is, I suppose, inevitable and surely if an actor could play Jolson, an actress can play Fannie Brice's Snooks. But to some of us it will seem a gross violation, particularly those who saw her play the part (perhaps in the Follies) many years before radio. The extraordinary quality of this characterization, which was apparently a straight formula job, lay in the sense one felt that Fannie was constantly "making up" Snooks, as a child makes up a rambling story when playing house. Snooks was constantly being created and re-created from moment to moment.

Once when I wrote of my admiration for one of the programs, she sent me a recording of Snooks reciting *The Three Little Kittens*. It is a masterpiece because it brings to life the little girl who is giving the recitation— shy, wilful, uncertain—then suddenly bold—and finally relieved at the words "the end." ᷒

These, too . . .

Remy de Gourmont has propounded, somewhere, an interesting theory. If life is worth anything *per se,* is the substance of the argument, then we do wrong to live it in a series of high moments separated by long hours of dulness. We ought to take the *amount* of energy, or ecstasy, we possess, and spread it as thin as possible, relishing each moment for itself, each being as good as any other. (I do not mean that Gourmont endorsed this philosophy; he discussed it.) It is, of course, the logical conclusion of burning *always* with a hard gemlike flame, for if one is to be always *anything* it is more likely to be calm and languorous and reserved; that is the difference between burning and burning up—of which Pater was aware.

We have all had these days of halcyon perfection, when the precise degree of warmth was a miracle, when the aroma of a wine seemed to have the whole fragrance of the earth, when one could do anything or nothing and be equally content. In the presence of great works of art we experience something similar. We are suspended between the sense of release from life, the desire to die before the image of the supremely beautiful, and a new-found capacity for living. Our daily existence gives us no such opportunity; we cannot live languorously because we have no leisure, and we are compelled to be intense at rare intervals if life isn't to be entirely a hoax and a bore. In the preoccupations of daily life a tragic incident or an outburst of temper or a perfectly

185

cut street dress or the dark-light before a storm, may give us, apart from our emotional lives, the intensity we require. We rather defend ourselves from the impact of great beauty, of nobility, of high tragedy, because we feel ourselves incompetent to master them; we preserve our individual lives even if we diminish them.

The minor arts are, to an extent, an opiate—or rather they trick our hunger for a moment and we are able to sleep. They do not wholly satisfy, but they do not corrupt. And they, too, have their moments of intensity. Our experience of perfection is so limited that even when it occurs in a secondary field we hail its coming. Yet the minor arts are all transient, and these moments have no lasting record, and their creators are unrewarded even by the tribute of a word. A moment comes when everything is exactly right, and you have an occurrence—it may be something exquisite or something unnamably gross; there is in it an ecstasy which sets it apart from everything else. The scene of the "swaree" in the *Pickwick Papers* has that quality; nearly the whole of *South Wind* has it (I choose examples as disparate as possible). The whole performance of *Boris* by Chaliapin (the second time he sang it at the Metropolitan on his second visit to the United States) had precisely the same exaltation—and Conrad Veidt as Cesare had one comparable moment: the breathless second when the draperies seem to cling to the ravished virgin in the hands of the Somnambulist. It is an unpredictable event; but there are those on whom one can count to approach it. All of those I am writing about here have given me that thrill at least once—and my memory goes back to these occasions, trying to catch the incredible moment again.

It will be impossible to communicate even the sense of it unless the material be dissociated from the event. Surely there is nothing exquisite in the roaring charwoman created by George Monroe. He had to an inspiring degree the capacity to be one of those vast figures in Dickens—Mrs

Gamp to perfection—and it is odd that another impersonator, Bert Savoy, should have created, in Margie, Mrs Gamp's own confidante and admirer, the devoted Mrs Harris. George Monroe's creation was huge and cylindrical—more like a drainpipe than a woman in shape. There was no effort at realism, for Monroe roared in a deep bass voice, and his "Be that as it ma-a-y" was a leer in the face of all logic, order, and decency. There was in it an unrestraint, a wildness, an independent commonness which rendered it immortal. The creation of Bert Savoy is at the other extreme. It is female impersonation and the figure is always the same—the courtesan whose ambition it is to be a demi-mondaine. Savoy makes capital of all his defects down to the rakish slanting hat over one eye. His repetitions, apparently so spontaneous, are beautifully timed and spaced; the buzz and pause in the voice—"you muzzt com'over . . . you don't know the ha-ff of it, dear-ie" fix themselves in memory. He is remembered for the excellent stories he tells, and they are worth it, but the interpolations are funnier than the climax. The audacity is colossal and disarming. The occurrence of a character out of Petronius on our stage is exceptional in itself, that it should at the same time be slightly vicious and altogether charming, funny and immoral and delicate, is the wonder.

Last year there was an added touch, when Savoy danced while he sang a stanza about the Widow Brown. It was as delicate, it passed as quickly, as breath on a windowpane.[1]

❧ Shortly after this was written Bert Savoy was killed (by a bolt of lightning, according to report) and the stage lost the last of the great female impersonators. In conversation, Savoy was a candid and, it seemed to me, remarkably cheerful, homosexual and was possessed of a macabre humor. His vocabulary was copious and dirty, his imagina-

[1] All this was written before Bert Savoy died. I haven't changed the verbs to the past tense. "How well could we have spared for him . . ."

tion fanciful. At a Thanksgiving party for people without families, at the house of Bob Chanler, Savoy denounced filial obligation in toto and said he envied foundlings because all they had to do was write an occasional letter to a doorstep. It was his capacity for creating images that made us *see* his Margie in all her unreality.

Perhaps because homosexuals are now more taken for granted, the art at which they excelled, female impersonation, has virtually ceased to exist on the stage. It still occurs in nightclubs.

Of the others mentioned here, Bobby Clark is far and away the greatest. I can't now separate his career into what I saw before and what after this was written. I know that the essentials of his act, if not the essence of his art, were present right from the start and that in the middle of the 1920's Clark and McCullough were among the great teams in musical shows. In recent years Clark has become a sort of Grand Old Man of comedy, appearing in Molière or musical shows with the same grace. Mishandling which can only be called imbecilic made his first goes at television disastrous and he was therefore spared the grueling labor of a weekly show which, however, he could have done with far more variety and skill than some of those whom the medium accepted.

Willie Howard was a genuinely great comedian. He used to appear with his brother, Eugene, who was like a parody of a straight man, but the great moments came when Willie would deliver lectures, especially his "French Taught in a Hurry." The recording of this is still procurable and once, several years ago, I saw it on film—a priceless treasure. ॐ

I repeat the material doesn't matter. For Leon Errol has nothing but the type drunkard to work with, and is wonderful. In his case it is easy to analyze the basis of the effect— it is in the loping dance step into which he converts the lurch of the drunkard. The tawdry moment—funny enough if you can bear it—is always Errol's breathing into someone else's face; the great moment comes directly after, when the lurch and the fall are worked up into a complete arc of dance steps, ending in three little hops as a sort of proof of sobriety. Jimmy Barton has the same quality in his skating scene—he uses less material and the movement round the rink is beautiful to watch. But of him it is useless to speak. Someone has pointed out that he can slap the bare back of a woman and make that funny!

It is interesting to see how many of the people who give this special quality arrive out of burlesque. Harry Kelly is another. I recall him first with Lizzie the Fish Hound in *Watch Your Step* and last in a quite useless musical comedy, *The Springtime of Youth* (textually that was the title—and in 1922!) For two acts he was wholly wasted. In the third he was magnificent. He was playing the obdurate father: "No son of mine shall ever marry a daughter of the Baxters" was his line. He was informed that she was, in fact, an adopted daughter and that her uncle had left her the bulk of his fortune. For precisely a minute and a half Kelly played with the word "bulk"—one saw it registered in his brain, saw an idea germinating, felt it working forward to the jaw before the cavernous voice gave it utterance—and again one felt the inner struggle *not* to say it a third time, one felt the conflict of pride and avarice. It was remarkably delicate and fine—so is all of Kelly's work when he has a chance. His spare figure, long hands, and unbelievable voice always create a character—and it isn't always the same character.

Bobby Clark's scene with the lion comes at once to mind (it is another burlesque act), and Bert Williams—in many scenes—always soft spoken, always understating his case. There were five minutes of Blanche Ring and Charles Winninger, once, at the Winter Garden; to my surprise, there were more than that for Eugene and Willie Howard at the same house, but they were gained in spite of the Winter Garden technique which underestimates even the lowest intelligence. Willie is rather like Fanny Brice at moments; when he cuts loose one has an agreeable sense of uncertainty. Joe Jackson,[1] actually a great clown, although one doesn't recognize this in the highly developed medium he chooses, has exactly the opposite effect—he doesn't cut loose at all; he develops. Everything he does is careful and nothing exaggerated, so you think at first that, although he will be funny, he will not quite reach that top notch on which an artist teeters perilously while you wonder whether he will fall over or keep his balance. Yet Jackson gets there. As the tramp cyclist his acrobatics are good, his make-up enchanting; but his expressed attitude of mind is his most precious quality. It becomes almost too much to watch him worrying with a motor horn which has become detached from the handlebars and which he cannot replace. He tries it everywhere; at the end he is miserably trying to hang it up on the air, and when it fails to catch there he is actually wretched. His movements are full of grace—like those of the grotesque, Alberto, among the Fratellini—and the ecstasy he gives comes by a surexcess of laughter. Another moment of great delicacy, without laughter, however, is that in which Fortunello and Cirrilino swing about on the broomstick. They are a lovely pair, and the little one seated on the palm of the other's hand is a beautiful picture.

Either few women are brought out of burlesque, or women haven't the exceptional quality I care for. In any case they have seldom given me the excess of emotion by what they have done. Their beauty is quite another matter on which I fail to commit myself. Ada Lewis, in her broad and grand way, has the stuff, and Florence Moore. And once in each performance you can be sure that Gilda Grey will utter a

[1] R. C. Benchley has written a just and sympathetic account of Jackson. It appeared in a magazine and is not, so far as I know, available in book form.

sound or tremble herself into a bacchanalian revel. For the most part her singing is undistinguished, and I do not care for the anxious way in which she regards her members, as if she fancied they would fall off by dint of shimmying. Yet I have never gone to a show of hers without hearing some echo of the nymphs pursued, or seeing a movement of abandon and grace. The dark shuddering voice is sub-human, the movement divinely animal.

Different in every way, but exquisite in every way, was Gaby Deslys. It is good form now to belittle her; she was so vulgar; she came so much on the crest of a revolution, she was such a bidder for our great precious commodity—news space. Ah, well! we have given publicity to less worthy causes. For she was perfect of her type, and in her hard, calculating, sublimely decent way she made us like the type. It was gently vicious—the whole manner. It was overdone —the pearls and the peacock feathers. But behind was a lovely person—lovely to look at and enchanting to all the senses. No, she couldn't act—how pitiable her loyal efforts; she sang badly; she wasn't one of the world's great dancers. But she had something irreducible, not to be hindered or infringed upon—her definite self. She was, to begin with, outcast of our moral system, and she made us accept her because she was an independent human being. She had a sound and accurate sense of her personal life, of her rights as an individual. Nothing could stand against her—and it is said that when she was at grips, at the end, with something more powerful than popular taste, she still held her own, and died rather than suffer the spoiling of her beauty. If that were true one could hardly wish even her beauty back again.

◄§ A few months after this book was published, I was writing about W. C. Fields and checked to make sure I wasn't repeating myself—and discovered that there wasn't a word about this great man in the text.

I shall not attempt to do him justice now. I note that he was the greatest comedian of his time, on the stage and in the movies. He created laughter far beyond Chaplin's intention and he created a limited, but perfectly understood, series of characters. Of his three careers, the one in the movies was the best and the best part of these consisted of a series of two-reel comedies in which all his wild imagination cut loose. Next come the long pictures he composed for himself, and finally the works of others in which he acted.

He was also one of the most exasperating and endearing of human beings. I add this note here not for his memory, but to make sure that at least one version of *The 7 Lively Arts* will not conspicuously lack his name. ॐ

The "vulgar" comic strip

Of all the lively arts the Comic Strip is the most despised, and with the exception of the movies it is the most popular. Some twenty million people follow with interest, curiosity, and amusement the daily fortunes of five or ten heroes of the comic strip, and that they do this is considered by all those who have any pretentions to taste and culture as a symptom of crass vulgarity, of dulness, and, for all I know, of defeated and inhibited lives. I need hardly add that those who feel so about the comic strip only infrequently regard the object of their distaste.

Certainly there is a great deal of monotonous stupidity in the comic strip, a cheap jocosity, a life-of-the-party humour which is extraordinarily dreary. There is also a quantity of bad drawing and the intellectual level, if that matters, is sometimes not high. Yet we are not actually a dull people; we take our fun where we find it, and we have an exceptional capacity for liking the things which show us off in ridiculous postures—a counterpart to our inveterate passion for seeing ourselves in stained-glass attitudes. And the fact that we do care for the comic strip—that Jiggs and Mutt-and-Jeff and Skinnay and the Gumps have entered into our existence as definitely as Roosevelt and more deeply than Pickwick— ought to make them worth looking at, for once. Certainly they would have been more sharply regarded if they had produced the counterpart of Chaplin in the comic film—a universal genius capable of holding the multitude and excit-

193

ing the speculations of the intellectuals. It happens that the actual genius of the comic strip, George Herriman, is of such a special sort that even when he is recognized he is considered something apart and his appearance among other strips is held to be only an accident.

It is by no means an accident, for the comic strip is an exceptionally supple medium, giving play to a variety of talents, to the use of many methods, and it adapts itself to almost any theme. The enormous circulation it achieves imposes certain limitations: it cannot be too local, since it is syndicated throughout the country; it must avoid political and social questions because the same strip appears in papers of divergent editorial opinions; there is no room in it for acute racial caricature, although no group is immune from its mockery. These and other restrictions have gradually made of the comic strip a changing picture of the average American life—and by compensation it provides us with the freest American fantasy.

In a book which appeared about two years ago, *Civilization in the United States*, thirty Americans rendered account of our present state. One of them, and one only, mentioned the comic strip—Mr Harold E. Stearns—and he summed up the "intellectual" attitude perfectly by saying that *Bringing Up Father* will repay the social historian for all the attention he gives it. I do not know in what satisfactions the social historian can be repaid. I fear that the actual fun in the comic strip is not one of them. *Bringing Up Father,* says Mr Stearns, "symbolizes better than most of us appreciate the normal relation of American men and women to cultural and intellectual values. *Its very grotesqueness and vulgarity are revealing*" (italics mine). (Query: Is it vulgar of Jiggs to prefer Dinty's café to a Swami's lecture? Or of Mrs Jiggs to insist on the lecture? Or of both of them to be rather free in the matter of using vases as projectiles? What, in short, is vulgar?) I am far from quarreling with Mr

194

Stearns' leading idea, for I am sure that a history of manners in the United States could be composed with the comic strip as its golden thread; but I think that something more than its vulgarity would be revealing.

The daily comic strip arrived in the early 'nineties—perhaps it was our contribution to that artistic age—and has gone through several phases. In 1892 or thereabouts Jimmy Swinnerton created *Little Bears and Tigers* for the San Francisco *Examiner;* that forerunner has passed away, but Swinnerton remains, and everything he does is observed with respect by the other comic-strip artists; he has had more influence on the strip even than Wilhelm Busch, the German whose *Max und Moritz* were undoubtedly the originals of the *Katzenjammer Kids.* The strip worked its way east, prospered by William Randolph Hearst especially in the coloured Sunday Supplement, and as a daily feature by the Chicago *Daily News,* which was, I am informed, the first to syndicate its strips and so enabled Americans to think nationally. About fifteen years ago, also in San Francisco, appeared the first work of Bud Fisher, *Mr Mutt,* soon to develop into *Mutt and Jeff,* the first of the great hits and still one of the best known of the comic strips. Fisher's arrival on the scene corresponds to that of Irving Berlin in ragtime. He had a great talent, hit upon something which took the popular fancy, and by his energy helped to establish the comic strip as a fairly permanent idea in the American newspaper.

The files of the San Francisco *Chronicle* will one day be searched by an enthusiast for the precise date on which Little Jeff appeared in the picture. It is generally believed that the two characters came on together, but this is not so. In the beginning Mr Mutt made his way alone; he was a race-track follower who daily went out to battle and daily fell. Clare Briggs had used the same idea in his *Piker Clerk* for the Chicago *Tribune.* The historic meeting with Little

Jeff, a sacred moment in our cultural development, occurred during the days before one of Jim Jeffries' fights. It was as Mr Mutt passed the asylum walls that a strange creature confided to the air the notable remark that he himself was Jeffries. Mutt rescued the little gentleman and named him Jeff. In gratitude Jeff daily submits to indignities which might otherwise seem intolerable.

The development in the last twenty years has been rapid, and about two dozen good comics now exist. Historically it remains to be noted that between 1910 and 1916 nearly all the good comics were made into bad burlesque shows; in 1922 the best of them was made into a ballet with scenario and music by John Alden Carpenter, choreography by Adolph Bolm; costumes and settings after designs by George Herriman. Most of the comics have also appeared in the movies; the two things have much in common and some day a thesis for the doctorate in letters will be written to establish the relationship. The writer of that thesis will explain, I hope, why "movies" is a good word and "funnies," as offensive little children name the comic pages, is what charming essayists call an atrocious vocable.

Setting apart the strip which has fantasy—it is practised by Frueh and by Herriman—the most interesting form is that which deals satirically with every-day life; the least entertaining is the one which takes over the sentimental magazine love-story and carries it through endless episodes. The degree of interest points to one of the virtues of the comic strip: it is a great corrective to magazine-cover prettiness. Only one or two frankly pretty-girl strips exist. *Petey* is the only one which owes its popularity to the high, handsome face and the lovely flanks of its heroine, and even there the pompous awkwardness of the persistent lover has a touch of wilful absurdity. Mrs Trubble, a second-rate strip unworthy of its originator, is simply a series of pictures dramatizing the vampire home-breaker; I am not even sure she is

196

intended to be pretty. When nearly everything else in the same newspapers is given over to sentimentality and affected girl-worship, to advice to the lovelorn and pretty-prettiness, it is notable that the comic strip remains grotesque and harsh and careless. It is largely concerned with the affairs of men and children, and, as far as I know, there has never been an effective strip made by, for, or of a woman. The strip has been from the start a satirist of manners; remembering that it arrived at the same time as the Chicago World's Fair, recalling the clothes, table manners, and conversation of those days, it is easy to see how the murmured satiric commentary of the strip undermined our self-sufficiency, pricked our conceit, and corrected our *gaucherie*. To-day the world of Tad, peopled with cake-eaters and finale-hoppers, the world of the *Gumps* and *Gasoline Alley*, of *Abie the Agent* and *Mr and Mrs* serve the same purpose. I am convinced that none of our realists in fiction come so close to the facts of the average man, none of our satirists are so gentle and so effective. Of course they are all more serious and more conscious of their mission; but—well, exactly who cares?

The best of the realists is Clare Briggs, who is an elusive creator, one who seems at times to feel the medium of the strip not exactly suited to him, and at others to find himself at home in it. His single pictures: *The Days of Real Sport* and *When a Feller Needs a Friend,* and the now rapidly disappearing *Kelly Pool* which was technically a strip, are notable recreations of simple life. Few of them are actively funny; some are sentimental. The children of *The Days of Real Sport* have an astonishing reality—and none are more real than the virtually unseen Skinnay, who is always being urged to "come over." They are a gallery of country types, some of them borrowed from literature—the Huck Finn touch is visible—but all of them freshly observed and dryly recorded. Briggs' line is distinctive; one could identify any square inch of his drawings. In *Kelly Pool* he worked close to Tad's *Indoor Sports,* and did what Tad hasn't done—created a character, the negro waiter George whom I shall be sorry to lose. George's amateur interest in pool was continually being submerged in his professional interest: getting tips, and his "Bad day . . . ba-a-ad day" when tips were low is a little classic. Deserting that scene, Briggs has made a successful comedy of domestic life in *Mr and Mrs.* No one has come so near to the subject—the grumbling, helpless, assertive, modest, self-satisfied, self-deprecating male, in his contacts with his sensible, occasionally irritable, wife. As often as not these episodes end in quarrels—in utter blackness with harsh bedroom voices continuing a day's exacerbations; again the reconciliations are mushy, again they are genuine sentiment. And around them plays the child whose one function is to say "Papa loves mamma" at the most appropriate time. It is quite an achievement, for Briggs has made the ungrateful material interesting, and I can recall not one of these strips in which he has cracked a joke. Tad here follows Briggs, respectfully. *For Better or Worse* is considerably more obvious, but it has Tad's special value, in sharpness of caricature. The surrounding types are brilliantly drawn; only the central characters remain stock figures. Yet the touch of romance in Tad, continually overlaid by his sense of the ridiculous, is precious; he seems aware of the faint aspirations of his characters and recognizes the *rôles* which they think they are playing while he mercilessly shows up their actuality. The finest of the *Indoor Sports* are those in which two subordinate characters riddle with sarcasm the pretentions of the others—the clerk pretending to be at ease when the boss brings his son into the office, the lady of the house talking about the new motor car, the small-town braggart and the city swell—characters out of melodrama, some, and others so vividly taken from life that the very names Tad gives them pass into common speech. He is an inveterate creator and manipulator of slang; whatever phrase he makes or picks up has its vogue

198

for months and his own variations are delightful. Slang is a part of their picture, and he and Walter Hoban are the only masters of it.

Ketten's *Day of Rest* is another strip of this *genre,* interesting chiefly as a piece of draughtsmanship. He is the most economical of the comic-strip artists, and his flat characters, without contours or body, have a sort of jack-in-the-box energy and a sardonic obstinacy. The Chicago School I have frankly never been able to understand—a parochialism on my part, or a tribute to its exceptional privacy and sophistication. It pretends, of course, to be simple, but the fate of every metropolis is to enter its small-town period at one time or another, to call itself a village, to build a town hall and sink a town pump with a silver handle. The Gumps are common people and the residents of Gasoline Alley are just folks, but I have never been able to understand what they are doing; I suspect they do nothing. It seems to me I read columns of conversation daily, and have to continue to the next day to follow the story. The campaign of Andy Gump for election to the Senate gave a little body to the serial story—he was so abysmally the ignorant Congressman that he began to live. But apart from this, apart from the despairing cry of "Oh, Min," one recalls nothing of the Chicago School except the amusing vocabulary of Syd Smith and that Andy has no chin. It is an excellent symbol; but it isn't enough for daily food.

The small-town school of comic strip flourishes in the work of Briggs, already mentioned, in Webster's swift sketches of a similar nature, and in Tom MacNamara's *Us Boys.* The last of these is an exceptional fake as small-town, but an amusing and genuine strip. It is people by creation of fancy —the alarmingly fat, amiable Skinny, the truculent Eaglebeak Spruder, the little high-brow Van with his innocence and his spectacles, and Emily, if I recall the name, the village vampire at the age of seven. Little happens in *Us Boys,* but MacNamara has managed to convey a genuine emotion in tracing the complicated relations between his personages—there is actual childhood friendship, actual worry and pride and anger—all rather gently rendered, and with a recognizable language.

It is interesting to note that none of these strips make use of the projectile or the blow as a regular *dénoûement.* I have nothing against the solution by violence of delicate problems, but since the comic strip is supposed to be exclusively devoted to physical exploits I think it is well to remark how placid life is in at least one significant branch of the art. In effect all the themes of the comic strip are subjected to a great variety of treatments, and in each of them you will find, on occasions, the illustrated joke. This is the weakest of the strips, and, as if aware of its weakness, its creators give it the snap ending of a blow, or, failing that, show us one character in consternation at the brillance of the other's wit, flying out of the picture with the cry of "Zowie," indicating his surcharge of emotion. This is not the same thing as the wilful violence of *Mutt and Jeff,* where the attack is due to the malice or stupidity of one character, the resentment or revenge of the other.

Mutt is a *picaro,* one of the few rogues created in America. There is nothing too dishonest for him, nor is there any chance so slim that he won't take it. He has an object in life: he does not do mean or vicious things simply for the pleasure of doing them, and so is vastly superior to the Peck's Bad Boy type of strip which has an apparently endless vogue—the type best known in *The Katzenjammer Kids.* This is the least ingenious, the least interesting as drawing, the sloppiest in colour, the weakest in conception and in execution, of all the strips, and it is the one which has determined the intellectual idea of what all strips are like. It is now divided into two—and they are equally bad. How happy one could be with neither! The other outstanding picaresque strip is *Happy Hooligan*—the type tramp—who with his brother, Gloomy Gus, had added to the gallery of our national mythology. *Non est qualis erat*—the spark has gone out of him in recent years.[1] Elsewhere you still find that exceptionally immoral and dishonest attitude toward the business standards of America. For the comic strip, especially after you leave the domestic-relations type which is itself realistic and unsentimental, is specifically more violent, more dishonest, more tricky and roguish, than America usually permits its serious arts to be. The strips of cleverness: *Foxy Grandpa*, the boy inventor, *Hawkshaw the Detective,* haven't great vogue. *Boob McNutt,* without a brain in his head, beloved by the beautiful heiress, has a far greater following, although it is the least worthy of Rube Goldberg's astonishing creations. But Mutt and Jiggs and *Abie the Agent,* and *Barney Google* and *Eddie's Friends* have so little respect for law, order, the rights of property, the sanctity of money, the romance of marriage, and all the other foundations of American life, that if they were put into fiction the Society for the Suppression of Everything would hale them incontinently to court and our morals would be saved again.

The Hall-room Boys (now known as *Percy and Ferdy,* I think) are also picaresque; the indigent pretenders to social eminence who do anything to get on. They are great bores, not because one foresees the denunciation at the end, but because they somehow fail to come to life, and one doesn't care whether they get away with it or not.

Abie and *Jerry on the Job* are good strips because they are self-contained, seldom crack jokes, and have each a significant touch of satire. Abie is the Jew of commerce and the man of common sense; you have seen him quarrel with a waiter because of an overcharge of ten cents, and, encouraged by his companion, replying, "Yes, and it ain't the principle, either; it's the ten cents." You have seen a thousand tricks by which he once sold Complex motor cars and

---

[1] A number of comic-strip artists, on achieving fame, stop drawing, leaving that work to copyists of exceptional skill. I do not know whether this is the case in the *Happy Hooligan* strip.

now promotes cinema shows or prize fights. He is the epitome of one side of his race, and his attractiveness is as remarkable as his jargon. Jerry's chief fault is taking a stock situation and prolonging it; his chief virtue, at the moment, is his funny, hard-boiled attitude toward business. Mr Givney, the sloppy sentimentalist who is pleased because some one took him for Mr Taft ("Nice, clean fun," says Jerry of that), is faced with the absurd Jerry, who demolishes efficiency systems and the romance of big business and similar nonsense with his devastating logic or his complete stupidity. The railway station at Ammonia hasn't the immortal character of *The Toonerville Trolley* (that meets all the trains) because Fontaine Fox has a far more entertaining manner than Hoban, and because Fox is actually a caricaturist—all of his figures are grotesque, the powerful *Katinka* or *Aunt Eppie* not more so than the Skipper. Hoban and Hershfield both understate; Fox exaggerates grossly; but with his exaggeration he is so ingenious, so inventive that each strip is funny and the total effect is the creation of character in the Dickens sense. It is not the method of *Mutt and Jeff* nor of *Barney Google* in which Billy de Beck has done much with a luckless wight, a sentimentalist, and an endearing fool all rolled into one.

These are the strips which come to life each day, without forcing, and which stay long in memory. I am stating the case for the strip in general and have gone so far as to speak well of some I do not admire, nor read with animation. The continued existence of others remains a mystery to me; why they live beyond change, and presumably beyond accidental death, is one of the things no one can profitably speculate upon. I do not see why I should concede anything more to the enemies of the strip. In one of *Life's* burlesque numbers there was a page of comics expertly done by j held in the manner of our most popular artists. Each of the half dozen strips illustrated the joke: "Who was that lady I seen you with on the street last night?" "That wasn't a lady; that was my wife." Like so many parodies, this arrived too late, for the current answer is, "That wasn't a street; that was an alley." Each picture ended in a slam and a cry—also belated. The actual demolition of the slam ending was accomplished by T. E. Powers, who touches the field of the comic strip rarely, and then with his usual ferocity. In a footnote to a cartoon he drew *Mike and Mike*. In six pictures four represented one man hitting the other; once to emphasize a pointless joke, twice thereafter for no reason at all, and finally to end the picture. It was destruction by exaggeration; and no comic strip artist missed the point.

At the extremes of the comic strip are the realistic school and the fantastic—and of fantasy there are but few practitioners. Tad has some of the quality in *Judge Rummy,* but for the most part the Judge and Fedink and the rest are human beings dressed up as dogs—they are out of Æsop, not out of LaFontaine. But the Judge is actually funny, and I recall an inhuman and undoglike episode in which he and Fedink each claimed to have the loudest voice, and so in midwinter, in a restaurant, each lifted up his voice and uttered and shouted and bellowed the word "Strawberries" until they were properly thrown into the street. This is the kind of madness which is required in fantasy, and Goldberg occasionally has it. He is the most versatile of the lot; he has created characters, and scenes, and continuous episodes—foolish questions and meetings of ladies' clubs and inventions (not so good as Heath Robinson's) and through them there has run a wild grotesquerie. The tortured statues of his *décors* are marvelous, the way he pushes stupidity and ugliness to their last possible point, and humour into everything, is amazing. Yet I feel he is *manqué,* because he has never found a perfect medium for his work.

Frueh is a fine artist in caricature and could have no such difficulty. When he took it into his head to do a daily strip

he was bound to do something exceptional, and he succeeded. It is a highly sophisticated thing in its humour, in its
subjects, and pre-eminently in its execution. His series on
prohibition enforcement had infinite ingenuity, so also his
commentaries on political events in New York city. He remains a caricaturist in these strips, indicating, by his use of
the medium, that its possibilities are not exhausted. Yet
for all his dealing with "ideas" his method remains fantastic,
and although he isn't technically a comic-strip artist he is
the best approach to the one artist whom I have only mentioned, George Herriman, and to his immortal creation.
For there is, in and outside the comic strip, a solitary and
incomprehensible figure which must be treated apart. The
Krazy Kat that Walks by Himself.

◦§ I face a blank wall here. Again and again, year after
year, I have tried to follow a comic strip—and failed. It
is as if I had grown blind. The nearest I came to success
was with Al Capp's work and when he caved in, yielding
to some pressure he couldn't himself properly identify,
and let Li'l Abner marry Daisy Mae, I gave him up. I was
told that *Barnaby* had the real stuff, I still am told that
Pogo is as imaginative and fanciful and great as I thought
Krazy Kat was—but I cannot focus on these or any other
strips as I turn the pages of my newspaper.

I have elsewhere paid my respects to Al Capp's prodigious talent and to the exceptional situation of his strip,
as political satire. I am afraid that anything I would say
here about the comic strip as a whole would be an ill-
natured description or analysis of those elements in current strips which make them uninteresting to me. This, it
strikes me, would be about as persuasive as an essay by a
blind man proving that color doesn't exist.

Two minor points: clearly one is sentimental about the
pleasures of one's youth and tends to overrate them in

comparison with the present. I do not find myself doing this in regard to the other entertainments about which I have been writing. The high water mark of the movies, for instance, comes for me some twenty years later. Second: I still enjoy one comic strip although I find it now only between the covers of a book: *Krazy Kat.* ॐ

The Krazy Kat
that walks by himself

Krazy Kat, the daily comic strip of George Herriman is, to me, the most amusing and fantastic and satisfactory work of art produced in America to-day. With those who hold that a comic strip cannot be a work of art I shall not traffic. The qualities of *Krazy Kat* are irony and fantasy—exactly the same, it would appear, as distinguish *The Revolt of the Angels;* it is wholly beside the point to indicate a preference for the work of Anatole France, which is in the great line, in the major arts. It happens that in America irony and fantasy are practised in the major arts by only one or two men, producing high-class trash; and Mr Herriman, working in a despised medium, without an atom of pretentiousness, is day after day producing something essentially fine. It is the result of a naïve sensibility rather like that of the *douanier* Rousseau; it does not lack intelligence, because it is a thought-out, a constructed piece of work. In the second order of the world's art it is superbly first rate—and a delight! For ten years, daily and frequently on Sunday, *Krazy Kat* has appeared in America; in that time we have accepted and praised a hundred fakes from Europe and Asia—silly and trashy plays, bad painting, woful operas, iniquitous religions, everything paste and brummagem, has had its vogue with us; and a genuine, honest native product has gone unnoticed until in the year of grace 1922 a ballet brought it a tardy and grudging acclaim.

Herriman is our great master of the fantastic and his early career throws a faint light on the invincible creation which is his present masterpiece. For all of his other things were comparative failures. He could not find, in the realistic framework he chose, an appropriate medium for his imaginings, or even for the strange draughtsmanship which is his natural mode of expression. *The Family Upstairs* seemed to the realist reader simply incredible; it failed to give him the pleasure of recognizing his neighbours in their more ludicrous moments. *The Dingbats,* hapless wretches, had the same defect. Another strip came nearer to providing the right tone: *Don Koyote and Sancho Pansy;* Herriman's mind has always been preoccupied with the mad knight of La Mancha, who reappears transfigured in *Krazy Kat.* And—although the inspirations are *never* literary—when it isn't Cervantes it is Dickens to whom he has the greatest affinity. The Dickens mode operated in *Baron Bean*—a figure half Micawber, half Charlie Chaplin as man of the world. I have noted, in writing of Chaplin, Mr Herriman's acute and sympathetic appreciation of the first few moments of *The Kid.* It is only fair to say here that he had himself done the same thing in his medium. Baron Bean was always in rags, penniless, hungry; but he kept his man Grimes, and Grimes did his dirty work, Grimes was the Baron's outlet, and Grimes, faithful retainer, held by bonds of admiration and respect, helped the Baron in his one great love affair. Like all of Herriman's people, they lived on the enchanted mesa (pronounced: macey) by Coconino, near the town of Yorba Linda. The Baron was inventive; lacking the money to finance the purchase of a postage stamp, he entrusted a love letter to a carrier pigeon; and his "Go, my paloma," on that occasion, is immortal.

Some of these characters are reappearing in Herriman's latest work: *Stumble Inn.* Of this I have not seen enough to be sure. It is a mixture of fancy and realism; Mr Stumble himself is the Dickens character again—the sentimental, endearing innkeeper who would rather lose his only patron than kill a favourite turkey cock for Thanksgiving. I have heard that recently a litter of pups has been found in the cellar of the inn; so I should judge that fantasy has won the day. For it is Herriman's bent to disguise what he has to say in creations of the animal world which are neither human nor animal, but each *sui generis*.

That is how the Kat started. The thought of a friendship between a cat and a mouse amused Herriman and one day he wrote them in as a footnote to *The Family Upstairs*. On their first appearance they played marbles while the family quarreled; and in the last picture the marble dropped through a hole in the bottom line. An office boy named Willie was the first to recognize the strange virtues of *Krazy Kat*. As surely as he was the greatest of office boys, so the greatest of editors, Arthur Brisbane, was the next to praise. He urged Herriman to keep the two characters in action; within a week they began a semi-independent existence in a strip an inch wide under the older strip. Slowly they were detached, were placed at one side, and naturally stepped into the full character of a strip when the *Family* departed. In time the Sundays appeared—three quarters of a page, involving the whole Krazy Kat and Ignatz families[1] and the flourishing town of Coconino—the flora and fauna of that enchanted region which Herriman created out of his memories of the Arizona desert he so dearly loves.

In one of his most metaphysical pictures Herriman pre-

[1] I must hasten to correct an erroneous impression which may have caused pain to many of Krazy's admirers. The three children, Milton, Marshall, and Irving, are of Ignatz, not, as Mr Stark Young says, of Krazy. Krazy is not an unmarried mother. For the sake of the record I may as well note here the names of the other principals: Offisa Bull Pupp; Mrs Ignatz Mice; Kristofer Kamel; Joe Bark the moon hater; Don Kiyoti, that inconsequential heterodox; Joe Stork, alias Jose Cigueno; Mock Duck; Kolin Kelly the brick merchant; Walter Cephus Austridge; and the Kat Klan: Aunt Tabby, Uncle Tom, Krazy Katbird, Osker Wildcat, Alec Kat, and the Krazy Katfish.

sents Krazy as saying to Ignatz: "I ain't a Kat . . . and I ain't Krazy" (I put dots to indicate the lunatic shifting of background which goes on while these remarks are made; although the action is continuous and the characters motionless, it is in keeping with Herriman's method to have the backdrop in a continual state of agitation; you never know when a shrub will become a redwood, or a hut a church) . . . "it's wot's behind me that I am . . . it's the idea behind me, 'Ignatz' and that's wot I am." In an attitude of a contortionist Krazy points to the blank space behind him, and it is there that we must look for the "Idea." It is not far to seek. There is a plot and there is a theme—and considering that since 1913 or so there have been some three thousand strips, one may guess that the variations are infinite. The plot is that Krazy (androgynous, but according to his creator willing to be either) is in love with Ignatz Mouse; Ignatz, who is married, but vagrant, despises the Kat, and his one joy in life is to "Krease that Kat's bean with a brick" from the brickyard of Kolin Kelly. The fatuous Kat (Stark Young has found the perfect word for him: he is crack-brained) takes the brick, by a logic and a cosmic memory presently to be explained, as a symbol of love; he cannot, therefore, appreciate the efforts of Offisa B. Pupp to guard him and to entrammel the activities of Ignatz Mouse (or better, Mice). A deadly war is waged between Ignatz and Offisa Pupp—the latter is himself romantically in love with Krazy; and one often sees pictures in which Krazy and Ignatz conspire together to outwit the officer, both wanting the same thing, but with motives all at cross-purposes. This is the major plot; it is clear that the brick has little to do with the violent endings of other strips, for it is surcharged with emotions. It frequently comes not at the end, but at the beginning of an action; sometimes it does not arrive. It is a symbol.

The theme is greater than the plot. John Alden Carpenter has pointed out in the brilliant little foreword to his ballet, that Krazy Kat is a combination of Parsifal and Don Quixote, the perfect fool and the perfect knight. Ignatz is Sancho Panza and, I should say, Lucifer. He loathes the sentimental excursions, the philosophic ramblings of Krazy; he interrupts with a well-directed brick the romantic excesses of his companion. For example: Krazy blindfolded and with the scales of Justice in his hand declares: "Things is all out of perpotion, 'Ignatz.'" "In what way, fool?" enquires the Mice as the scene shifts to the edge of a pool in the middle of the desert. "In the way of 'ocean' for a instinct." "Well?" asks Ignatz. They are plunging head down into midsea, and only their hind legs, tails, and words are visible: "The ocean is so innikwilly distribitted." They appear, each prone on a mountain peak, above the clouds, and the Kat says casually across the chasm to Ignatz: "Take 'Denva, Kollorado' and 'Tulsa, Okrahoma' they ain't got no ocean a tall—" (they are tossed by a vast sea, together in a packing-case) "while Sem Francisco, Kellafornia, and Bostin, Messachoosit, has got more ocean than they can possibly use"—whereon Ignatz properly distributes a brick evenly on Krazy's noodle. Ignatz "has no time" for foolishness; he is a realist and Sees Things as They ARE. "I don't believe in Santa Claus," says he; "I'm too broad-minded and advanced for such nonsense."

But Mr Herriman, who is a great ironist, understands pity. It is the destiny of Ignatz never to know what his brick means to Krazy. He does not enter into the racial memories of the Kat which go back to the days of Cleopatra, of the Bubastes, when Kats were held sacred. Then, on a beautiful day, a mouse fell in love with Krazy, the beautiful daughter of Kleopatra Kat; bashful, advised by a soothsayer to write his love, he carved a declaration on a brick and, tossing the "missive," was accepted, although he had nearly killed the Kat. "When the Egyptian day is done it has become the Romeonian custom to crease his lady's bean with a brick laden with tender sentiments . . . through the tide of dusty years" . . . the tradition continues. But only Krazy knows this. So at the end it is the incurable romanticist, the victim of acute Bovaryisme, who triumphs; for Krazy faints daily in full possession of his illusion, and Ignatz, stupidly hurling his brick, thinking to injure, fosters the illusion and keeps Krazy "heppy."

Not always, to be sure. Recently we beheld Krazy smoking an "eligint Hawanna cigar" and sighing for Ignatz; the smoke screen he produced hid him from view when Ignatz passed, and before the Mice could turn back, Krazy had handed over the cigar to Offisa Pupp and departed, saying "Looking at 'Offisa Pupp' smoke himself up like a chimly is werra werra intrisking, but it is more wital that I find 'Ignatz' "—wherefore Ignatz, thinking the smoke screen a ruse, hurls his brick, blacks the officer's eye, and is promptly chased by the limb of the law. Up to this point you have the usual technique of the comic strip, as old as Shakespeare. But note the final picture of Krazy beholding the pursuit, himself disconsolate, unbricked, alone, muttering: "Ah, there him is—playing tag with 'Offisa Pupp'—just like the boom compenions wot they is." It is this touch of irony and pity which transforms all of Herriman's work, which relates it, for all that the material is preposterous, to something profoundly true and moving. It isn't possible to retell these pictures; but that is the only way, until they are collected and published, that I can give the impression of Herriman's gentle irony, of his understanding of tragedy, of the *sancta simplicitas,* the innocent loveliness in the heart of a creature more like Pan than any other creation of our time.

Given the general theme, the variations are innumerable, the ingenuity never flags. I use haphazard examples from 1918 to 1923, for though the Kat has changed somewhat since the days when he was even occasionally feline, the essence is the same. Like Charlot, he was always living in a world of his own, and subjecting the commonplaces of actual life to the test of his higher logic. Does Ignatz say that "the bird is on the wing," Krazy suspects an error and after a careful scrutiny of bird life says that "from rissint obserwation I should say that the wing is on the bird." Or Ignatz observes that Don Kiyote is still running. Wrong, says the magnificent Kat: "he is either still or either running, but not both still and both running." Ignatz passes with a bag containing, he says, bird-seed. "Not that I doubt your word, Ignatz," says Krazy, "but could I give a look?" And he is astonished to find that it is bird-seed, after all, for he had all the time been thinking that birds grew from eggs. It is Ignatz who is impressed by a falling star; for Krazy "them that don't fall" are the miracle. I recommend Krazy to Mr Chesterton, who, in his best moments, will understand. His mind is occupied with eternal oddities, with simple things to which his nature leaves him unreconciled. See him entering a bank and loftily writing a check for thirty million dollars. "You haven't that much money in the bank," says the cashier. "I know it," replies Krazy; "have you?" There is a drastic simplicity about Krazy's movements; he is childlike, regarding with grave eyes the efforts of older people to be solemn, to pretend that things are what they seem; and like children he frightens us because none of our pretensions escapes him. A king to him is a "royal cootie." "Golla," says he, "I always had a ida they was grend, and megnifishint, and wondafil, and mejestic . . . but my goodniss! It ain't so." He should be given to the *enfant terrible* of Hans Andersen who knew the truth about kings.

He is, of course, blinded by love. Wandering alone in springtime, he suffers the sight of all things pairing off; the solitude of a lonesome pine worries him and when he finds a second lonesome pine he comes in the dead of night and transplants one to the side of the other, "so that in due course, Nature has her way." But there are moments when the fierce pang of an unrequited passion dies down. "In these blissfil hours my soul will know no strife," he confides to Mr Bum Bill Bee, who, while the conversation goes on, catches sight of Ignatz with a brick, flies off, stings Ignatz from the field, and returns to hear: "In my Kosmis there will be no feeva of discord . . . all my immotions will function in hominy and kind feelings." Or we see him at peace with Ignatz himself. He has bought a pair of spectacles, and seeing that Ignatz has none, cuts them in two, so that each may have a monocle. He is gentle, and gentlemanly, and dear; and these divagations of his are among his loveliest moments; for when irony plays about him he is as helpless—as we are.

To put such a character into music was a fine thought, but Mr Carpenter must have known that he was foredoomed to failure. It was a notable effort, for no other of our composers had seen the possibilities; most, I fear, did not care to "lower themselves" by the association. Mr Carpenter caught much of the fantasy; it was exactly right for him to make the opening a parody—The Afternoon Nap of a Faun. The "Class A Fit," the Katnip Blues were also good. (There exists a Sunday Krazy of this very scene—it is 1919, I think, and shows hundreds of Krazy Kats in a wild abandoned revel in the Katnip field—a rout, a bacchanale, a satyr-dance, an erotic festival, with our own Krazy playing the viola in the corner, and Ignatz, who has been drinking, going to sign the pledge.) Mr Carpenter almost missed one essential thing: the ecstasy of Krazy when the brick arrives at the end; certainly, as Mr Bolm danced it one felt only the triumph of Ignatz, one did not feel the grand leaping up of Krazy's heart, the fulfilment of desire, as the brick fell upon him. The irony was missing. And it was a mistake for Bolm to try it, since it isn't Russian ballet Krazy requires; it is American dance. One man, one man only can do it right, and I publicly appeal to him to absent him from felicity awhile, and though he do it but once, though but a small number of people may see it, to pay tribute to his one compeer in America, to the one creation equalling his own—I mean, of course, Charlie Chaplin. He has been urged to do many things hostile to his nature; here is one thing he is destined to do. Until then the ballet ought to have Johnny and Ray Dooley for its creators. And I hope that Mr Carpenter hasn't driven other composers off the subject. There is enough there for Irving Berlin and Deems Taylor to take up. Why don't they? The music it requires is a jazzed tenderness—as Mr Carpenter knew. In their various ways Berlin and Taylor could accomplish it.

They may not be able to write profoundly in the private idiom of Krazy. I have preserved his spelling and the quotations have given some sense of his style. The accent is partly Dickens and partly Yiddish—and the rest is not to be identified, for it is Krazy. It was odd that in *Vanity Fair's* notorious "rankings," Krazy tied with Doctor Johnson, to whom he owes much of his vocabulary. There is a real sense of the colour of words and a high imagination in such passages as "the echoing cliffs of Kaibito" and "on the north side of 'wild-cat peak' the 'snow squaws' shake their winter blankets and bring forth a chill which rides the wind with goad and spur, hurling with an icy hand rime, and frost upon a dreamy land musing in the lap of Spring"; and there is the rhythm of wonder and excitement in "Ooy, 'Ignatz' it's awfil; he's got his legs cut off above his elbows, and he's wearing shoes, and he's standing on top of the water."

Nor, even with Mr Herriman's help, will a ballet get quite the sense of his shifting backgrounds. He is alone in his freedom of movement; in his large pictures and small, the scene changes at will—it is actually our one work in the expressionistic mode. While Krazy and Ignatz talk they move from mountain to sea; or a tree stunted and flattened with odd ornaments of spots or design, grows suddenly long and thin; or a house changes into a church. The trees in this enchanted mesa are almost always set in flower pots with Coptic and Egyptian designs in the foliage as often as on the pot. There are adobe walls, fantastic cactus plants, strange fungus and growths. And they *compose designs.*

For whether he be a primitive or an expressionist, Herriman is an artist; his works are built up; there is a definite relation between his theme and his structure, and between his lines, masses, and his page. His masterpieces in colour show a new delight, for he is as naïve and as assured with colour as with line or black and white. The little figure of Krazy built around the navel, is amazingly adaptable, and Herriman economically makes him express all the emotions with a turn of the hand, a bending of that extraordinary starched bow he wears round the neck, or with a twist of his tail.

And he has had much to express for he has suffered much. I return to the vast enterprises of the Sunday pictures. There is one constructed entirely on the bias. Ignatz orders Krazy to push a huge rock off its base, then to follow it downhill. Down they go, crashing through houses, uprooting trees, tearing tunnels through mountains, the bowlder first, Krazy so intently after that he nearly crashes into it when it stops. He toils painfully back uphill. "Did it gather any moss?" asks Ignatz. "No." "That's what I thought." "L'il fillossiffa," comments Krazy, "always he seeks the truth, and always he finds it." There is the great day in which Krazy hears a lecture on the ectoplasm, how "it soars out into the limitless ether, to roam willy-nilly, unleashed, unfettered, and unbound" which becomes for him: "Just imegine having your 'ectospasm' running around, William and Nilliam, among the unlimitliss etha—golla, it's imbillivibil—" until a toy balloon, which looks like Ignatz precipitates a heroic gesture and a tragedy. And there is the greatest of all, the epic, the Odyssean wanderings of the door:

Krazy beholds a dormouse, a little mouse with a huge door. It impresses him as being terrible that "a mice so small, so dellikit" should carry around a door so heavy with weight. (At this point their Odyssey begins; they use the door to cross a chasm.) "A door is so useless without a house is hitched to it." (It changes into a raft and they go down stream.) "It has no ikkinomikil value." (They dine off the

216

door.) "It lecks the werra werra essentials of helpfilness." (It shelters them from a hailstorm.) "Historically it is all wrong and misleading." (It fends the lightning.) "As a thing of beauty it fails in every rispeck." (It shelters them from the sun and while Krazy goes on to deliver a lecture: "You never see Mr Steve Door, or Mr Torra Door, or Mr Kuspa Door doing it, do you?" and "Can you imagine my li'l friends Ignatz Mice boddering himself with a door?") his li'l friend Ignatz has appeared with the brick; unseen by Krazy he hurls it; it is intercepted by the door, rebounds, and strikes Ignatz down. Krazy continues his adwice until the dormouse sheers off, and then Krazy sits down to "concentrate his mind on Ignatz and wonda where he is at."

Such is our Krazy. Such is the work which America can pride itself on having produced, and can hastily set about to appreciate. It is rich with something we have too little of—fantasy. It is wise with pitying irony; it has delicacy, sensitiveness, and an unearthly beauty. The strange, unnerving, distorted trees, the language inhuman, un-animal, the events so logical, so wild, are all magic carpets and faery foam—all charged with unreality. Through them wanders Krazy, the most tender and the most foolish of creatures, a gentle monster of our new mythology.

◄§ George Herriman was one of the most endearing men I have ever known. Once, while he was living in New York, which was not where he wanted to be, he said he hoped to end his life on the mesa, lying down on a giant cactus leaf until he shriveled up and was blown away by the wind. He almost had his wish. Although he sounded rather sad the last time I talked to him, out West, he was approaching death as sweetly as he had approached life.

A collection of *Krazy Kat* daily and Sunday strips has been published, with an introduction by E. E. Cummings. The book is unfortunately not well-proportioned and the strips have been reduced a little too much, so that it isn't easy to read the text. But anyone who doubts the position I have given to Herriman can get an inkling, at least, from the collection. ઠ✒

Following is the text, originally printed in an appendix of John Alden Carpenter's programme note on his Krazy Kat ballet, the piano score of which—illustrated by Herriman—is published.

To all lovers of Mr. Herriman's ingenious and delightful cartoons it must have seemed inevitable that sooner or later Krazy Kat and Ignatz Mouse would be dragged by some composer into music. I have tried to drag them not only into music but on to the stage as well, by means of what I have called, for obvious reasons, a Jazz Pantomime.

To those who have not mastered Mr Herriman's psychology it may be explained that Krazy Kat is the world's greatest optimist—Don Quixote and Parsifal rolled into one. It is therefore possible for him to maintain constantly at white heat a passionate affair with Ignatz Mouse, in which the gender of each remains ever a delightful mystery. Ignatz, on the other hand, condenses in his sexless self all the cardinal vices. If Krazy blows beautiful bubbles, Ignatz shatters them; if he builds castles in Spain, Ignatz is there with a brick. In short, he is meaner than anything, and his complex is cats.

After a few introductory bars the curtain is raised and Krazy is discovered asleep under a tree. Officer Pup passes, swinging his club. All is well. Then comes Bill Poster, a canine relative of Officer Pup, with his bucket and brush, and pastes upon the wall an announcement of the grand ball which will shortly be given for all the animals. The job finished, Bill departs.

Krazy wakes up; he rubs his eyes and reads the exciting poster. He is moved to try his steps; he finds his feet heavy and numerous. Of a sudden he spies on a clothes line which the moving scenery has brought into view, a *ballet skirt*. Undoubtedly it is ·his costume for the ball. He approaches the clothes line, first with restraint, then with eagerness. He snatches the skirt from the line, claps it on, and comes bounding forward in high abandon.

He is interrupted by the appearance of Old Joe Stork, drilling by with his bundle on his back. He passes on, but he has carelessly dropped his pack. Krazy sniffs at it, filled with curiosity. He picks it up and carries it triumphanly to his tree in the corner. He opens the bundle, and finds that it contains not what you thought it would, but a vanity case, mirror, rouge, powderpuff, lip-stick and all, complete, including a beautiful pair of white cotton gloves.

He abandons himself to the absorbing task of make-up for the ball. Meanwhile the moving scenery has brought into view the house of Ignatz Mouse. The door opens, and Ignatz' head appears. Opportunity has knocked. The Mouse steals forward and is about to seize an inviting brick when Officer Pup (thank heaven!) arrives in the very nick of time and drives him from the scene. The unsuspecting Kat, in the meantime, has completed his make-up. He now arises, draws on his white cotton gloves, and then by way of further preparatory exercise, he indulges in a bit of a Spanish dance.

At its conclusion Krazy is suddenly confronted by the *Mysterious Stranger*. The sophisticated audience will observe that it is none other than Ignatz disguised as a catnip merchant. Very formidable indeed! The Stranger steps briskly forward and holds out to the ever-receptive Kat a bouquet—an enormous bouquet of catnip. Krazy plunges his nose into the insidious vegetable, inhales deeply to the very bottom of his lungs, and then goes off at once into what Mr Herriman calls a *Class A fit*. It is a fit progressive, a fit *de luxe*, the Katnip Blues, in which the wily Ignatz joins as additional incitement. When the frenzy has achieved its climax, the Mouse throws off his disguise, seizes his brick, dashes it full in the face of the Kat, and escapes. Krazy staggers back, stunned and exhausted, but yet undaunted. There is the moment of ecstatic recognition—Ignatz Dahlink— as he totters and reels back to his little tree. He sinks down wearily under its protecting boughs. The moon comes out. Krazy sleeps. Krazy dreams. Indominatable Kat!

The damned effrontery
of the two-a-day

The narrator of the following episode is Mr Percy Ham-
mond of the New York *Tribune;* the stars are Montgomery
and Stone; the Mr Mansfield is Richard himself again, the
actor who played *Dr Jekyll and Mr Hyde* better than
Thomas E. Shea did:

"As the stars appeared in the last act in evening dress,
Mr Mansfield turned to me and with venomous indignation
said, 'That is damned effrontery!' It seemed to be Mr Mansfield's belief that mere dancers had no right to wear the
vestments of refined society."

To me that is a very funny story and the humour of it
has nothing to do with upon what meat has this our Cæsar
fed that he is grown so great. The eminence of Mansfield
and the worthlessness of Montgomery and Stone may be
assumed; the recrudescence of the mediæval attitude toward
strolling players, even if it be in the mind of another player,
is also conceivable; snobbism is always conceivable and often
interesting. The story is funny because it so perfectly illustrates the genteel tradition in America. (I am rather
freely applying Mr Santayana's phrase, without any effort
to do it justice.) Montgomery and Stone were in revue or
extravaganza, and were therefore outcast; they didn't count
as Art. Whereas Mr Mansfield played Shakespeare and high-
school girls went to see him, and so he was Art. The ap-

plication to vaudeville is immediate, because vaudeville is considered on Broadway as the grave of artistic reputations. An actor of established prestige *may* venture into vaudeville; he usually makes his audience feel exactly how far he has condescended to appear before them and accept, even if he doesn't earn, a salary three times as great as usual; but the actor in the middle distance very well knows that if he goes into vaudeville he is digging his own grave, because there is a stigma attached to the two-a-day. Vaudeville players, in short, are not entitled to "the vestments of refined society." About every ten years the corrupt desire to be refined takes hold of vaudeville itself; but it dies out quickly and vaudeville remains simple and good.

It is in one of the stages of simple goodness now, and I propose to discuss it without reference to a possibly more noble past. I am well acquainted with the other method, which was founded, I believe, by Arthur Symons, and beautifully practised by him. To him we owe the peculiarly attractive attitude of sentimental reminiscence which, invented or borrowed by him, has become classic. It leads to excellent prose at times, and by showing that there was a golden age even in vaudeville sometimes creates the suspicion that vaudeville itself need not be all brass. But the attitude is unsatisfactory because it invokes, in dealing with the most immediate of the minor arts, more than a share of the pathos of distance. Vaudeville is brightly coloured, zestful, with sharp outlines; and the classic attitude softens and blurs. It is required of you to name and describe the acts and numbers of a better day; one *must* say "music-hall" or be slain in the passages of the Jordan; in America a reference to the *commedia dell'arte* is, as scientists say, indicated. Yet the time must come when it is possible to say, "Vaudeville is. Surely it could never have been worse than this—or for that matter, never better. Let us regard it as it is." The moment must come in the history of general culture when vaudeville can be taken without comparisons. That is, it happens, the only way I can take it, for in my youth I saw little of it and cared less. I recall a skit called *Change Your Actor Go Back to the Woods;* there were Fours and among them were Cohans; there was, I remember, The Man Who Made the Shah of Persia Laugh; once I saw an artist in pantomime. Yet I am not moved to beat my breast and begin *Einst in meinen Jugendjahren.* Nothing I have heard leads me to believe that there were better days in vaudeville than those which open benignant and wide over Joe Cook and Fanny Brice and the Six Brown Brothers, over the two Briants and Van and Schenck and the four Marxes and the Rath Brothers and the team of Williams and Wolfus; over Duffy and Sweeney and Johnny Dooley and Harry Watson, Jr., as Young Kid Battling Dugan, and Messrs Moss and Frye, who ask how high is up.

I shall arrive in a moment at the question of refined vaudeville, a thing I dislike intensely; there is another sort of refinement in vaudeville which demands respect. It is the refinement of technique. It seems to me that the unerring taste of Fanny Brice's impersonations is at least partly due to, and has been achieved through, the purely technical mastery she has developed; I am sure that the vaudeville stage makes such demands upon its artists that they are compelled to perfect everything. They have to do whatever they do swiftly, neatly, without lost motion; they must touch and leap aside; they dare not hold an audience more than a few minutes, at least not with the same stunt; they have to establish an immediate contact, set a current in motion, and exploit it to the last possible degree in the shortest space of time. They have to be always "in the picture," for though the vaudeville stage seems to give them endless freedom and innumerable opportunities, it holds them to strict account; it permits no fumbling, and there are no reparable errors. The materials they use are trivial, yes; but the treatment must be accurate to a hair's breadth; the wine they serve is light, it must fill the goblet to the very brim, and

223

not a drop must spill over. There is no great second act to redeem a false entrance; no grand climacteric to make up for even a moment's dulness. The whole of the material must be subsumed in the whole of the presentation, every page has to be *written,* every scene *rendered,* every square inch of the canvas must be *painted,* not daubed with paint. It is, of course, obvious, that the responsibility in this case is exactly that of the major arts. It is at least tenable that in this case, as in the major arts, the responsibilities are fulfilled.

And nothing could be more illuminating than the moments in vaudeville when the tricky and the bogus appear. I face here willingly the protest of intelligent men and women who have gone to vaudeville to see or hear one turn and have sat through some of the dreariest æsthetic dancing,[1] have heard the most painfully polite vocalism, have witnessed "drama." If vaudeville requires half of what I have said, how do these things get in and get by? Largely as a concession to debased public taste. Note well that all the cuture elements in vaudeville, the dull and base and truly vulgar ones, are importations. The dance appropriate to the vaudeville stage is the stunt dance; its proper music is ragtime or jazz; the playlet which belongs to it (witness the success of *A Slice of Life*) is burlesque. Yet like every other popular art in America, vaudeville is required, by the tradition of gentility, to be cultural; and its dull defenders often make it their boast that it does give culture to the masses (the same sort of thing is heard in connexion with the music played at moving-picture houses) because among its native acts appear *tableaux vivants* out of Landseer or because a legitimate actor brings to the common herd scraps and snatches of *Les Misérables.* The process continues, regrettably, and extends to the spoiling of good vaudeville material. It isn't a loss of anything precious, except time which

[1] Heywood Broun has discovered that everybody in vaudeville is an "artist" except the trained seal.

224

could be filled by something better, when Mr Lou Tellegen struts about on the variety stage; it is a defamation of something good in the major line and equally a loss of moments when the *"Affairs of" Anatol* are inexpertly and tastelessly produced "for vaudeville." But what shall we say of such a real disaster as the return of Miss Ethel Levey to vaudeville, still so rich in attraction that she plays four weeks at the Palace in New York, wholly spoiled for variety because she has had a triumph abroad and has become a "great actress" or is it "an *artiste*"? There was in Miss Levey something roughly elemental, something common and pure; whatever she did had broadness and sharpness both. Corrupted by her success abroad, she returns still magnificent, the voice still throbbing, the form heavy but dominant—yet no longer vaudeville. She has the grandeur of a star and appears in full stage with a grand piano and silk-shaded lamps and draperies and sings *All by Myself* with shocking bad sentimental *acting,* and gets all she can out of *Love's Old Sweet Song* before the touch of her old spirit protests—and recites a dramatic monologue entitled *Destiny!* Now and again flashes of burlesque reveal her ancient flavour; but it is an axiom in vaudeville that you can't be good in it if you are too good for it.

I omit the people who aren't, simply, good enough; there are second-rate people in vaudeville as in everything else, and first-rate people of *its* second order. The part that is pure, I am convinced, is rarely matched on our other stages. Certainly not in the legitimate, nor in the serious artistic playhouse where knowing one's job perfectly and doing it simply and unpretentiously are the rarest things in the world. Revue and musical comedy require and often attain the pitch of technical accuracy which vaudeville sets as a standard, and these two forms draw heavily upon vaudeville for material and stars, whom they incorporate only in so far as the stars are not pure variety themselves. They are as much entitled to the jazz bands as any other stage, but to me a jazz band is not essentially variety, although it has a legitimate place there. That is why I reject Mr Walter Haviland's ranking of Ted Lewis as one of the greatest of vaudeville acts, for the great acts in vaudeville are those which could not be perfectly appreciated elsewhere. (The æsthetics of the question have been canvassed in Laokoön, I believe.) Johnny Dooley, who always breaks up the show in musical comedy, is a real vaudeville player, and Jack Donahue, who was the sole attraction of another such piece, is always right, his fumbling for words is inspired, and so is his dancing, and altogether it is a completely realized act. Among the most popular of the big-time acts I am left cold by Van and Schenck, who are perpetually stopping short of perfection; their songs are funny, but not witty; their music is current, no more; their rendition is always near enough right to be passed. The Four Marx Brothers do better in creating their special atmosphere of low comedy; the Six Brown Brothers are at the very top with their saxophones. It is an independent act, wholly self-contained, not nearly so appropriate in any other framework, except possibly a one-ring circus; it is a real variety turn where a jazz band is only half and half; and in the case of these performers everything they do is exquisite.

It isn't possible to describe the acts, nor even to suggest the distinctive quality of the head-liners. There are inexplicable things in vaudeville, things no rational explanation can touch, such as the persistence of sawing a woman in half, or the terrific impact of the singing of Belle Baker, who destroys you with *Elie! Elie!* Houdini is variety as all magicians are and all tricksters—the circus side of vaudeville, to be sure, and the sensational side. Here belong the acrobats; I have written elsewhere of the Rath Brothers, who alone are in the spirit and tone of vaudeville, without any intrusion of the circus. At the present moment nearly everything in vaudeville which is best has a touch of parody; not infrequently it burlesques itself. Herbert Williams, of

226

Williams and Wolfus, exaggerates wholly in the manner of a clown; his despairing cry for the "spot*li-i-i-ght*," his wail of unhappiness, with his appearance, his gesture, his shambling walk, make him a figure out of the *commedia dell'arte* —one of the few in vaudeville. Duffy and Sweeney are parodists of their *métier;* their whole fun is in their elaborate pretense of not caring to amuse the audience. Harry Watson, Jr., has taken out of burlesque the accentuated form, the built-up face, the wide and fatuous gesture peculiar to that type, and in his broken-down prize-fighter has created a real character with his jumping the rope "fi' thousand conseggitive times" and "tell 'em what I did to Philadelphia Jack O'Brien." I am dragged into a catalogue of names, which I want to avoid; but I cannot omit the macabre Moving-Man's Dream of the Briants, the rustic studies of Chic Sale, the elaborate burlesque of melodrama by Charles Withers, and the exceptional mad magician of Frank Van Hoven. Van Hoven carries farther than anyone else the appearance of not knowing the audience is to be amused. He complains in a mutter of the presence of human beings, individually probably all right, but *en masse* . . . ! He leaves the stage and passes out of the auditorium, bidding the audience amuse itself while he's gone. And his great finale, with a bowl of goldfish, a handkerchief in a trunk, a table covered with a cloth, an inflated paper bag, and a revolver shot—at the sound of which exactly nothing happens, is the last word in destroying the paraphernalia of the magician and all his works.

I have committed myself to the statement that Joe Cook is perfect and am in no mood to withdraw it. As vaudeville he is perfect; I can see him in no other *milieu* because he lacks the gift—not needed in vaudeville, though useful there—of holding the audience in his hand. He is liked, not loved; his act is met with continuous chuckles, smiles, and laughter; seldom with guffaws. This is not necessarily to his credit; it means that he does one sort of thing, and does it extremely well. It happens to be just the thing for which vaudeville is made. As Ethel Levey is what most vaudeville players aspire to be, so Cook is what they ought to be. He is exactly right. Yet to give the quality of his rightness is difficult. To recognize it is easier.

He is versatile, but not in the manner of Sylvester Schaeffer. He is a master of parody and burlesque, yet not in the fashion of Charles Withers; his delicate impersonations have an ease and certainty far beyond the studies of Chic Sale. Essentially what distinguishes Joe Cook is that he is very wise and slightly mad, and his madness is not the "dippy" kind so admirably practised by Frank Van Hoven. It is structural. Mr Cook's is probably the longest single act in vaudeville, and after it is over he saunters into one or more of the acts that follow his on the programme, as his fancy takes him.

His own starts as a running parody of old-time vaudeville, beginning with the musicians coming out of the pit, through the magician and the player of instruments to—but no one has ever discovered where it does go to. For after the card tricks—the ace of spades is asked for and, as he remarks after five minutes of agonized fumbling behind his back, the ace of spades is asked for and practically at a moment's notice the ace of spades is produced; and it never is—Mr Cook finds it necessary to explain to the audience in one of the most involved pieces of nonsense ever invented why he will not imitate four Hawaiians playing the ukulele. After that literally nothing matters. He might be with Alice in Wonderland or at a dada ballet or with the terribly logical clowns of Shakespeare. I think that Chaplin would savour his humours.

In an art which is hard and bright and tends to glitter rather than radiate, he has a gleam of poetry; but he is like the best of poets because there are no fuzzy edges, no blurred contours; he is exact and his precision is never cold. He

228

holds conversations of an imbecile gravity: How are you? How are *you?* Fine, how's yourself? Good. And you? Splendid. How's your uncle? I haven't got an uncle. Fine, how is he? He's fine. How are *you?* He is amazingly inventive, creating new stunts, writing new lines, doing fresh business from week to week. His little bits are like witty epigrams in verse, where the thing done and the skill of the method coincide and pleasing separately please more by their fusion. His sense of the stage is equalled by but one man I have ever seen: George M. Cohan.

Had I had any doubts about vaudeville as we practice it in the United States they would have been dispelled in the past two years by one great success and one notable failure: the *Chauve-Souris* of Balieff and the show of the Forty-niners. Balieff seemed for a moment to be destroying B. F. Keith; here was something certainly vaudeville, with turns and numbers, appealing to every grade of intelligence; here were good music, exciting scenery, and good fun; here were voices caressing the ear and dancers dazzling the eye; here was a gay burlesque and a sophisticated *conférencier*. Now if our native product were only like that . . . (the implication was, Wouldn't we just go every day to the nearest vaudeville house!). Then, to be sure, a reaction. Put Ed Wynn and Leon Errol and . . . I omit the list—Wynn was almost unanimously chosen as *conférencier*—and we could give the Russians at least a good run for the money—and it *was* money, loads of it, much to their surprise. And then, without Ed Wynn and the list, the attempt; for the Forty-niners were cheerfully setting out to be a company of Americans stranded in Russia, giving the Russians to understand what the folk and popular arts of America were. Months earlier the thing had been perfectly done, as a game, in the *No-Siree,* a wholly amateur single performance which was without doubt the gayest evening of the year in New York.

229

(The tribute is not exactly wrung from me, for friends of mine were concerned in it; it was the high moment of the Algonquin Circle and they should have disbanded the following morning. Since I was not an adherent of the group, my advice was not asked; I do not know whether it still exists, has passed to further triumphs, or has repeated the Forty-niners.) Put on professionally, high class vaudeville showed all the weaknesses of the commercial kind, and had a dulness of its own. The Dance of the Small-town Mayors was exactly right, but most of the parodies were outdated, the burlesques were too *voulus,* the strain too great. There was lacking that technical proficiency which is essential to vaudeville, and the adjustment of means to material was sloppy. One fell back on Balieff and discovered, as the exoticism wore off, that he too had his weak points. Sentimental songs in however beautiful voices, the choreographics of figures come to life from Copenhagen plate however accurately the footfall coincided with Anitra's Dance, and a number of other things suggested that in Russia, too, refinement could corrupt and stultify. There remained elements we could not match: we hadn't encouraged our legitimate stage sufficiently to be justified in expecting cubist settings in vaudeville; nor when we heard American folk music (and its contemporary form in ragtime) did we so earnestly applaud as to keep them fresh in variety shows. Balieff never was "variety," and we asked of variety that it be like him; we missed the meaning of Balieff as surely as we appreciated the fun. For he was a lesson not to vaudeville, but to us, to those of us who left vaudeville in the hands of the least cultivated audiences. We have asked nothing of vaudeville simply because we haven't suspected what it had to give. Yet week after week at the Palace Theatre in New York there have been bills equal in entertainment to the average Balieff programme; there has been evident an expertness in technique, a skill in construction, a naturalness

230

of execution, a soundness of sense and judgement, which ought to have appealed to all who had taste and discrimination. The people who do go there have something, at least; and lack snobbism generally. If the audiences of the Theatre Guild and the Neighborhood Playhouse were to add themselves to their number, were to accept what is given and be receptive to something more, it could not hurt vaudeville. Because like everything else variety must grow, and there is no reason why it should shut itself off from the direction of civilized life. It can exist very well without the Theatre Guild audience; I wonder whether that audience can exist as well without variety.

❧ Everyone knows what happened to vaudeville: it has become the most consistently popular form of entertainment of the American people. It has done this by a resolute pretence that nothing happened in entertainment after 1900, by refusing to adapt itself to any apparent change, by following the maxim: if you don't pay attention to it, it'll go away.

To be sure, the vaudeville circuit no longer exists, "playing the Palace" is a sentimental phrase, and for a vaudeville artist to face his audience is no longer possible. But as a component of television, the old acts are as successful as they ever were. It was a graduate of vaudeville, Ed Sullivan, who managed the transfer best and for years his program has flourished until stealing first-place from him, in the battle of the ratings, becomes the criterion of success—which few manage to achieve.

Missing from my list, perhaps because I confused them with Moss and Frye, is the team of Moran and Mack, blackface comedians whose work is available on records. They were going strong when Amos and Andy came along and the difference between these two couples is a perfect illustration of the difference between the two forms. Moran and Mack were droll, sharp, instantly funny; Amos and Andy were, I always felt, overworking their material, rather slow-witted. But they were exactly right for radio and it was fitting that through them the American public first became aware of the revolution radio was bringing about. ❧

They call it dancing

One of the most tiresome of contemporary intellectual senti-
mentalities is the cult of "the dance"—a cult which has almost nothing in the world to do with dancing. "The dance"
is "art"; dancing is a form of popular entertainment, one
of the very few which can be practised by its admirers. It
is also one of the arts which can be "polite" without danger
of atrophy, the danger in this case being that the technical
refinement may eventually make dancing a trick, a rather
graceful sort of juggling.

In any case, we shall not have in America anything corresponding to folk dances; the ritual dance, the dance as
religion, simply isn't our type, and none of the tentatives
in favour of that kind of dancing has made me regret our
natural bent toward ballroom and stunt dancing as a mode
of expression. In the rue Lappe in Paris nearly every other
house is a *Bal Musette* and in all but one of these dance
halls the floor is taken by men and women of that quarter,
working men and women who come in and dance and pay
a few *sous* for each dance. They do this every night and
enjoy it; they enjoy the sometimes wheezing accordeon and
the bells which, on the right ankle of the player, accentuate
the beat. They dance waltzes and polkas and, since the Java
is forbidden, the mazurka. Once I saw two couples rise and
dance the *bourrée,* presumably as it was danced in their
native province of Auvergne; it is possible to see other provincial dances of France, as they are remembered, in the Bal

233

Musette of this district and elsewhere—occasionally and not by pre-arrangement. The ancient dances of America haven't such roots, nor such vitality; and we may have to become much more simple, or much more sophisticated, before we will proceed naturally to buck-and-wing and cake-walk and the ordinary breakdown on the floor of the Palais Royal. There are Kentucky mountain and cowboy dances which the moving picture inadequately reconstructs, and I am afraid that even negro levee dancing has lost much of its own character in the process of influencing the steps of the ordinary American dance. Undoubtedly those who can should preserve these provincial and rooted dances; but it is idle to pretend that dancing itself can be a subject for archæology. It is essentially for action, not for speculation.

꙳ A good part of the following—until I begin to describe the dancing I care for—mystifies me. Clearly I am attacking something—but what?

I suspect myself of cowardice, if not of dishonesty in this. In the rest of this book I name names, I say exactly what I think, and am rather belligerent about it all. Here I retreat into obscurity. I am—so far as I can make out—deriding the kind of dance that used to be called "interpretive." But why do I leave it faceless and anonymous? Who did this irritating thing? Why did it annoy me so much? Why did I wrap what I had to say in a meaningless mumble?

Any amateur analyst could explain it: I really admired the art I pretended to dislike. Or, I yearned to do interpretive dancing myself and, consequently, belittled those who could do what I could not. I'm dubious about these explanations.

I still dislike those forms of dancing which are presented in a quasi-religious form, those which uplift the soul before they enchant the eye. I disliked the school of Mary Wigman and I dislike the psychological gloss over

234

the work of Martha Graham. The unnamed offenders I am dealing with here were not as impressive as these founders of styles and I suspect that some of them were remote followers of Isadora Duncan for whom, as I recall it, I had a great admiration when I first saw her. She was, however, the inspiration for a vast amount of sleazy dancing which asked to be forgiven because it was "natural" or "expressed" something profound in the breast of the dancer. I think I turned against a sloppy emotionalism, identified it with a style of dancing, and then, for some reason, was intimidated. Or perhaps all I was concealing here was ignorance—of styles, techniques, and intentions. ૬∾

I do not belittle dancing when I attempt to deprive it of the cachet of "Art." Nothing so precise, so graceful, so implicated with music, can escape being artistic; in the hands of its masters it becomes an intuitive creative process, but this happens most frequently when the dancer gives himself to the music and seldom when he tries to interpret the music. From the waltz to the tango, from the tango to the current fox-trot or one-step, polite dancing has held more of what is essentially artistic than the art-dance, and it has had no pretensions. The old tango and the maxixe were the only ones which could not easily be danced by those who applauded them on the stage; classic dancing, on the contrary, has always been an art of professionals—almost a contradiction in terms in this case, for it is the essence of the dance that it can be danced. It is not the essence of the dance that it can be staged, or made into a pantomime. The Russian Ballet has no reference to the subject for it is essentially the work of mimes and the dancing is either folk dance or choreography.

The reason politeness is not fatal to the dance is that there is only one standard of vulgarity in dancing, which is ugliness. Vulgarity means actively disagreeable postures and steps not exceptionally adapted to the music. The relation of the dancers to one another is the basis of their relation to the music, and that is why the shimmy has little to do with dancing, whereas the cheek-to-cheek position—the *bête-noire* of chaperons a few weeks, or is it years, ago?—is fundamentally not objectionable, since it brings two dancers to as near a unit, with the same centre of gravity, as the dance requires. One doesn't dance the fox-trot as one danced the Virginia reel, and the question of morals has little to do with the case. The "indecencies" of the turkey-trot, as we used to phrase it, disappeared not because we are better men and women, but because we are dancing more beautifully.

Two influences have worked to accomplish this. One is that our music has become more interesting and is written specifically to be danced, as the waltz-song always was and as our older ragtime was not. The other is the effect of the stage (through which we have, recently, learned a vast amount from negro dancing, an active influence for the last fifteen years at least, touching the dance at every point in music, and tending always to prevent the American dance from becoming cold and formal.) Dancing masters go to the stage to perform the dances they have elaborated in their studios; from the stage the dance is adapted to the floor. This is what makes it so unnerving to go through a year seeing nothing but men jumping over their own ankles, or to witness Carl Randall dancing himself into his evening clothes. One doesn't know how soon one will be called upon to do the same sort of thing in the semi-privacy of the night club. Acrobatic dancing is interesting as all acrobatics are—brutally for the stunt and æsthetically for the picture formed while doing the trick. The dancing of choruses has something of the same interest. The Tiller or Palace Girls do very little that would merit attention if done by one of them; done by sixteen, it is entertaining; so are the ranks of heads appearing over the top step of the Hippodrome or at the New Amsterdam, and the ranks of knees rhythmically bending as row follows row down the stairs. But none of these affect actual dancing appreciably.

Acrobatic or stunt dancing has a tendency to corrupt good exhibition dancing—the desire to do something obviously difficult displaces the more estimable desire to do something beautiful. Yet some of our best stunt dancers can and do combine all the elements and to watch them is to experience a double delight. George M. Cohan always danced interestingly; he has sardonic legs and he is, I suppose, the repository of all the knowledge we have of the 1890-1910 dance. Frisco took up the same work near the place where Cohan dropped it; he is (but where I do not know) a character dancer with a specific sense of jazz, and was, for a moment, the symbolic figure of what was coming. His eccentricities were premature, his comparative disappearance unmerited. Eccentric also, and not chiefly dancers, are Leon Errol and Jimmy Barton. Eccentric and essentially a dancer is the fine comic Johnny Dooley. The difference is that almost all of Dooley's comedy is *in* his dancing, whereas the others are great comedians and their dances are also funny. It seems to be Dooley's natural mode to walk on the side of his feet and to catch a broken, wholly American rhythm in every movement—to create dances, therefore, which are untouched by the Russian Ballet and other trepaks and hazzazzas. The foreign influence has touched Carl Randall, a gain in expertness, a loss in freshness. There seems to be nothing he cannot do, nothing he doesn't do well, nothing he does superbly.

The dancing team which ought to have been the best of our time and wasn't is that of Julia Sanderson and Donald Brian.[1] The suppleness of Miss Sanderson's body, the breathless sway of the torso on the hips, the suggestion of languor in the most rapid of her movements, are not to be equalled; and Brian was always smart, decisive, accurate. It

[1] I do not know enough of Carl Hyson and Dorothy Dickson or of the Astaires to judge their place.

is difficult to define the defect which was always in their work; probably a reserve, a not giving themselves away to the music, a shade too much of the stiffness which dancing requires. Miss Sanderson gets along quite well without the lyric knees (as they were—one doesn't see them now) of Ann Pennington; nor has she the exceptional height which makes the grace of Jessica Brown so surprising and her curve of beauty so exceptional. Miss Brown, I take it, is one of the best dancers of the stage, and, unlike Charlotte Greenwood, has nothing to do with grotesque. Miss Greenwood makes a virtue of her defect—the longest limbs in the world. Miss Brown is unconscious of hers as defects at all; like most people's, her legs are long enough to reach the ground. It is marvellous to see what she can do when she lifts them off the ground.

I choose these names as examples, fully aware that I may be omitting others equally famous. But what remains is deliberate: two groups of dancers who were at the very top, I think, of their profession, of their art. Of Doyle and Dixon only Harland Dixon is now visible; the team is broken, but Dixon continues to be a wonderful dancer, in the tradition rather of Fred Stone, and with recent leanings toward acting. It was 1915 or so when I saw them dance Irving Berlin's *Ragtime Melodrama,* and although I have never seen that equalled, I have never seen the team or Dixon alone dance anything unworthy of that piece. It was a beautiful duo, perfectly cadenced, creating long grateful lines around the stage; it was full of tricks and fun and character. And gradually the duo resolved itself into feats of individual prowess, in which Dixon slowly surpassed his partner and became a miracle of acrobatics in rhythm. He is agile, never jerky, with a nice sense of syncopation; he requires Berlin rather than Kern for his full value.

Kern gives all (and more) that Maurice can require, and whether with Florence Walton or Leonora Hughes the dancing of Maurice is always icily regular, and nearly null.

His type of mechanism is exactly wrong and he sets off in bold relief the accuracy, the inspired rightness of Irene and Vernon Castle. That these two, years ago, determined the course dancing should take is incontestable. They were decisive characters, like Boileau in French poetry and Berlin in ragtime; for they understood, absorbed, and transformed everything known of dancing up to that time and out of it made something beautiful and new. Vernon Castle, it is possible, was the better dancer of the two; in addition to the beauty of his dancing he had inventiveness, he anticipated things of 1923 with his rigid body and his evolutions on his heel; but if he were the greater, his finest creation was Irene.

No one else has ever given exactly that sense of being freely perfect, of moving without effort and without will, in more than accord, in absolute identity with music. There was always something unimpassioned, cool not cold, in her abandon; it was certainly the least sensual dancing in the world; the whole appeal was visual. It was as if the eye following her graceful motion across a stage was gratified by its own orbit, and found a sensuous pleasure in the ease of her line, in the disembodied lightness of her footfall, in the careless slope of her lovely shoulders. It was not—it seemed not to be—intelligent dancing; however trained, it was still intuitive. She danced from her shoulders down, the straight scapular supports of her head were at the same time the balances on which her exquisitely poised body depended. There were no steps, no tricks, no stunts. There was only dancing, and it was all that one ever dreamed of flight, with wings poised, and swooping gently down to rest. I put it in the past, I hardly know why; unless because it is too good to last.

&⁊ Between the time this was written and the date of publication I achieved a dubious distinction. I refused to dance with Irene Castle. I met her at a dinner party, she

239

told me the Astaires were more wonderful than I knew, and when everyone else had gone to the dance floor, asked me if I didn't want to dance with her. I didn't because I didn't know how to dance. I began taking lessons the next day, but I never met Irene Castle again.

If I were writing a new chapter on the dance in America, I would have the Charleston and the Black Bottom to parallel the turkey trot and Ray Bolger and Paul Draper and the great Bill Robinson to place with the Bartons and Dooleys. Once in a while, in a movie or on the stage, a partner of Fred Astaire's seems entirely captivating—but my loyalty to Irene Castle has never diminished.

But, of course, if I were writing such a chapter the two names most featured would be those of Agnes de Mille and Lincoln Kirstein. His championing of American ballet and her integration of it into *Oklahoma!* are the turning points in our dance-history. When I began writing in *Esquire,* in 1933, the editors, following their admirable policy of letting me do what I pleased, indulged my whim to devote one piece a year to ballet which was then beginning in America, but was still shrouded in a snobbish mystery. Then, seeing a straight ballet in the midst of a musical, the American public discovered you could like it without having to speak French. It was a cultural revolution—and all to the good. It deprived the intellectuals of a piece of private property they were running into the ground and shook the ground under the feet of the reverse-snobs who held that the intellectuals were incapable of doing anything the public really liked. ठ॰

St Simeon stylites

◄§   The only embarrassment in the following report is
the too-frequent and still inconsistent spelling of the word
"column—colyum." My recollection is that F.P.A. used
the misspelling, with some justification, because a newspaper column is any column of print, whereas the kind of
thing he was doing had a special character and deserved
a private name. One of the characteristics of these "col-
yums" was a private vocabulary which became rapidly
obsolete. By the time the book was printed, the word was
a banality.

Throughout these comments on what I wrote years ago,
I have tried to identify nostalgia, to separate the delight
of life in one's youth from the judgments, which have
their own delight, of maturity. I may have made wrong
guesses; I am willing to make another. In spite of the
excesses of the highly personal, tricky column of wit and
tangential comment, it was a good thing and its disappearance, while falling short of a major disaster, is regrettable.
The breadth of interest, the range and variety, the good
and bad humor, the sheer intelligence of Adams and Bert
Leston Taylor and Don Marquis and Baird Leonard,
were relatively high intellectual pleasures for newspaper
readers. Their place was not taken by Walter Lippmann
and Max Lerner; they were simply dropped because newspapers wanted gossip columns or couldn't give space to

the elegant trifling, the sniping from behind well-cultivated rose-bushes of the wits.

This was to be expected. Newspapers were losing circulation and the natural thing was to cut down those features which were known to have an appeal to small minorities. In the surveys of readers' taste conducted by the Hearst papers, *Krazy Kat* always came in last among the comics, but the enthusiasm of Brisbane and Hearst kept the strip going. Other proprietors couldn't apparently afford the luxury of a column on the editorial page which attracted more readers than the editorials.

Some of F.P.A.'s contributors and some of his readers, too, went over to *The New Yorker*. It is, by intention, a minority publication, determined on an editorial policy which will attract a number of readers which will grow, but never grow big enough to impose its own standards.

The situation of considerable minorities becomes of importance in the later development of the popular arts. What right they have to satisfaction in the movies and television is a question that can stand more discussion than it now gets. I did not foresee the question when I wrote this book and try to persuade myself that it didn't exist. I was looking the other way: I was discovering for myself vast pleasures which, it seemed to me, other intellectuals (minorities of one, every single intellectual of them) might enjoy. The movies, like the newspapers in general, were out for the masses, but the search for the lowest of all the low common denominators hadn't yet become a scientific enterprise, studios took chances just as newspapers did. The change came some ten years after radio began.

About this I have written a great deal, some of it in terms of profound gloom. My present approach is relatively optimistic. I think that the mass media into which the lively arts turned can still perform reasonably in a democratic society. All they need is some ten million inde-pendent-minded people being eternally vigilant about them. ?~

The most sophisticated of the minor arts in America is that of the colyumist. It is, except for occasional lapses into the usual journalistic disrespect for privacy, a decent art, and if it never rises to the polish and wit of such an outstanding colyumist as La-Fourchardière of *l'Œuvre,* it never sinks to the pretentious pseudo-intelligent vulgarity of the English counterpart. The colyumist is, to begin with, a newspaper humorist, and there are times, when questions of art and letters are discussed, when one wishes he had remained one. Phillips, who is now with the *Sun and Globe* in New York, sticks to his game manfully; he tells nothing about himself, discusses no plays, and his colyum, which he illustrates with grotesque little drawings, is self-contained. You do not have to be in the secret to read him. His usual manner is to take a notable or obscure item of news and play with it, in the manner of Mark Twain. When Ambassador Harvey made a speech on the topic, "Have women Souls?" Phillips reported the proceedings and the aftermath:

"Latest bulletins from Europe and Asia on the conduct of other American diplomats follow:

"Warren G. Harding,
  President, United States:
Excellency:—
  American ambassador here has brought about grave crisis by speech, "Are Bananas a Fruit or a Flower?" and "Can Fresh Roasted Peanuts Think?" Understand he has stated publicly his opinion that John McCormack is greater singer than Caruso. People are near uprising. Will you recall him or shall we give him the bum's rush?

                                                  KING OF ITALY

and so on.

It is horseplay; but when he is in form it achieves a wild carelessness and gaiety which the intellectual colyumist entirely forswears. He has for compeer Arthur "Bugs" Baer, by all odds the funniest of the colyumists and a too-much-neglected creator of American humour. There is, also, a considerable number of colyumists of the Phillips type in other cities. I make no apology for not knowing them, for a colyum correctly conceived is written for the readers of its paper. It ought to be partly private, and wholly provincial. Even Mencken when the ran the colyum of the Baltimore *Sun,* and gathered much material for *The American Language,* and told of each new consignment of German beer after the blockade began in 1915, even he was not all things to all men.

The last man who kept his colyum balanced between the high and low comic touch was Bert Leston Taylor. He was a very wise and humane person, wise and humane enough to appreciate and to publish fun of a sort differing by much from the humour he created. There was something unnervingly oblique in his vision of the world, perfectly illustrated by the captions he wrote for clippings from rustic journals. He would take an item, "Our popular telegraphist Frank Dane had a son presented to him last week. Frank says he is going to stay home nights hereafter," and write over it, "How the Days Are Drawing In." There was nothing incongruous in the appearance side by side of his own expert parodies and the horseplay humour of some of his contributors. Taylor's touch made everything light, everything right. In his house there were indeed many mansions. After him—before his death even—the colyumists divided and went separate ways. The Chicago *Tribune* continues the Field-Taylor tradition indifferently well. Riq of the Chicago *Evening Post* comes near the golden mean, but his own character as a colyumist is jeopardized by his contributors; when he gets a good theme—such as the necessity for keeping the seam of a stocking straight, he can be counted on.

Calverley indicated his difficulty—or almost: Themes are so scarce in this world of ours.

The colyumists are sophisticated, or *faux-naïfs,* or actually *naïf.* Of the first, F. P. A. of the New York *World* is the most notable and Baird Leonard of the *Morning Telegraph* the best. F. P. A. has all the virtues of the colyumist in the highest degree; unfortunately he has almost all the faults, in nearly the same measure. He is a defeated Calverley, writing the best light verse in America, and the best parodies in verse. His Persicos Odi, one of several (published in the quarterly "1910"), seems to me better than Field's—which had the lines, "And as for roses, Holy Moses, they can't be got at living prices." Adams', as I recall it, ran:

> The pomp of the Persian I hold in aversion;
> I hate all their gingerbread tricks;
> Their garlicky wreathings and lindeny tree-things
> Nix.
> Boy, us for plain myrtle while under this fertile
> Old grapevine myself I protrude
> For your old bibacious Quintus Horatius
> Stewed.

and his treatment of the same poem according to Service is perfect parody. Algernon St. John Brenon used to quarrel magisterially with Adams about Latin quantities, but he could never undermine Adams' feeling for the ease and urbanity of Horace—and Adams isn't in the business of preserving the tradition of dignity.

His trick verse is not exceptional; he has no Dobsonian feeling for form; in prose parody he is a duffer. His own prose has the one essential quality for wit—it is not diffuse.[1] His actual character is that of a civilized man who cannot be imposed upon by the bunk, and as he is fairly in-

[1] For example: "Ours is a sincere doubt as to whether the question 'And what did *you* do during the Great War?' might not embarrass, among others, God."

dependent he recognizes fake—in the world of politics, business, and society—wherever it occurs. This is what prevents him from being a good radical (type: Heywood Broun; other things in his nature keep him from the insolence of martyrdom), and what makes his work sympathetic to mature and disillusioned minds. His exceptional good sense—he seems to have no sensibility—make stupidity an irritation to him; he follows half of the biblical precept and does not suffer fools gladly. The habit of pontificating has grown on him, and from expressing himself with justifiable arrogance on minor matters he has proceeded to speak with assurance on manners, art, and letters. It would be more accurate to say that he speaks without the humility becoming to one who for many months boosted W. B. Maxwell in opposition to Joseph Conrad. He hasn't, essentially, any idea of his great influence; for if he knew that a vast number of semi-intelligent people were guided by him he would not so rapidly praise and damn (or praise with faint damns, if I may quote another colyum). He is the most exasperating of colyumists; and his triviality when confronted by things he does not understand—I am thinking of his comment on *The Waste Land*—is appalling. Yet this same quality is what makes him precious; he is a gadfly to an exceptionally sluggish beast—the New York intellectual. He has, inevitably, become the patron saint of the smart. At any rate, he has done something to destroy the tradition that what is witty is unsound. It is only when he is serious that he becomes a little ridiculous.

I quarrel as much with Baird Leonard's judgment on art and letters, but I am not irritated because Miss Leonard (who writes for a paper devoted to horse-racing and the theatre) is almost always willing to indicate the path by which she arrives at her discriminations. She hasn't F. P. A.'s weak fear of the common, and her own mind is as far removed as his from the commonplace, it has movements of grace and lightness, and her humour is smooth and wholly urban. Too often for me she fills her column with Bridge Table Talk, a sardonic report of fake intellectualism done with vigour and ferocity, but hampered by the framework which is not adaptable. I do not, at this moment, recall a line she has written; I recall the tone of her whole work—it is unaffected, not self-conscious, brightly aware of everything, keen and curious and always on the alert. If the stage were what it seems from out in front, Miss Leonard would be well placed on a theatrical paper. She is writing for people wise enough to know the place of wit. Adams, I fear, is beginning to write for people witty enough (and no more) to despise wisdom.

The creator of an American legend—I quote from the advertisements—is certainly a wise man. Don Marquis, who now writes his colyum alone, has always had a good second-rate talent for verse, and a good first-rate understanding of humanity. It is the second quality which makes him appreciate the memoirs of William Butler Yeats, and helps him create *The Old Soak*. "Here's richness"! It was right for him to make an entire second act of that play an ode to hard liquor, with lyric interludes about the parrot, for he is on the side of humanity, against the devils and angels alike. Hard liquor, loafing, decency, are his gods, and he fights grimly, with a tendency to see the devil in modern art. He is against a great many American fetiches: efficiency and Y. M. C. A. morality and getting on; and he has a strong, persistent sentiment for common and simple things. All of these together would not make him a good colyumist without some expressive gift. He has enough to render his most endearing qualities fully. And beyond them he has at times a bitterness which drives him to write like Swift and a fantasy which creates archie and Captain Fitz-Urse, and these also are parts of his wisdom.

Christopher Morley, like Rolla (not, however, Rollo), has come too late into a world too old, and daily dreams himself back into the time when a gentle essayist was the

247

noblest man of letters and William McFee a great novelist. His latest work is bound in Gissing Blue Leather, is admired by Heywood Broun, and has been compared to nearly everything except the Four Gospels. Little children should not be permitted to read his colyum in the New York *Evening Post,* for it is a sort of literary *boy-scoutisme,* and very wrong! (It has recently ceased to exist.)

The influence of the daily column is so great that by this time a goodly portion of the literary criticism—or book-reviewing—appears in that form. Keith Preston is partly colyumist, partly literary critic, estimable if not always just in both departments, and a writer of excellent verse. Of the literary colyumists Broun is the most interesting case. He has a peculiar mind, apt to find a trifling detail the clue to too many great things; he has a great sense for the pompous and the pretentious; he is actually a humorist when he lets go. But a strange thing has happened to him. While he was ac-quiring a reputation as arbiter of taste in New York by putting down his simple feelings about books and other things, he was slowly becoming aware of the existence of the intellect. It was borne in upon him, as I believe the phrase is, that a work of art is the product of an intellect working upon materials provided by a sensibility. The discovery un-nerved him—I might almost say deflowered. For Broun has lost his native innocence; he is a little frightened by the hard young men who suddenly let loose the jargon of æs-thetics, of philosophy, of the intellect in general—and what is worse, he *thinks* that they may not be bluffing. He has gone manfully to work, but the middle distance is danger-ous. It is likely to produce more dicta like his notorious dis-missal of rhythmic prose by a reference to verse rhythms in prose. His characteristic statement is, however, apropos of a flying catch by Aaron Ward, of which, Broun said that no book had ever so affected him with the sense that the hu-manly impossible had been accomplished. He seems to wonder, now, whether discovering the mind will ever console him if he loses the catch, whether being an amiable, intelligent, courageous, radical humorist, with sufficient taste to dislike the third-rate and a jocular respect for the first-rate—whether all this isn't enough. And all the while the young men of three nations are giving him to believe that the really new movement is going to be intellectual. In the moment of hesitation he does one thing which may save him—slowly renouncing literature, he digs into his humour and works it hard. He or it will be exhausted presently; when that happens he will be out of the woods—on either side.

But I doubt whether Broun ever was as simple as Bugs Baer. His is called roughneck humour—for all I care. The truth is that Baer is one of the few people writing for the newspapers who have a distinct style. K. C. B. has a form which becomes a formula—it is exasperating to read it— one continues as one continues to read the Bull Durham signs along a railroad track. Baer writes like the speech of Falstaff and his companions, with a rowdy exaggeration. His comparisons are far fetched, his conceptions utterly fantastic. His daily commentaries on sport are concise and entertaining, his best work occurs there,[1] but in *The Family Album,* a Sunday feature of the Hearst papers, he succeeds, despite the subject and the length, in communicating his peculiar quality. It is mingled with banalities like "he was hunting quail on toast up in Canada," but you also get:

So he felt better and met a friend of his and they skipped the Eighteenth Amendment a couple of times and uncle came home and challeneged pop to anything. Pop wanted to know what, and uncle said, "Anything at all. There ain't one thing that you can do that I can't do better than you."

He kept up his anonymous boasting and pop said to mom, "You're escaped brother is loose again. That's him. He takes one drink of that radio liquor and he starts broadcasting."

[1] He said of Firpo that when he came up after the sixth or seventh knock-down, his face looked like a slateful of wrong answers.

Uncle said, "I'll broadcast you for a row of weather-beaten canal boats. I'm mad and hungry. I'm as hot and hollow as a stovepipe."

Mom said to pop, "Don't turn Abimelech away hungry. What does the Good Book say about—"

Pop said, "Oh! That's been vetoed by the President."

There follows what he calls "another quaint tribal quarrel" in which "pop laughed a whole octave above sarcastic" and "Mom said, 'Stop that debate before I take the negative.'"

Everything of Bugs Baer is foreshortened; he is elliptical, omits the middle step. His language is syncopation. His points of reference are all in the common life; I don't suppose that he has ever touched a book or a play in his column. For all that, he impresses me as a naturally subtle spirit. I may be wrong. He is certainly a joyful one.

Burlesque, circus,
clowns, and acrobats

This is a footnote in the interest of justice more than any-thing else. The general scheme of this book is that it is to be an outline, for each of its major chapters is devoted to a subject about which a book ought to be written—but not by me. In such an outline there is no specified allotment of space, and I have written most on the lively arts in which I myself take the liveliest pleasure. Burlesque is not of these —and I confess to enjoying it most in the person of those artists who come out of it into revue, or vaudeville, or any other framework with which I am familiar and which I admire. I can understand an enthusiast feeling the same way about them as I feel about revue and vaudeville players who try to enter the legitimate stage—that they are cor-rupted by a desire to be refined. The great virtues of bur-lesque as I (insufficiently) know it are its complete lack of sentimentality in the treatment of emotion and its treatment of appearance. The harsh ugliness of the usual burlesque make-up is interesting—I have seen sinister, even macabre, figures upon its stage—and the dancing, which has no social refinement, occasionally develops angular positions and lines of exciting effect. I find the better part of burlesque else-where, notably in clowns. And instead of trying to be fair to a medium I do not know well, nor care too much about, I have put in a picture which I greatly admire and which probably is more to the point than anything I could write.

◄§ This was a picture by E. E. Cummings of a comedian at the National Winter Garden Burlesque. For the circus, I reproduced the famous Toulouse-Lautrec painting of the equestrienne and the riding-master at the Cirque Medrano.

Although the smaller tent-shows continue, the biggest of them all has given up playing under canvas and there was even some doubt, in 1957, whether it would play the big cities. It opened in New York and seemed to be totally unchanged. The effort to make it new and sophisticated, which was resented by old-timers some years previously, had left no mark. I found myself still entranced by the trajectory of bodies bouncing off the trampolin and by the effect noted below in connection with the Hippodrome: sheer reduplication adds a new dimension to an act. One girl half way up a rope, doing gymnastics, is so-so; a girl doing the same thing on every rope around the whole Garden area, at intervals of fifty feet, is exciting.

The year before, there was a remarkable act: three men and one woman mounted to the top of poles which nearly touched the top tier of seats and then, swaying the poles, exchanged places. It had that quality of danger which, on the whole, I think I can do without, but it also had skill and a certain finish, which made it quite a beautiful act.

For the rest, a big circus is largely a big bore. Parents not only have to attend, they have to pretend they like nothing better. It is for children and for those artists who have, to our advantage, distilled the essential beauty of the acts so that we can have them always with us, without having to go see them. §►

I shall try to find a picture for the circus, too. Because the circus is a mixed matter and some of it is superb. The *jeux icariens* I have never seen except in France: they are really exquisite. They are usually performed by a whole family. The training is exceedingly arduous, must be begun in childhood, and the art is dying out. In this act the essential thing is the use of human bodies as maniable material. The small boy I saw rolled himself into a tight round ball and was caught on the upturned feet of his father, flat on his back, and tossed to another grownup in the same position, the little rolled-up body spinning like a ball through the air. The beauty of the movements, the accuracy and the finesse of the exploitation of energy, delighted. Trained elephants, however, haven't exactly this quality; and trained seals, agreeable to watch because they are graceful and supple of body, lack something. I have seen a diabolo player who was beautiful to follow, and a juggler who placed two billiard cues end to end on his forehead, threw a ball and caught it at the top of the cues, then dislodged the ball and put it into play with three others. This extraordinary mixture of good and dull things, this lack of character, makes the circus easy to like and useless to think about. The special atmosphere of the circus, the sounds and sights, and smells, are, of course, another matter.

Two of its actual features justify speculation: acrobats and clowns. The American vaudeville player can say nothing worse of an audience than "they like the acrobats." When they hang by their teeth I cannot respect them; the development of any part of the human body is interesting, no doubt, and I do not wish to insist that there *must* be an æsthetic interest in every act. But I feel about them as the Chinese philosopher felt about horse-racing: that it is a well-established fact that one horse can beat another, and the proof is superfluous. But there are trapeze workers whose technique is a joy to see and who exploit all the possible turns, leaps, somersaults in air, so that one is pleased and dazzled. I do not wonder that painters in every age have found them a lovely subject. But a lady balanced on one leg of a trapeze bar, smoking a cigarette, fanning herself, *not holding on to anything*—means exactly nothing to me unless it is accomplished with some other quality than nerve. I am sure she will never fall and do not care to be present when she does.

Clowns are different. Even those poor nameless ones who dash in between major acts and with noise and toy balloons divert little children, have some quality. They partake of our tradition about masks, they can't help having background. Everything exaggerated and ugly in burlesque is here put to the uses of laughter; even the dullest has some gaiety in make-up, in a mechanical contrivance, in gait or gesture. Marceline helping the attendants with Powers' Elephants at the *Hippodrome,* so busy, so in the way, so unconscious of hindering, always created a little world around himself. Grock is incredible in the faultlessness of his method; as musical-eccentric he surpasses all other clowns, and his simple attitude before chairs and pianos and the other complications of life is a study in creativeness. I have written elsewhere of Fortunello and Cirillino, also great clowns; and they complete this sketchy footnote, since for the greatest clowns I have ever seen, nothing short of a separate title will suffice.[1]

[1] A footnote to a footnote is preposterous. Perhaps the very excess of its obscurity will give it prominence and render faint justice to the old New York *Hippodrome*. It is a fine example of handling of material, and of adjustment, spoiled occasionally by too much very loud singing and a bit of art. It is part of New York's small-townness; but it is so vast in its proportions that it can never acquire the personal following of a small one-ring circus like the Medrano in Paris. I adore the *Hippodrome* when it is a succession of acts: the trained crow and Ferry who plays music on a fence and the amazing mechanical and electrical effects. Joe Jackson, one of the greatest of clowns, played there, too, and had ample scope. I like also the complete annihilation of personality in the chorus. When you see three hundred girls doing the same thing it becomes a problem in mass—I recall one instance when it was a mass of white backs with black lines indicating the probable existence of clothes—the whole thing was quite unhuman. And one great scene in which, I believe, the whole of the personnel participated: there were, it seemed, hundreds of tumblers and scores of clowns, and a whole toy shop in excited action. Oddly enough, one finds that the weakness of the *Hip* is in its humour; there is plenty of it, but it is not concentrated, and there is no specific *Hippodrome* "style." What it will become under the new Keith régime remains to be seen.

The true and inimitable
kings of laughter

Clowns are the most traditional of all entertainers and one of the most persistent of the traditions about them is that those who have just died were better than those one has laughed at a moment ago. A very obvious reason is that the clowns of the recent past are the clowns of our own childhood. It is my fortunate position never to have seen a clown when I was a child, and all those I have ever laughed at are alive and funny. One of them, the superb Grock, was a failure in New York; the remarkable Fortunello and Cirillino who arrived with the *Greenwich Village Follies* of 1922 are acrobats of an exceptional delicacy and humour; there isn't a touch of obvious refinement about them and they are exquisite. And the real thing in knockabout grotesquerie are the three who call themselves, justifiably, the true and inimitable kings of laughter, the brothers Fratellini at the Cirque Medrano in Paris.

The Cirque Medrano is a one-ring circus in a permanent building near the Place Pigalle; ten times a week it fills the vast saucer of its seating capacity at an absurdly low price— the most expensive seats, I believe, are six francs—and presents something a little above the average European circus bill. There are more riding and a few more stunts than at others, and there are less trained animals. And ten times weekly the entire audience shouts with gratification as Francesco Fratellini steps gracefully over the ring, hesitates, retreats, and finally sits down in a ringside seat and begins a conversation with the lady sitting beside him.

The thing which distinguishes the Fratellini and makes them great is a sort of internal logic in everything they do. When the spangled figure with the white-washed face sits down by the ring and chats a moment it is merely disconcerting; at once the logic appears—he is waiting for the show to begin. An attendant approaches and tells him to stop stalling, that the people are waiting to be amused. He replies in an odd English that he has paid his "mawney" and why doesn't the show begin. Promptly another attendant repeats the message of the first in English; Francesco replies in Italian. By the time the process has been gone through in five languages the clown has changed his tack entirely; you realize that since he doesn't understand what all these uniformed attendants are saying to him, he thinks that *they* are the show and he is trying to conceal his own irritation at being made the object of their addresses and at the same time he is pretending to be amused at their antics. The last time he speaks in what seems to be gibberish (it is credibly reported to be rather fair Turkish) and the attendants fall back. From the opposite entrance to the ring arrives a figure of unparralleled grotesqueness—garments vast and loose in unexpected places, monstrous shoes, squares like windowpanes over his eyes, a glowing and preposterous nose. His gait is of the utmost dignity, he senses the situation and advances to Francesco's seat; and as a pure matter of business he delivers a terrific slap, bows nobly, and departs. Francesco enters the ring. At the same time a third figure appears—a bald-headed man in carefully arranged clothes, a monocle, and a high hat, a stick. The three Fratellini are on the scene.

It is impossible to say what happens there, for the Fratellini have an inexhaustible repertoire. The materials are always of the simplest, and the effects, too; they have hardly any "props," the costumes, the smiles, the movements, the gestures, are almost exactly alike from day to day. Much of their material is old, for they are the sons and grandsons of clowns as far back as their family memory can carry; I have seen them once appear armed for a fight with inflated bladders, looking precisely like contemporary pictures in Maurice Sand's book about the *commedia dell'arte,* and on another occasion have seen them so carried away with the frenzy of their activity that they actually improvised and proved their descent from this ancient form. They do burlesque sketches—a barber shop, a bull fight, a human elephant, a magician, or a billiard game; the moment they stop the entire audience roars for "la musique," the most famous of their acts, remarkable because it has a minimum of physical violence.

La Musique is all a matter of construction and is a wonderful example of the use of material. For at bottom it consists of the efforts of two men to play a serenade and the continual intrusion of a third. Francesco and Paolo arrive, each carrying a guitar or a mandoline, and place two chairs close together exactly in the centre of the ring. They step on the chairs and prepare to sit on the backs, but even this simple process is difficult for them, as neither is willing to sit down before the other, nor to remain seated while the other is still erect, and they must be continually rising and apologizing until one flings the other down and keeps him there until he himself is seated. Ready then, they blow out the electric lights and strike the first notes; but the spotlight deserts them; they are left in the dark and puzzled; they regard one another with dismay and suspicion. Suddenly they see it across the ring and, descending with great gravity, carry their chairs across. Again they start, and again the spotlight goes; their irritation mounts, but their dignity remains and they follow it. It flits back to where they had come from.

There is a consultation and the two chairs are returned to their original place in the centre of the ring. Then the two musicians take off their coats, prowl around the ring stalking the light, and fall upon it; then slowly and with much labour they lift the light by its edges and carefully carry it back to their chairs. And as they begin to play the grotesque marches in behind them, unconscious of them, intent only upon his vast horn and the enormous musical score he carries. Unseeing and unseen, he prepares himself, and at about the tenth bar the great bray of his horn shatters the melody of the strings. The two musicians are dismayed, but as they cannot see the source of the disturbance, they try again; again the horn intrudes. This time there is expostulation and argument with the grotesque, but, as he reasonably points out, music was desired and he is doing his share. There is only one issue for such a scene, and it takes places, in a riot.

The preparation of these riots is a work of real delicacy, for the Fratellini know that two things are equally true: violence is funny and violence ceases to be funny. Like Chaplin, they infuse into their violence the sense of reason— they are violent only when no other means will suffice. In the photographer scene they call into action the "august" a stock character of the European circus, played at the Medrano with exceptional skill by M Lucien Godart. The august is a man of great dignity whose office it is to parley with clowns, be the butt of their jokes, and in M Godart's version, set off their grotesque appearance by an excellent figure and the most correct of evening clothes. (He is in addition a rather good tumbler, and it is part of the Medrano tradition for the audience to hiss him until he grows seemingly furious and turns twenty difficult somersaults around the ring.) The Fratellini, armed with a huge black box and a cloth, ask him to sit for his photograph. Francesco takes it upon himself to explain the apparatus, Paolo stand-

258

ing close by with the three fence posts which represent the tripod, and Alberto, the grotesque waiting near by. Suddenly the tripod falls on Alberto's feet and he howls with pain; Paolo picks the posts up again, and again they fall, and again he howls. It is unbelievable that this should be funny, yet it is funny beyond any capacity to describe it for one reason which the spectator senses long before he sees it. That is that the tripod is not intentionally thrown on the feet of the grotesque. The fault is Francesco's, for he is explaining the machine and making serious errors, and every time he makes a mistake Paolo gets excited and forgets that he has the tripod in his hand, and simply lets it drop. One senses his acute regret, and at the next moment one realizes that his scientific zeal, his respect for his profession of photographer, simply does not permit him to let a misstatement pass; his gesture as he turns to set the matter right is so eager, so agonized, that one doesn't see what has happened to the tripod until it has fallen. And to point the moral of the matter, when the grotesque Alberto after the fifth time picks the tripod up and attempts to slay Paolo, Paolo is again turning toward the others and the blow goes wide.

What the Fratellini are doing here is, to be sure, what every great actor does—they are presenting their effects indirectly. The difficulty for them is that in the end they must give their effects with the maximum of directness—they have to strike a man in the face and make the sound tell. In the scene of the photograph the august is "he who gets slapped" (the phrase is a common one) and the scene is carefully built up through his reluctance and stupidity in posing. At first it is only an exaggeration of the customary difficulties between a photographer and a little child; but as the august becomes more and more suspicious of the intentions of the photographer, the clowns become more and more insistent that he, and nobody but he, shall have his picture taken. Gradually an atmosphere of hostility is built

259

up; the august tries to escape from the ring and is hauled back; then dragged, then forced to sit; the opposing wills grow more and more violent; the audience senses the good will of the clowns, the obstinacy of the august; not a push or shove is given without reason and meaning. And when they see that there is nothing else for it, the three hurl themselves upon the clown in a frenzy of destructiveness and he is rent limb from limb. (In actual fact only his exquisite evening clothes were rent, but the effect is the same.)

In these scenes and almost all their others, the Fratellini escape the reproach of being nothing but violent, while they hold every good element which violence in action can give them. To them are comparable the best (and only the best) of Eddie Cantor's scenes—when he applied for the job of policeman and when he was examined for the army—where there is a play of motive and a hidden logic. In their world everything must be sensible, and the most sensible thing in the world is to hit out. Behind them is a dual tradition— centuries of laughter and centuries of refining the instruments by which simple laughter can be produced. For it is opposed to their sense of fitness (as it is to ours) that the clown should create an effect of subtlety.[1] The kind of laughter they produce *must* involve the whole body, but not the mind. They have to be active all the time, so that you are dazzled and cannot think; and they must shake the solid ground under your feet, so that you may shake with laughter. What the critical observer discovers as method must reach the actual average spectator only as effect. All of this the Fratellini have accomplished—"these three brothers who constitute one artist" are the complete and perfect exemplars of their art. Seeing them sometimes twice a week, and nearly two dozen times, I find their qualities inexhaustible. Even in the descriptions of acts noted above it can be seen that they have a definite sense of pace; their changes

[1] They nevertheless played exquisitely, I am told, in the Cocteau-Milhaud *Bœuf sur le Toit*.

from fast to slow in the middle of an act, their variations from violence to trickery, their complete mastery of climax, their fertility of invention, are all elements of superiority. But they are only elements in a composition based on something fundamentally right—the knowledge that we have almost forgotten how to laugh in the actual world, and that to make us laugh again they must create a world of their own.

The Great God Bogus

᳇ The manifesto in the nine statements which follow probably accounted for most of the rancor this book inspired and also, I suspect, for its good repute among young people who were reading Mencken and took me as a collaborator of his, working a special field. It may indicate premature hardening of the intellectual arteries, but the simple fact is that I am still moved by the same preferences and prejudices. The reader of to-day will not be aware of the contemporary reputations of some of the individuals mentioned. Ethel Barrymore, for instance, redeemed half a lifetime of appearing, without much distinction, in second-rate plays, by a career in the movies which has been admirable. Her tragic brother John had begun brilliantly as a romantic hero on the stage, had progressed to do a superb Hamlet, and was beginning a long decline when I wrote. Cabell and Hergesheimer were among the favorites of H. L. Mencken and were considered great artists, with a special bow to Hergesheimer because he put his art over on the editors of The Saturday Evening Post. David Belasco gave himself insufferable airs as an artist in the theatre to which he had contributed a needed dash of realism a generation earlier and nothing of much value after that. Cecil de Mille is discussed later— nothing in his distinguished career persuades me that the movies are any the better for it and I am quite willing to uphold the contrary.

All of these comparisons were made, obviously, for purposes of shock. In that, they apparently succeeded. ❧

If there were an Academy I should nail upon its doors the following beliefs:

That Al Jolson is more interesting to the intelligent mind than John Barrymore and Fanny Brice than Ethel;
That Ring Lardner and Mr Dooley in their best work are more entertaining and more important than James B. Cabell and Joseph Hergesheimer in their best;
That the daily comic strip of George Herriman (*Krazy Kat*) is easily the most amusing and fantastic and satisfactory work of art produced in America to-day;
That Florenz Ziegfeld is a better producer than David Belasco;
That one film by Mack Sennet or Charlie Chaplin is worth the entire *œuvre* of Cecil de Mille;
That *Alexander's Ragtime Band* and *I Love a Piano* are musically and emotionally sounder pieces of work than *Indian Love Lyrics* and *The Rosary*;
That the circus can be and often is more artistic than the Metropolitan Opera House in New York;
That Irene Castle is worth all the pseudo-classic dancing ever seen on the American stage; and
That the civic masque is not perceptibly superior to the Elks' Parade in Atlantic City.

Only about half of these are heresies, and I am quite ready to stand by them as I would stand by my opinion of Dean Swift or Picasso or Henry James or James Joyce or Johann Sebastian Bach. But I recognize that they are expressions of personal preference, and possibly valueless unless related to some general principles. It appears that what I care for in the catalogue above falls in the field of the lively arts; and that the things to which I compare them

264

(for emphasis, not for measurement) are either second-rate instances of the major arts or first-rate examples of the peculiarly disagreeable thing for which I find no other name than the bogus. I shall arrive presently at the general principles of the lively arts and their relation to the major. The bogus is a lion in the path.

Bogus is counterfeit and counterfeit is bad money and bad money is better—or at least more effective—than good money. This is not a private paradox, but a plain statement of a law in economics (Gresham's, I think) that unless it is discovered, bad money will drive out good. Another characteristic of counterfeit is that, once we have accepted it, we try to pass it off on some one else; banks and critics are the only institutions which don't—or ought not to—continue the circulation. In the arts counterfeit is known as *faux bon*—the apparently good, essentially bad, which is the enemy of the good. The existence of the bogus is not a serious threat against the great arts, for they have an obstinate vitality and in the end—but only in the end—they prevail. It is the lively arts which are continually jeopardized by the bogus, and it is for their sake that I should like to see the bogus go sullenly down into oblivion.

Namely: vocal concerts, pseudo-classic dancing, the serious intellectual drama, the civic masque, the high-toned moving picture, and grand opera.

The first thing about them is that a very small percentage of those who make the bogus arts prosperous really enjoy them. I recall my own complete stultification after hearing my first concert; and the casual way in which I made it evident to all my companions that I had been to a concert is my only clue to the mystery. For at bottom there is a vast snobbery of the intellect which repays the deadly hours of boredom we spend in the pursuit of art. We are the inheritors of a tradition that what is worth while must be dull; and as often as not we invert the maxim and pretend that what is dull is higher in quality, more serious, "greater art" in short than whatever is light and easy and gay. We suffer fools gladly if we can pretend they are mystics. And the fact that audiences at concerts and opera, spectators at classic dances and masques, are suffering, is the final damnation, for it means that these arts are failures. I do not found my belief on any theory that all the arts ought to be appreciated by all the people. I do mean that most of those who read *Ulysses* or *The Pickwick Papers* do so because they enjoy it, and they stop the moment they are bored. There is no superiority in having read a book. The lively anticipation of delights which one senses in those going to the *Follies* or to a circus is wholly absent in the lobby of the Metropolitan or at a performance of *Jane Clegg.* And the art which communicates no ecstasy but that of snobbism is irretrievably bogus.

⋞ A far clearer insight into the psychology of the art-snob is needed. I. A. Richards has (in another connection) supplied a clue. Whenever we have worked hard to understand a work of art, it irritates us to have someone else apparently enjoy it just as much with none of the labor. The music student cannot believe that the amateur gets as much out of a performance, the man who has read Berenson or Malraux must see something in a painter which the unlettered spectator does not. We have a vested interest—we must insist that many things are too good for the average man. ⋟

There is something hopeless about opera as we know it in the United States; and the fact that ten or fifteen operas are among the permanent delights of civilized existence does not alter the fact. (Three of them: *Chovanstchina, The Marriage of Figaro,* and *Don Giovanni,* are not in the repertoire of the Metropolitan; nor are *Falstaff* and *Otello;* nor does the ballet proceed beyond *Coq d'Or;* nor it seems would the Metropolitan hold it within its dignity to produce *The*

266

Mikado, although Schumann-Heink was ready to sing Katisha.) Here is an art-form hundreds of years old, prospered by an enormous publicity, favoured by extraordinary windfalls—the voice of Caruso, the "personality" of Farrar—able to set into motion nearly every appeal to the senses in colour, tone, movement—it has song and action and dance—and what exactly is the final accomplishment? The pale maunderings of Puccini, the vulgarity of Massenet, and the overpowering dulness of our domestic try-outs. Wagner? A philosopher drunk with divine wisdom is reported (by Goethe) to have cried out that he could discern shortcomings even in God; and the melancholy truth is that the welding of three arts into one succeeded only in Wagner's brain, for on the boards we lose Wagner as we attend to the stage, and regain him as we return to the music. This is not true of *Boris* or of *Figaro*—so much less pretentious, both; and the director may arise who will know how to fuse Wagner into one harmonious and beautiful object. At the moment, one takes the Metropolitan with its vast seating capacity, its endless sources of appeal to the multitude, and one knows that it isn't a success. If it isn't losing money it is paying its way through social subventions. Eighty per cent of the music heard there is trivial in comparison with either good jazz or good symphonic music; ninety per cent of the acting is preposterous; and the settings, costumes, and properties are so far below popular musical comedy standards that in the end Urban and Norman-Bel Geddes have had to be called in to save them, and haven't been given scope or freedom enough to succeed. The Metropolitan is, I am told, the finest opera house in the world and loses money because it is still several leaps ahead of its clientèle which insists on more Puccini and no *Coq d'Or.* Also I have had the supreme pleasure of hearing Chaliapin there and I am not ungrateful. The Metropolitan has difficulties happily unknown to us and is unquestionably an eminent institution. It is opera as we know it, that calls down the curse, opera which has to

267

call itself "grand" to distinguish itself from the popular, superior, kind. For it is pretentious and it appeals not to our sensibilities but to our snobbery. It neither excites nor exalts; it does not amuse. Over it and under it and through it runs the element of fake; it is a substitute for symphonic music and an easy expiatory offering for ragtime. *Ecrasez l'infâme!*

◖ The Metropolitan has come a long way, but it should have accepted the proposals made, at least half seriously, which would have handed the direction over to Billy Rose. (Not that I would want him to waste his time on half of the trash he'd be compelled to produce.) ◗

Audiences at the opera have, however, been thrilled by a voice. What is there to say for the uncommunicative, uninspired, serious-minded intellectual drama which without wit, or intensity, "presents a problem" or drearily holds the mirror up to nature? Those little scenes from domestic life, those second-hand expositions of other people's philosophies, those unflinching grapplings with "the vital facts of existence" which year by year are held to be great plays? Let me be frank; let me face my vital facts. I have never found my brain inadequate to grapple with their grapplings, for it is almost in the nature of the case that if a man has anything profound to express he will flee from the theatre where everything is dependent upon actors usually unintelligent and is reduced to the lowest common factor of human intelligence. Bernard Shaw writes his ideas into his prefaces because they can't be fully stated on the stage; Henry James tried to be delicate and failed. It remains for Ferencz Molnar and Augustus Thomas to succeed—with borrowed and diminished ideas. Still speaking of modern serious plays (because the *Medea* of Euripides and the tragedy of *Othello* are not involved) what is bogus in them is their spurious appeal to our sentimentality or our snobbery. It is their

268

pretence to be a great and serious art when they are simply vulgarizations. I have no quarrel with any man for the subject matter of his work of art, and I should allow every freedom to the artist. The whole trouble with our modern serious drama is that it is usually such bad drama; the tedium of three hours of *Jane Clegg* isn't worth sitting through because of the desperate effort of the dramatist and the producer to create the illusion of reality by reproducing the rhythm of reality. The essential distortion, caricature, or transposition which you find in a serious work of art or in a vaudeville sketch, is missing here. And the efforts to ram this sort of play home by pretending that only morons do not like it is exactly and precisely bunk. Most plays fail because they are bad plays; and the greater part of the intellectual drama following this divine LAW, fails. A good manipulator of the theatre like Molnar can put over *Liliom*, which has no more of a great idea than *Seven Keys to Baldpate* and is almost as good drama, if he knows in what proportion to mingle his approaches to our meaner and higher sensibilities. For we are not altogether lost yet.

⋙ I find here the same wooly thinking as in the chapter on the dance. The enemy is not identified—it can't be one miserable play, *Jane Clegg*. Some of Eugene O'Neill's plays had been produced by the time I wrote this—not his great ones, but the one-acters which are surely parts of our "serious drama." There was probably a lull in the theatre before the brightness of the later 1920's was to come and the Theatre Guild may have been having one of its arty spells.

But I did my case little good by going off into a denunciation of theatrical realism and equating that style with the intellectual drama as a whole. The only thought here which I can still endorse is the position "that only morons do not like it" is an improper critical gambit. There was a lot of pretentiousness going on at the time

269

and I was against it. But I may have been overawed by the critical acclaim which the serious drama was getting, so I pulled my punches.

In these days, when the theatre is the last remaining place in which anything serious can be said to a great many people at the same time, this snarling of mine is woefully out of place. It had no effect at the time, for which I am grateful. ❧

If the civic masque and classic dancing continue much longer we will be lost entirely. These arty conglomerations of middle-high seriousness and bourgeois beauty are not so much a peril as a nuisance. The former is the "artistic" counterpart of the Elks Parade and since I cannot speak with decent calm about its draperies and mummery, I recommend Mr R. C. Benchley's chapter on the same subject in *Of All Things!* The civic masque is fake mediævalism, the sort of thing which, if ridicule could kill, should have gone out after W. S. Gilbert's couplets appeared in *Patience*. Alas the instinct for trumpery art persists and on it has been grafted the astounding idea of communal artistic effort—a characteristic thing, too, for the communal efforts of ancient Greece were war and Bacchanalia, and of the middle ages, the crusades; the municipal celebrations after which the civic masque is patterned were created in cities which were unself-conscious and were doing something out of vanity and joy. I cannot imagine the six million of New York or the six thousand of Vineland, Arkansas, growing suddenly mad with joy over the fact that they live in no mean city. I neither like the civic consciousness nor believe deeply in its honest existence. And when it takes to expressing itself as the symbol of the corn and such-like idiocy it isn't as funny as the induction scene of the Ziegfeld Follies (which the Forty-niners took off as "I am the spirit of Public School Number 146") and it isn't any more moving or intelligent.

Certainly it has never been so beautiful. Faced with the vast myths of the American pasts, our poets simply haven't found the medium for projecting them. The dime novel and the Wild West film both failed for lack of imaginative power, and that treasure remains undisturbed. It is sealed and guarded and the civic masque nibbles at it, dislodges a fragment, and comes dancing awkwardly into the foreground waving the shadow of an illusion like a scarf over its head.

For obviously classic dancing is the natural form of expression for this pseudo-civism. I have never had the patience to discover the beginnings of the fatuous craze for imitations of presumably ancient dances. Certainly the first of the notable dancers I saw was not before 1907—in the person of Isadora Duncan. It would be absurd to recall those renditions of the *Seventh Symphony* and what not at this date. If Miss Duncan is a great artist and a great personality now, so much the better, for her early success had much to do with breaking down the gates of our decent objection to fake and her imitators swept over us like a flood. Bogus again, these things; they interpret in dance things which had already been all too clear in music or drama. They know, it seems, the science of eurhythmics, which ought to mean good rhythm, and they employ it to produce in pantomime an obvious, brutally flat version of the Fall of Troy. They haven't as yet added one single thing to our stock of interest and beauty—as the Russian Ballet did, as the old five-position ballet dance did, as modern ballroom and stage dancing does. The costuming is almost always silly; the music chosen is almost always obvious; and the postures assumed are lethally monotonous. The old ballet, based on five definite positions, made each slight variation count, and Pavlowa with her stricken face and tenderness of movement knew it by heart, or by instinct. The new dancers have no internal discipline and no freedom; and only the accident that the human body is at times not displeasing to look

271

upon makes them tolerable. One could forgive them much if the pretensions were not so unutterably lofty and the swank so ignorant and the results so ugly. Fat women leaping with chaplets in their hair, in garments of grey gauze, are not the poetry of motion, and Irene Castle in a black evening dress dancing Irving Berlin's music is—just as surely as Nijinsky was. What is more, these two dancers, whom I choose at the extremes of the dance, both have reference to our contemporary life; and the classic dancing of Helen Moeller and Marion Morgan and Mr Chalif and the rest have absolutely nothing to say to us. We've lost that "simplicity," thank God, or haven't found it yet. We are an alert and lively people—and our dance must actually express that spirit as no fake can do.

Our existence is hard, precise, high spirited. There is no nourishment for us in the milk-and-water diet of the bogus arts, and all they accomplish is a genteel corruption, a further thinning out of the blood, a little extra refinement. They are, intellectually, the exact equivalent of a high-toned lady, an elegant dinner or a refined collation served in the saloon, and the contemporary form of the vapours. Everything about them is supposed to be "good taste," including the kiss on the brow which miraculously "ruins" a perfect virgin—and they are in the physical sense of the word utterly tasteless. The great arts and the lively arts have their sources in strength or in gaiety—and the difference between them is not the degree of intensity, but the degree of intellect. But the bogus arts spring from longing and weakness and depression.[1] A happy people creates folk songs or whistles rag; it does not commit the vast atrocity of a "community singsong"; it goes to Olympic games or to a race track, to *Iphigenia* or to Charlie Chaplin—not to hear a "vocal concert."

The bogus arts are corrupting the lively ones—because

[1] *Quanto più, un' arte porta seco fatica di corpo, tanto più è vile!* Pater, who quotes this of Leonardo, calls it "princely."

an essential defect of the bogus is that they pretend to be better than the popular arts, yet they want desperately to be popular. They borrow and spoil what is good; they persuade people by appealing to their snobbery that they are the real thing. And as the audience watches these arts in action the comforting illusion creeps over them that at last they have achieved art. But they are really watching the manifestations of the Great God Bogus—and what annoys me most is that they might at that very moment be hailing Apollo or Dionysos, or be themselves participating in some of the minor rites of the Great God Pan.

An open letter
to the movie magnates

Ignorant and unhappy People:

The Lord has brought you into a narrow place—what you would call a tight corner—and you are beginning to feel the pressure. A voice is heard in the land saying that your day is over. The name of the voice is Radio, broadcasting nightly to announce that the unequal struggle between the tired washerwoman and the captions written by or for Mr Griffith is ended. It is easier to listen than to read. And it is long since you have given us anything significant to see.

You may say that radio will ruin the movies no more than the movies ruined the theatre. The difference is that your foundation is insecure: you are monstrously over-capitalized and monstrously undereducated; the one thing you cannot stand is a series of lean years. You have to keep on going because you have from the beginning considered the pictures as a business, not as an entertainment. Perhaps in your desperate straits you will for the first time try to think about the movie, to see it steadily and see it whole.

❧ Three years later the movies were in even worse straits. Warner Brothers, in desperation, tried out Vitaphone—and the whole industry was saved. The beneficent

275

workings of the bankruptcy act under the New Deal saved the studios. How they would have fared if sound had not come in is too gruesome to contemplate. ॐ

My suggestion to you is that you engage a number of men and women: an archæologist to unearth the history of the moving picture; a mechanical genius to explain the camera and the projector to you; a typical movie fan, if you can find one; and above all a man of no practical capacity whatever: a theorist. Let these people get to work for you; do what they tell you to do. You will hardly lose more money than in any other case.

If the historian tells you that the pictures you produced in 1910 were better than those you now lose money on, he is worthless to you. But if he fails to tell you that the pictures of 1910 pointed the way to the real right thing and that you have since departed from that way, discharge him as a fool. For that is exactly what has occurred. In your beginnings you were on the right track; I believe that in those days you still looked at the screen. Ten years later you were too busy looking at, or after, your bank account. Remember that ten years ago there wasn't a great name in the movies. And then, thinking of your present plight, recall that you deliberately introduced great names and chose Sir Gilbert Parker, Rupert Hughes, and Mrs Elinor Glyn. If I may quote an author you haven't filmed, it shall not be forgiven you.

Your historian ought to tell you that the moving picture came into being as the result of a series of mechanical developments; your technician will add the details about the camera and projector. From both you will learn that you are dealing with *movement governed by light*. It will be news to you. You seem not to realize the simplest thing about your business. Further, you will learn that everything you need to do *must* be by these two agencies: movement and light. (Counting in movement everything of pace and in

276

light everything which light can make visible to the eye, even if it be an emotion: do you recall the unnatural splash of white in a street scene in *Caligari*?) It will occur to you that the cut-back, the alternating exposition of two concurrent actions, the vision, the dream, are all good; and that the close-up, dearest of all your finds, usually dissociates a face or an object from its moving background and is the most dangerous of expedients. You will learn much from the camera and from what was done with it in the early days.

I warn you again they were not great pictures except for *The Avenging Conscience* and—one you didn't make—*Cabiria*. To each of these a poet contributed. (Peace, Mr Griffith; the poet in your case was E. A. Poe; and the warrior poet of Fiume contributed the scenario for the second.) Mr Griffith contrived in his picture to project both beauty and terror by combining *Annabel Lee* with *The Telltale Heart*. A sure instinct led him to disengage the vast emotion of longing and of lost love through an *action* of mystery and terror. (I think he made a happy ending somehow—by having the central portion of his story appear as a dream. How little it mattered since the *real* emotion came through the story.) The picture was projected in a palpable atmosphere; it was *felt*. After ten years I recall dark masses and ghostly rays of light. And if I may anticipate the end, let me compare it with a picture of 1922, a picturization as you call it, of Annabel Lee. It was all scenery and captions; it presented a detestable little boy and a pretty little girl doing æsthetic dancing along cliffs by the sea; one almost saw the Ocean View Hotel in the background. Mercilessly the stanzas appeared on the screen; but nothing was allowed to *happen* except a vulgar representation of calf love. I cannot bear to describe the disagreeable picture of grief at the end; I do not dare to think what you may now be preparing with a really great poem. The lesson is not merely one of taste; it is a question of knowing the camera, of realizing that you

277

must project emotion by movement and by picture combined.

I am trying to trace for you the development of the serious moving picture as a *bogus* art, and I can't do better than assure you that it was best before it was an "art" at all. (Or I can indicate that slap-stick comedy, which you despise, is not bogus, is a real, and valuable, and delightful entertainment.) I believe that you went out West because the perpetual sun of southern California made taking easy; there you discovered the lost romance of America, its Wild West and its pioneer days, its gold rush and its Indians. You had it in your hands, then, to make that past of ours alive; a small written literature and a remnant of oral tradition remained for you to work on. On the whole you did make a good beginning. You missed fine things, but you caught the simple ones; you presented the material directly, with appropriate sentiment. You relied on melodrama, which was the rightest thing you ever did. Combat and pursuit, the last-minute rescue, were the three items of your best pictures; and your cutting department, carefully alternating the fight between white men and red with the slow-starting, distant, approaching, arriving, victorious troops from the garrison appealed properly to our soundest instincts. You went into the bad-man period; you began to make an individual soldier, Indian, bandit, pioneer, renegade, the focus of your interest: still good because you related him to an active, living background. Dear Heaven! before you had filmed Bret Harte you had created legendary heroes of your own.

Meanwhile Mr Griffith, apparently insatiable, was developing small *genre* scenes of slum life while he thought of filming the tragic history of the South after the war. Other directors sought other fields—notably that of the serial adventure film. Since they made money for all concerned, you will not be surprised to hear these serials praised: *The Exploits of Elaine,* the whole Pearl White adventure, the thirty minutes of action closing on an impossible and unresolved

278

climax were, of course, infinitely better pictures that your version of Mr Joseph Conrad's *Victory,* your *Humoreske,* your *Should a Wife Forgive?* [1] They were extremely silly; they worked too closely on a scheme: getting out of last week's predicament and into next week's can hardly be called a "form." But within their limitations they used the camera for all it was worth. It didn't matter a bit that the perils were preposterous, that the flights and pursuits were all fakes composed by the speed of the projector. You were back in the days of Nick Carter and the Liberty Boys; you hadn't heard of psychology, and drama, and art; you were developing the camera. You bored us when your effects didn't come off and I'm afraid amused us a little even when they did. But you were on the right road.

There was very little *acting* in these films and in the Wild West exhibitions. There was a great deal of *action.* I can't recall Pearl White *registering* a single time; I recall only movement, which was excellent. It was later that your acting developed; up to this time you were working with people who hadn't succeeded in or were wholly ignorant of the technique of the stage; they moved before the camera gropingly at first, but gradually developing a technique suited to the camera and to nothing else. I am referring to days so far back that the old Biograph films used to be branded with the mark AB in a circle, and this mark occurred in the photographed sets to prevent stealing. In those days your actors and actresses were exceptionally naïve and creative. You were on the point of discovering mass and line in the handling of crowds, in the defile of a troop, in the movement of individuals. Mr Griffith had already discovered that four men running in opposite directions along the design of a figure 8 gave the effect of sixteen men—a discovery lightly comparable to that of Velasquez in the crossed spears of the Surrender of Breda. You would have done well to continue

[1] It is not too late for you to film Mr D. Taylor's *Should a Brother-in-Law Give a Damn?*

your experiments with nameless individuals and chaotic masses; but you couldn't. You developed what you called personalities—and after that, actresses.

Before *The Birth of a Nation* was begun Mary Pickford had already left Griffith. I have heard that he vowed to make Mae Marsh a greater actress—as if she weren't one from the start, as if acting mattered, as if Mary Pickford ever could or needed to act. Remember that in *The Avenging Conscience* at least four people: Spottiswood Aiken, Henry Walthall, Blanche Sweet, and another I cannot identify—the second villain—*played* superbly without acting. Conceive your own stupidity in not knowing what Vachel Lindsay discovered: that "our Mary" was literally "the Queen of my People," a radiant, lovely, childlike girl, a beautiful figurehead, a symbol of all our sentimentality. Why did you allow her to become an actress? Why is everything associated with her later work so alien to beauty? You did not see her legend forming; you began to advertise her salary; you have, I believe unconsciously, tried to restore her now by giving her the palest rôle in all literature, that of Marguerite in *Faust*. You are ten years too late. In the same ten years Blanche Sweet has almost disappeared and Mae Marsh has not arrived; Gishes and Talmadges and Swansons and other fatalities have triumphed. You have taken over the stage and the opera; you have filmed Caruso and Al Jolson, too, for all I know. You now have acting and no playing.

This is a matter of capital importance and I am willing to come closer to a definition. Acting is the way of impersonating, of rendering character, of presenting action which is suitable to the stage; it has, in the first place, a specific relation to the size of the stage and to that of the auditorium; it has also a second important relation to the lines spoken. Good actors—they are few—will always suit the gesture to the utterance in the sense that their gesture will be on the beat of the words; failure to know this ruined several of John Barrymore's soliloquies in *Hamlet*. Neither of these two primary and determinant circumstances affect the moving picture. It should be obvious that if good acting is adapted to the stage, nothing less than a miracle could make it also suitable to the cinema. The same thing is true of opera, which is in a desperate state because it failed to develop a type of representation adapted to musical instead of spoken expression. Opera and the pictures both needed "playing"—by which I cover *other forms* of representation, of impersonation, characterization, without identifying them. It is unlikely that opera and pictures require the same kind of playing; but neither of them can bear acting. Chaplin, by the way, is a player, not an actor—although we all think of him as an actor because the distinction is tardily made. I should say that Mae Marsh, too, was a player in *The Birth*. So was H. B. Warner in a war play called *Shell 49* (I am not sure of the figure); and there have been others. I have never seen Conrad Veidt or Werner Kraus on the stage; in *Caligari* they were players, not actors. Possibly since Kraus is considered the greatest of German actors, he acted so well that he seemed to be playing. But that requires genius and the Gishes have no genius.

The emergence of Mary Pickford and the production of *The Birth of a Nation* make the years 1911-14 the critical time of the movies. Nearly all your absurdities began about this time, including your protest against the word movies as no longer suited to the dignity of your art. From the success of *The Birth* sprang the spectacle film which was intrinsically all right and only corrupted Griffith and the pictures because it was unintelligently handled thereafter. From the success of Mary Pickford came the whole tradition of the movie as a genteel intellectual entertainment. The better side is the spectacle and the fact that in 1922 the whole mastery of the spectacular film has passed out of your hands ought to be sufficient proof that you bungled somewhere. Or, to drive it home, what can you make of the circumstance that one of the very greatest successes, in America and abroad, was *Nanook of the North,* a spectacle film to which the producer and the artistic director contributed nothing—for it was a picture of actualities, made, according to rumour, in the interests of a fur-trading company? You will reply that my assertions are pure theory. It is true that I have never filmed a scenario in my life. But as a spectator I am the one who is hard headed and you the theorists. What I and several million others know is that something wrong crept into the spectacle film. We know absolutely that the overblown idea of *Intolerance* was foisted on the simple tale of *The Mother and the Law,* and that while single episodes of this stupendous picture were excellent, the whole failed of effect. In *The Birth* Mr Griffith had two stories with no perceptible internal relation, but with sufficient personal interest to carry; even here not one person in ten thousand saw the significance of the highfalutin title. But after the time of *Intolerance* Mr Griffith receded swiftly, and his latest pictures are merely lavish. It is of no significance that Mr Griffith treats Thomas Burke as though the latter were a great writer instead of a good scenario writer; the prettifying of *Broken Blossoms* was so consistent, and the fake acting such good fake, that the picture almost succeeded. Everywhere Mr Griffith now gives us excesses—everything is big: the crowds, the effects, the rainstorms, the ice floes, and everything is informed with an overwhelming dignity. He has long ago ceased to create beauty—only beautiful effects, like set pieces in fireworks. And he was the man destined by his curiosity, his honesty, his intelligence, to reach the heights of the moving picture.

◆§ D. W. Griffith is nowadays so much *the* great man of the movies that I find my premature iconoclasm refreshing and wonder whether I would feel free to criticize him so harshly now. I think it is fair to say that the pictures after *Intolerance* marked a decline in his imagination, but I failed to note the astonishing technical virtuosity of that picture, the "hail of images" with which Griffith assaulted us—and inspired the *montage* of the great Russian period. ❧

It is a hard thing to say, but it is literally true that something in Mr Griffith has been corrupted and died—his imagination. *Broken Blossoms* was a last expiring flicker. Since then he has constructed well; I understand that his success has been great; I am not denying that Mr Griffith is the man to do *Ben-Hur*. But he has imagined nothing on a grand scale, nor has he created anything delicate or fine. People talk of *The Birth* as if the battle scenes were important; they were very good and a credit to Griffith, who directed, and to George Bitzer, who photographed them; the direction of the ride of the Klansmen was better, it had some imagination. And far better still was a moment earlier in the piece, when Walthall returned to the shattered Confederate home and Mae Marsh met him at the door, wearing raw cotton smudged to resemble ermine—brother and sister both pretending that they had forgotten their dead, that they didn't care what happened. And then—for the honours of the scene went to Griffith, not even to the exquisite Mae Marsh—then there appeared from within the doorway the arm of their mother and with a gesture of unutterable loveliness it enlaced the boy's shoulders and drew him tenderly into the house. To have omitted the tears, to have shown nothing but the arm in that single curve of beauty, required, in those days, high imagination. It was the emotional climax of the film; one felt from that moment that the rape and death of the little girl was already understood in the vast suffering sympathy of the mother. So much Mr Griffith never again accomplished; it was the one moment when he stood beside Chaplin as a creative artist—and it was ten years ago.

ɛ§   This scene remains for me one of the most memorable
in the films—after a lapse of some 30 years. A parallel
occurs in *Camille* when, toward the end of the picture,
Garbo is in Robert Taylor's arms, her face averted from
us, her hand visible over his shoulder. Then the hand
droops—and you know that she is going to die.   ɛ∾

Of course if Griffith hasn't come through there is hardly
anything to hope for from the others. Mr Ince always beat
him in advertized expenditure; Fox was always cheaper and
easier and had Annette Kellerman and did *The Village
Blacksmith*. The logical outcome of Griffithism is in the
pictures he didn't make: in *When Knighthood Was in
Flower* and in *Robin Hood,* neither of which I could sit
through. The lavishness of these films is appalling; the camera runs mad in everything but action, which dies a hundred
deaths in as many minutes. Of what use are sets by Urban
if the action which occurs in them is invisible to the naked
eye? The old trick of using a crowd as a background and
holding the interest in the individual has been lost; the
trick of using the crowd as an individual hasn't been found
because we must have our love story. The spectacle film is
slowly settling down to the level of the stereopticon slide.
Comparison with German films is inevitable. They are
as much on the wrong track as we are; and the exception,
Caligari, is defective because in a proper attempt to relieve
the camera from the burden of recording actuality, the
producers gave it the job of recording modern paintings for
background. The acting was, however, playing; and the destruction of realism, even if it was accomplished by a questionable expedient, will have much to do with the future of
the film. Yet even in the spectacle film the Germans managed to do something. *Passion* and *Deception* and the Phar-
aoh film and the film made out of *Sumurun* were not lavish.
And in the manipulation of material (not of the instrument,
where we know much more than they) there came occasion-

284

ally flashes of the real thing. In *Deception* there was a scene where the courtyard had to be cleared of an angry mob. Every American producer has handled the parallel scene and every one in the same way, centring in the mêlée between civilians and police. What Lubitsch did was to form a single line of pike staffs and to show a solid mass of crowd—the feeling of hostility was projected in the opposition of line and mass. And slowly the *space behind* the pike staffs opened. The bright calm sunlight fell on a wider and widening strip of the courtyard. One was hardly aware of struggle; all one saw was that gradually broadening patch of open, uncontested *space in the light.* And suddenly one knew that the courtyard was cleared, one seemed to hear the faint murmur of the crowd outside, and then silence. I am lost in admiration of this simplicity which involves *every correct principle of the æsthetics of the moving picture.* The whole thing was done with movement and light—the movement massed and the light on the open space. That is the true, the imaginative camera technique, which we failed to develop.[1]

The object of that technique is *the indirect communication of emotion*—indirect because that is the surest way, in all the arts, of multiplying the degree of intensity. The American spectacle film still communicates a thrill in the direct way of a highwayman with a blackjack. But the American serious film drama communicates not even this: it is at this moment entirely dead, or in other words, wholly bogus. I may be wrong in thinking that our present position develops out of the creation of Mary Pickford as a star. The result is the same.

For as soon as the movie became "the silent drama" it took upon itself responsibilities. It had to be dignified and

---

[1] I haven't seen *The Covered Wagon.* Its theme returns to the legendary history of America. There is no reason why it should not have been highly imaginative. But I wonder whether the thousands of prairie schooners one hears about are the film or the image. In the latter case there is no objection.

artistic; it had to have literature and actors and ideals. The simple movie plots no longer sufficed, and stage and novel were called upon to contribute their small share to the success of an art which seriously believed itself to be the consummation of all the arts. The obligation remained to choose only those examples which were suitable to the screen. It was, however, not adaptability which guided the choice, but the great name. Eventually everything was filmed because what couldn't be adapted could be spoiled. The degree of vandalism passes words; and what completed the ruin was that good novels were spoiled not to make good films, but to make bad ones. *Victory* was a vile film in addition to being a vulgar betrayal of Conrad; even the good Molnar with his exciting second-rate play, *The Devil*, found himself so foully, so disgustingly changed on the screen that the whole idea, not a great one, was lost and nothing remained but a sentimental vulgarity which had no meaning of its own, quite apart from any meaning of his. In each of these the elements are the same: a psychological development through an action. By corrupting the action the producers changed the idea; bad enough in itself, they failed to understand what they were doing and supplied nothing to take the place of what they had destroyed. The actual movies so produced refused to project any consecutive significant action whatsoever.

It would be futile to multiply examples—as futile as to note that there have been well-filmed novels and plays. The essential thing is that nearly every picture made recently has borrowed something, usually in the interest of dignity, gentility, refinement—and the picture side, the part depending upon action before the camera, has gone steadily down. Long subtitles explain everything except the lack of action. Carefully built scenes are settings in which nothing takes place. The climax arrives in the masterpieces of the de Mille school. They are "art." They are genteel. They offend nothing—except the intelligence. High life in the de Mille manner is not recognizable as decent human society, but it is refined, and the picture with it is refined out of existence. Ten years earlier there was another type of drama: the vamp, in short, and Theda Bara was its divinity, I have little to say in its defense because it was unalterably stupid (I don't say I didn't like it). But it wasn't half so pretentious as the de Mille social drama, and not half so vulgar. What it had to say, false or banal or ridiculous, it said entirely with the camera. It appealed to low passions and it truckled to imitative morality; there was in it a sort of corruption. Yet one could resist that frank ugliness as one can't resist the polite falsehood of the new culture of the movies.

⋖§ The vamp went her way, superseded by the It-girl. But Cecil de Mille remains, absorbing into his person everything that makes the movie not worth thinking about. "It is a solemn thought," he once solemnly thought, "that the decisions we make at our desks here in Hollywood may affect the lives of every man and woman and child throughout the world." §⋗

It would be easy to exaggerate your failures. Your greatest mistake was a natural one—in taking over the realistic theatre. You knew that a photograph can reproduce actuality without significantly transposing it, and you assumed that that was the duty of the film. But you forgot that the rhythm of the film was creating something, and that this creation adapted itself entirely to the projection of emotion by means *not realistic;* that in the end the camera was as legitimately an instrument of distortion as of reproduction. You gave us, in short, the pleasure of *verification* in every detail; the Germans who are largely in the same tradition—they should have known better because their theatre knew better—improved the method at times and counted on significant detail. But neither of you gave us the pleasure of *recognition.* Neither you nor they have taken the first step (except in

Caligari) toward giving us the highest degree of pleasure. that of escaping actuality and entering into a created world, built on its own inherent logic, keeping time in its own rhythm—where we feel ourselves at once strangers and at home. That has been done elsewhere—not in the serious film.

I would be glad to temper all of this with praise: for Anita Loos' captions and John Emerson's occasionally excellent direction; for George Loane Tucker, for Monte Katterjohn's flashes of insight into what makes a scenario. I have liked many more films than I have mentioned here. But you are familiar with praise and there remains to say what you have missed. The moving picture when it became pretentious, when it went upstage and said, "dear God, make me artistic" at the end of its prayers, killed its imagination and foreswore its popularity. At your present rate of progress you will in ten years—if you survive—be no more a popular art than grand opera is. You had in your hands an incalculable instrument to set free the imagination of mankind— and the atrophy of our imaginative lives has only been hastened by you. You had also an instrument of fanstsy— and you gave us Marguerite Clark in films no better than the "whimsy-me" school of stage plays. Above all, you had something fresh and clean and new; it was a toy and should have remained a toy—something for our delight. You gave us problem plays. Beauty you neither understood nor cared for; and although you talked much about art you never for a moment tried to fathom the secret sources, nor to understand the secret obligations, of art.

Can you do anything now? I don't know and I am indifferent to your future—because there is a future for the moving picture with which you will have nothing to do. I do not know if the movie of the future will be popular—and to me it is the essence of the movie that it should be popular. Perhaps there will be a period of semi-popularity—it will be at this time that you will desert—and then the new

288

picture will arrive without your assistance. For when you and your capitalizations and your publicity go down together, the field will be left free for others. The first cheap film will startle you; but the film will grow less and less expensive. Presently it will be within the reach of artists. With players instead of actors and actresses, with fresh ideas (among which the idea of making a lot of money may be absent) these artists will give back to the screen the thing you have debauched—imagination. They will create with the camera, and not record, and will follow its pulsations instead of attempting to capture the rhythm of actuality. It isn't impossible to recreate exactly the atmosphere of Anderson's *I'm a Fool;* it isn't impossible (although it may not be desirable) to do studies in psychology; it is possible and desirable to create great epics of American industry and let the machine operate as a character in the play—just as the land of the West itself, as the corn must play its part. The grandiose conceptions of Frank Norris are not beyond the reach of the camera. There are painters willing to work in the medium of the camera and architects and photographers. And novelists, too, I fancy, would find much of interest in the scenario as a new way of expression. There is no end to what we can accomplish.

The vulgar prettiness, the absurdities, the ignorances of your films haven't saved you. And although the first steps after you take away your guiding hand may be feeble, although bogus artists and culture-hounds may capture the movie for a time—in the end all will be well. For the movie is the imagination of mankind in action—and you haven't destroyed it yet.

&§ The movies were not saved by independents working on small budgets. They were saved, as corporate entities, by the coming of sound. They were saved again a generation later by the wide-screen. In the interval, they had again gone through a phase of great interest and had again fallen into the doldrums. Now, having sold their backlog to television—the very pictures whose routine staleness had begun to discourage customers at the box-office—the studios are making huge spectacles and experimenting with small and simple two-dimensional pictures on low budgets. Most of them are solvent because they can always rent their space and equipment for the manufacture of TV-movies. It seems a sad end—but it may not, it need not, be the end. ❧

Before a picture by Picasso

> For there are many arts, not among those we con-
> ventionally call "fine," which seem to me fundamental
> for living.
>
> *Havelock Ellis.*

It was my great fortune just as I was finishing this book to
be taken by a friend to the studio of Pablo Picasso. We had
been talking on our way of the lively arts; my companion
denied none of their qualities, and agreed violently with
my feeling about the bogus, what he called *le côté Puccini.*
But he held that nothing is more necessary at the moment
than the exercise of discrimination, that we must be on our
guard lest we forget the major arts, forget even how to appreciate them, if we devote ourselves passionately, as I do,
to the lively ones. Had he planned it deliberately he could
not have driven his point home more deeply, for in Picasso's
studio we found ourselves, with no more warning than our
great admiration, in the presence of a masterpiece. We were
not prepared to have an unframed canvas suddenly turned
from the wall and to recognize immediately that one more
had been added to the small number of the world's greatest
works of art.

I shall make no effort to describe that painting. It isn't
even important to know that I am right in my judgment.
The significant and overwhelming thing to me was that I
held the work a masterpiece and knew it to be contemporary.

It is a pleasure to come upon an accredited masterpiece which preserves its authority, to mount the stairs and see the Winged Victory and *know* that it is good. But to have the same conviction about something finished a month ago, contemporaneous in every aspect, yet associated with the great tradition of painting, with the indescribable thing we think of as the high seriousness of art and with a relevance not only to our life, but to life itself—that is a different thing entirely. For of course the first effect—after one had gone away and begun to be aware of effects—was to make one wonder whether it is worth thinking or writing or feeling about anything else. Whether, since the great arts are so capable of being practised to-day, it isn't sheer perversity to be satisfied with less. Whether praise of the minor arts isn't, at bottom, treachery to the great. I had always believed that there exists no such hostility between the two divisions of the arts which are honest—that the real opposition is between them, allied, and the polished fake. To that position I returned a few days later: it was a fortunate week altogether, for I heard the *Sacre du Printemps* of Strawinsky the next day, and this tremendous shaking of the forgotten roots of being gave me reassurance.

&§ The friend whose thoughts are reported above was Clive Bell. The particular picture is totally out of Picasso's more famous styles—it is a rather sentimental one, generally called *The Lovers*, which he did right after his Roman period. I remember that Picasso showed us, that day, a dozen others to which, I suspect, I would now turn. It was, indeed, the cumulative effect of seeing one magnificent work after another, of hearing Picasso's modest, "I tried this—to see if it would work," and of being in his compulsive presence, that so stirred me. When we left, Bell said, "I never know what to say to an artist when he shows you his own work"—and this, coming from a professional art critic, relieved my mind, for I had been entirely speechless in admiration. ૐ

More than that, I am convinced that if one is going to live fully and not shut oneself away from half of civilized existence, one must care for both. It is possible to do well enough with either, and much depends on how one derives pleasure from them. For no one imagines that a pedant or a half-wit, enjoying a classic or a piece of ragtime, is actually getting all that the subject affords. For an intelligent human being knows that one difference between himself and the animals is that he can "live in the mind"; to him there need be present no conflict between the great arts and the minor; he will see, in the end, that they minister to each other.

Most of the great works of art have reference to our time only indirectly—as they and we are related to eternity. And we require arts which specifically refer to our moment, which create the image of our lives. There are some twenty workers in literature, music, painting, sculpture, architecture, and the dance who are doing this for us now—and doing it in such a manner as to associate our modern existence with that extraordinary march of mankind which we like to call the progress of humanity. It is not enough. In addition to them—in addition, not in place of them—we must have arts which, we feel, are for ourselves alone, which no one before us could have cared for so much, which no one after us will wholly understand. The picture by Picasso could have been admired by an unprejudiced critic a thousand years ago, and will be a thousand years hence. We require, for nourishment, something fresh and transient. It is this which makes jazz so much the characteristic art of our time and Jolson a more typical figure than Chaplin, who also is outside of time. There must be ephemera. Let us see to it that they are good.

The characteristic of the great arts is high seriousness—it occurs in Mozart and Aristophanes and Rabelais and Molière as surely as in Æschylus and Racine. And the essence of the minor arts is high levity which existed in the *commedia dell'arte* and exists in Chaplin, which you find in the music of Berlin and Kern (not "funny" in any case). It is a question of exaltation, of carrying a given theme to the "high" point. The reference in a great work of art is to something more profound; and no trivial theme has ever required, or had, or been able to bear, a high seriousness in treatment. Avoiding the question of creative genius, what impresses us in a work of art is the intensity or the pressure with which the theme, emotion, sentiment, even "idea" is rendered. Assuming that a blow from the butt of a revolver is not exactly artistic presentation, that "effectiveness" is not the only criterion, we have the beginning of a criticism of æsthetics. We know that the method does count, the creativeness, the construction, the form. We know also that while the part of humanity which is fully civilized will always care for high seriousness, it will be quick to appreciate the high levity of the minor arts. There is no conflict. The battle is only against solemnity which is not high, against ill-rendered profundity, against the shoddy and the dull.

I have allowed myself to catalogue my preferences; it is possible to set the basis of them down in impersonal terms, in propositions:

That there is no opposition between the great and the lively arts.

That both are opposed in the spirit to the middle or bogus arts.

That the bogus arts are easier to appreciate, appeal to low and mixed emotions, and jeopardize the purity of both the great and the minor arts.

That except in a period when the major arts flourish with exceptional vigour, the lively arts are likely to be the most intelligent phenomena of their day.

That the lively arts as they exist in America to-day are entertaining, interesting, and important.

That with a few exceptions these same arts are more interesting to the adult cultivated intelligence than most of the things which pass for art in cultured society.

That there exists a "genteel tradition" about the arts which has prevented any just appreciation of the popular arts, and that these have therefore missed the corrective criticism given to the serious arts, receiving instead only abuse.

That therefore the pretentious intellectual is as much responsible as any one for what is actually absurd and vulgar in the lively arts.

That the simple practitioners and simple admirers of the lively arts being uncorrupted by the bogus preserve a sure instinct for what is artistic in America.

§ This series of propositions corresponds, in general terms, to the specific likes and dislikes listed at the beginning of *The Great God Bogus*. (It is, in fact, a fault of construction in the book that the two chapters were not integrated.) I find here, for the second time in the book, a reference to the "genteel tradition" and also a clue to the resentment the book aroused. It is in the next-to-last proposition, the idea that the pretentious intellectual, because he failed to respect and criticize the popular arts, was in some way responsible for their faults with the implication that this same intellectual was being taken in by the bogus. The critics had to destroy everything the book stood for unless they were willing to accept my impeachment. They tried—and if the actual arts I was discussing hadn't had superabundant vitality, they might have succeeded. Aid and comfort came to my side, however, from abroad. Particularly the French enthusiasm for our movies and our music had a decisive effect on native critics. *ठ*

And now a detour around two of the most disagreeable words in the language: high- and low-brow. Pretense about these words and what they signify makes all understanding of the lively arts impossible. The discomfort and envy which make these words vague, ambiguous, and contemptuous need not concern us; for they represent a real distinction, two separate ways of apprehending the world, as if it were palpable to one and visible to the other. In connexion with the lively arts the distinction is clear and involves the third division, for the lively arts are created and admired chiefly by the class known as lowbrows, are patronized and, to an extent enjoyed, by the highbrows; and are treated as impostors and as contemptible vulgarisms by the middle class, those who invariably are ill at ease in the presence of great art until it has been approved by authority, those whom Dante rejected from heaven and hell alike, who blow neither hot nor cold, the Laodiceans.

Be damned to these last and all their tribe! There exists a small number of people who care intensely for the major and the minor arts and they are always being accused of "not caring really" for the lively ones, of pretending to care, or of running away from "the ancient wisdom and austere control" of Greek architecture or from the intense passion of Dante, the purity of Bach, the great totality of what humankind has created in art. It is claimed, and here the professional lowbrow agrees, that these others *cannot* care for the lively arts, unless they romanticize them and find things in them which aren't there—at least not for the "real" patrons of those arts—those who observe them without thinking about them.

Aren't they there, these secondary qualities? I take for example a sport instead of an art. Nothing about baseball interests me except the newspaper reports of the games, so I speak without prejudice. In the days of Babe Ruth I took the sun in the bleachers once and saw that heavy hitter do exactly what he had to do on his first appearance for the day—a straight, businesslike home run, much appreciated by the crowd, as any expert well-timed job is appreciated by Americans. The game that day went against the Yankees; they were two runs behind in the ninth, and with two men on base Ruth came up again. Again he hit a home run. And the crowd roaring its joy in victory exhaled two sighs, for the dramatic quality of the blow and for the lovely spiralling of the ball in its flight over the fence. "A beauty—a beauty"— you heard the expression a thousand times—and "He knows *when* to hit them." They would have roared, too, if he had hit a single, which, muffed, would have brought in the winning run. But they would not have said, "a beauty"—and as far as I am concerned that is proof enough that the appreciation of æsthetic qualities is universal. It isn't, thank Heaven, always put into words.

Take as another instance the fame of the Rath Brothers. They are acrobats who do difficult things, but there are others doing much the same sort of thing without approaching the *réclame* of these two. Their appearance of ease is a delight; there is no strain, no swelling muscles, no visible exploitation of strength. The Hellenic philosopher who held that the arrow shot from the bow is never in motion, but at rest from second to second at the succeeding points of its trajectory, might have seen some ancient forerunners of these athletes, for each of their movements seems at once a sculptured rest and a passage into another pose. And that is precisely the quality which vaudeville and revue audiences care for, and in a groping way recognize as distinctive and fine. They may think that Greeks have been candy-vendors since the beginning of time and that Marathon was a racecourse; but they *know* what they like.

I do not see, therefore, that recognition of these aspects of the gay arts can in any way detract from actual enjoyment—on the contrary it adds. You see Charlie about to throw a mop; the boss enters; without breaking the line of his movement Charlie swoops to the floor and begins to scrub. The first, the essential thing, is the fun in the dramatic turn; but what makes it funny is that there is no jerk, no break in the line—the two things are so interwoven that you cannot separate them. And if anyone were actually entirely unconscious of the line, the fun would be lost; it would be Ham and Bud, not Charlie, for such a spectator. The question is only to what degree one can be conscious of it—for I have known intellectuals who so reduced Charlie to angles that the angles no longer made them laugh. They have done the same with Massine and Nijinsky; they have followed the score so closely that they haven't heard the music and they correspond exactly to the man who bets on the game and doesn't see the play.

The life of the mind is supposed to be a terrible burden, ruining all the pleasures of the senses. This idea is carefully supported by "mental workers" (as they call themselves) and by the brainless. The truth is, of course, that when the mind isn't afflicted by a desire to be superior, it does nothing but multiply all the pleasures, and the intelligent spectator, in all conscience, feels and experiences more than the dull one. To such a spectator the lively arts have a validity of their own. He cares for them for themselves, and their relation to the other arts does not matter. It is only because the place of the common arts in decent society is always being called into question that the answer needs to be given. I do not suppose that my answer is final; but I feel sure that it must be given, as mine is, from the outside.[1]

It happens that what we call folk music, folk dance, and the folk arts in general have only a precarious existence among us; the "reasons" are fairly obvious. And the popular substitutes for these arts are so much under our eyes and in our ears that we fail to recognize them as decent contribu-

[1] I wrote once, and was properly rapped over the knuckles for writing, that it wasn't to escape Bach, but to escape Puccini, that one played Berlin. Mr Haviland, whom I have quoted frequently, replied that those who really cared for jazz cared for it, not as an escape from any other art. I had not intended to write an apology; only, since I was replying to the usual attack on the jazz arts, I wanted to indicate that in addition to their primary virtues they have this great secondary one, that when we are too fed up with bad drawing, bad music, bad acting, and second-rate sentiment, we can be sure of consolation in the lively arts.

tions to the richness and intensity of our lives. The result, strange as it may appear to devotees of culture, is that our major arts suffer. The poets, painters, composers who withdraw equally from the main stream of European tradition and from the untraditional natural expressions of America, have no sources of strength, no material to work with, no background against which they can see their shadows; they feel themselves disinherited of the future as well as the past.

At the same time the contempt we have for the lively arts hurts them as much as it hurts us. We have all heard of the "great artist of the speaking stage" who will not lower himself by appearing on the screen; as familiar is the vaudevillian who will call himself an artist and has hankerings for the legit; we have seen good dancers become bad actors, good black-face comedians develop alarming tendencies toward singing sentimental ballads in whisky-tenor voices, good comic-strip artists beginning to do bad book illustrations. The "step upward" is never in the direction of superior work, but toward a more rarefied acclaim. They are like a notable novelist who has for years tried unsuccessfully to write a failure, because he has only one standard of artistic success: popularity—but in reverse.

◄§ The allusion here is to Sinclair Lewis and is inaccurate. When he had finished *Main Street,* Lewis was convinced he had written an American counterpart of *Madame Bovary,* and expected it to be denounced by his victims. As the sales of the book mounted, as he was forced to admit that the Main Streeters were reading it, his opinion of the book wavered. He began to fear that he had written just the sort of book Main Street wanted to read—hence a bad book. He was right in the last respect, but for the wrong reasons. And he made up for it later. §►

As these artists suffer under opprobrium and try to avoid it by touching the field of the *faux bon,* their work becomes more and more refined and genteel. The broadness, rough play, vitality, diminish gradually until a sort of Drama League seriousness and church-sociable good form are both satisfied. And all the more's the pity, for the thinning out of our lives goes on from day to day and these lively arts are the only things which can keep us hard and robust and gay. In America, where there is no recognized upper class to please, no official academic requirements to meet, the one tradition of gentility is as lethal as all the conventions of European society, and unlike those of Europe our tradition provides no nourishment for the artist. It is negative all the way through.

In spite of gentility the lively arts have held to something a little richer and gayer than the polite ones. They haven't dared to be frank, for a spurious sense of decency is backed by the police, and this limitation has hurt them; but it has made them sharp and clever by forcing their wit into deeper channels. There still exists a broadness in slap-stick comedy and in burlesque, and once in a while vast figures of Rabelaisian comedy occur. For the most part the lively arts are inhibited by the necessity to provide "nice clean fun for the whole family"—a regrettable, but inevitable penalty for their universal appeal. For myself, I should like to see a touch more of grossness and of license in these arts; it would be a sign that the blood hadn't gone altogether pale, and that we can still roar cheerfully at dirty jokes, when they are funny.

What Europeans feel about American art is exactly the opposite of what they feel about American life. Our life is energetic, varied, constantly changing; our art is imitative, anæmic (exceptions in both cases being assumed). The explanation is that few Europeans see our lively arts, which are almost secret to us, like the mysteries of a cult. Here the energy of America does break out and finds artistic expression for itself. Here a wholly unrealistic, imaginative presentation of the way we think and feel is accomplished. No

300

single artist has yet been great enough to do the whole thing —but together the minor artists of America have created the American art. And if we could for a moment stop wanting our artistic expression to be *necessarily* in the great arts— it will be that in time—we should gain infinitely.

◄§ There are two conflicting theories about the position of the popular arts in the Twenties. One holds that they were "discovered" by intellectuals who then made a great fuss over them, exaggerating their virtues, using them as a weapon against gentility in the arts, and probably robbing them of their innocence in the process. There is something to be said for this position, but it seems to me that the other, simpler, explanation is preferable. It is that a remarkable outburst of creative vigor did come about in the popular arts right after the first World War and that the critics perceived this, that the arts were worth all the attention they got and more, and that the critics were far less influential in putting them over than the practitioners of the arts themselves.

Note first that an explosion of creativity could be expected after the war—it occurred in every country—and the only thing we couldn't count on was *where* it would take place. The Keynes-Strachey axis in London, the Joyce-Pound-Eliot international, Dada in Paris, Der Sturm in Berlin which ultimately created *Caligari,* were parallel manifestations. Where should the lightning strike in the United States if not where the native art flourished—especially as the intellectuals who followed the fine arts were decamping to Europe as fast as the boats would take them over.

At the same time, the average man was turning against Europe. Our contact with ally and enemy had not always been satisfactory, the victory in which we participated left us with a tremendous reservoir of unused power, we had made our foray to foreign shores and now we wanted to stay home and cultivate our enormous garden. Within a few years the debunkers of our social system would catch up with us and prove, to our own delight, that Main Street wasn't the Champs Elysées and the good humor with which we embraced our traducers was only another demonstration of our strength. The time was right for something native to flower. It happened in our architecture and in fiction: Fitzgerald and Sinclair Lewis, among those who died young, and Faulkner, Hemingway, and Dos Passos were all establishing themselves at the time. Something more was needed because all of them, each in his own way, were affected by Europe and on the edge of Europe lay Russia which was even then beginning to disturb us. We needed something for ourselves alone.

The popular arts supplied it. It didn't matter that our music and our movies invaded Europe—they were made for us. They said something we couldn't express in the fine arts. They were insular, almost parochial—and we wanted it that way.

I don't pretend that the average man knew this and I am quite sure the exceptional critic didn't, either. All we saw was something easy to enjoy, untroubled, full of vitality. It seemed good to us.

I am suggesting that the twenties were really exceptional. Certainly it is noteworthy that high points were reached in several of the popular arts at the same time. And we have another proof: the individuals who gave this era its distinction continued on. The music that was then moving up from New Orleans was to be transformed in Chicago and New York, but it still dominates our basic mode to-day; in the dance, Fred Astaire, who was only a footnote to me, is having a new success in a movie as I write this; the songs written by Berlin and Gershwin and Kern and Rodgers are heard, Chaplin has not been dislodged and the movies have several times tried to catch up with D. W. Griffith . . . it is so in every field.

There has been a great change, to be sure. The moment radio arrived a revolution began and all the popular arts became much bigger business than they had been before. Perhaps the Twenties were the last flowering of our simple arts. 🙣

Because, in the first place, the lively arts have never had criticism. The box-office is gross; it detects no errors, nor does it sufficiently encourage improvement. Nor does abuse help. There is good professional critics in journals like *Variety, The Billboard,* and the moving-picture magazines—some of them. But the lively arts can bear the same continuous criticism which we give to the major, and if the criticism itself isn't bogus there is no reason why these arts should become self-conscious in any pejorative sense. In the second place the lively arts which require little intellectual effort will more rapidly destroy the bogus than the major arts ever can. The close intimacy between high seriousness and high levity, the thing that brings together the extremes touching at the points of honesty and simplicity and intensity—will act like the convergence of two armies to squeeze out the bogus. And the moment we recognize in the lively arts our actual form of expression, we will derive from them the same satisfaction which people have always derived from an art which was relevant to their existence. The nature of that satisfaction is not easily described. One thing we know of it—that it is pure. And in the extraordinarily confused and chaotic world we live in we are becoming accustomed to demand one thing, if nothing else—that the elements presented to us however they are later confounded with others, shall be of the highest degree in their kind, of an impeccable purity.

🙢 I have acknowledged the pleasure this book has given to me and my satisfaction in knowing that it was read by young people who later had some effect on the direction taken by the lively arts. It interests me to find that before swinging into my grand finale, I was appealing for more solid criticism of these arts and there are times when I think the only direct effect of the book was the encouragement of criticism. Even that took some time. Radio was left almost unexamined for years after it burst on the air; but by the time television arrived, genuine criticism of all the popular arts had become a regular feature of many newspapers and the exploitation of them was a staple of the large-circulation magazines.

I think that a great deal of what I called "the bogus" has been discarded. The danger to us now is that, with the shift of all entertainment into the area of big business, we are being engulfed in a mass-produced mediocrity. An idea for a single play of fifty years ago becomes the base-theme of several hundred half-hours in television, the creative artist in the mass media doesn't have to be lively more than once in five years—he has only to be copious. We listen by formula to entertainment produced by formula.

My own work, at the moment, is to effect a change in the way we receive what the mass media give us. I have still a good deal of faith in the power of criticism, but it will never be fully effective until it begins, itself, to use the media. Unlike the managers of the popular arts, I believe that the various audiences which make up the public have more appetites than are now satisfied. Among them, I firmly believe, is an appetite for precisely those qualities— vigor and impudence and gaiety among them—which were, when I wrote this book, the marks and the distinguished merits of the lively arts. ॐ

Acknowledgments

I owe so much to others in connexion with this book that
if I were to set down the names and the reasons it would
appear, quite properly, that I have done little except collect
and theorize about material presented to me; it might also
appear that I wish to make others responsible. Virtually
everyone I know has contributed something—and in many
cases they did so before I had thought of writing this book.
I can therefore make only specific acknowledgments. Above
all to two managing editors, John Peale Bishop and Edmund
Wilson, Jr., of *Vanity Fair* and to their editor, Frank Crowninshield; they published several essays which later served
as the raw material for chapters here, published portions of
other chapters written expressly for this book, and otherwise
encouraged and prospered me—to such an extent that I owe
to them and to my fellow-editors of the *Dial* the holiday
which made it possible for me to write at all.

For technical information and exceptionally painstaking criticism I am indebted to Sara and Gerald Murphy,
Martin Brown, Alexander Steinert, Deems Taylor, Lewis
Galantière, H. K. Moderwell, and Dorothy Butler; for helping me find some obscure materials, to Charles Chaplin,
Irving Berlin, Bushnell Dimond, Walter Hoban, and Sophie
Wittenberg. My indebtedness to those whom I do not know—
those I have written about—is too apparent to need emphasis,
and too great to be adequately acknowledged.

◖§ It is no longer possible for me to thank some of the people mentioned above. The preparation of this new edition has been pretty much a private concern and the thanks I have to give are professional—to those who have given me pleasure, to those who have clarified my mind. I cannot name them all. ᏽ